FRANCKEN MANUSCRIPT
1783

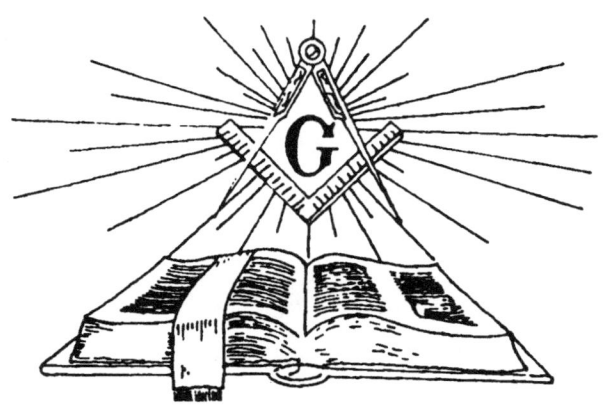

CONTENTS

The 7 classes of antient and Modern Masonry; Laws and regulations for a Lodge of Perfection; Statutes and Regulations for a Lodge of Perfection; Further Instructions for a Lodge of Perfection; 4°, Secret Master; 5°, Perfect Master; 6°, Intimate Secretary by Curiosity; 7°, Provost and Judge; 8°, Intendant of the Buildings; 9°, Master Elected of Nine; 10°, Illustrious Elected of Fifteen; 11°, Sublime Knights Elected; 12°, Grand Master Architect; 13°, Knights of the Royal Secret; 14°, Perfection; 15°, Knights of the East; 16°, Princes of Jerusalem; 17°, Knights of East and West; 18°, Knights of White Eagle or Pelican; 19°, Grand Pontif; 20°, Sovereign Prince of Masonry or Master ad Vitam; 21°, Prussian Knight or Noachite; 22°, Knights of the Royal Ax; 23°, Knights of the Sun; 24°, Knights of Kadoch & the Ne plus ultra of Masonry; 25°, The Royal Secret.; Form of submission to be signed by all those who are initiated.

Henry Andrew Francken

ISBN 1-56459-365-7

Kessinger Publishing's
Rare Mystical Reprints

THOUSANDS OF SCARCE BOOKS ON THESE AND OTHER SUBJECTS:

Freemasonry * Akashic * Alchemy * Alternative Health * Ancient Civilizations * Anthroposophy * Astrology * Astronomy * Aura * Bible Study * Cabalah * Cartomancy * Chakras * Clairvoyance * Comparative Religions * Divination * Druids * Eastern Thought * Egyptology * Esoterism * Essenes * Etheric * ESP * Gnosticism * Great White Brotherhood * Hermetics * Kabalah * Karma * Knights Templar * Kundalini * Magic * Meditation * Mediumship * Mesmerism * Metaphysics * Mithraism * Mystery Schools * Mysticism * Mythology * Numerology * Occultism * Palmistry * Pantheism * Parapsychology * Philosophy * Prosperity * Psychokinesis * Psychology * Pyramids * Qabalah * Reincarnation * Rosicrucian * Sacred Geometry * Secret Rituals * Secret Societies * Spiritism * Symbolism * Tarot * Telepathy * Theosophy * Transcendentalism * Upanishads * Vedanta * Wisdom * Yoga * *Plus Much More!*

DOWNLOAD A FREE CATALOG AT:
www.kessinger.net

OR EMAIL US AT:
books@kessinger.net

Introduction

This is a complete typescript of the rituals of all twenty-five degrees of Etienne (Stephen) Morin's Masonic Rite which became the foundation of the Ancient and Accepted (Scottish) Rite.

Soon after the development of 'Ecossais' Masonry in France, Morin was appointed 'Grand Inspector in all parts of the New World' by the Council of the Grand and Sovereign Lodge of St. Jean de Jerusalem in either Bordeaux or Paris. Morin, who had access to many high grade rituals, then apparently created a set of Masonic regulations called the 'Constitutions of 1762' to assist him in establishing High-Grade Masonry in the New World; he also organized these 'haut grades' into a Masonic rite. Armed with his patent, Morin traveled to Kingston, Jamaica, and between 1762 and 1767 conferred his rite upon H.A. Francken, whom he also appointed Deputy Inspector-General in 1769.

Francken wrote out the rituals in at least three manuscripts—the most complete set being the 1783 manuscript. In 1767 Francken authorized a 'Lodge of Perfection' in Albany, New York, and the seeds of Scottish Rite Masonry were planted on the East Coast. By 1800 some fifty men had been appointed Deputy Inspectors, and several resolved to establish a governing body of the Rite. A document, known as the 'Constitutions of 1786' authorized an increase from Morin's 25-degree system to one of 33 degrees. On May 31, 1801, the first Supreme Council, 33°, of the Ancient and Accepted Scottish Rite was organized in Charleston, South Carolina, which survives today as the Supreme Council, 33°, (Mother Council of the World) A\A\S\R\, Southern Masonic Jurisdiction, USA.

This is a complete copy of Francken's best manuscript, and is the single most important document relating to the Ancient and Accepted (Scottish) Rite, because it the lineal predecessor of the Rite. The rituals of this manuscript represent their authentic form at the birth of Scottish Rite, before they were modified by Carson, Gourgas, Yates, Pike, etc.

To whatever extent the rituals may have changed in any jurisdiction, all owe their existence to the rituals of this magnificent document. CONTENTS: The 7 classes of antient and Modern Masonry; Laws and regulations for a Lodge of Perfection; Statutes and Regulations for a Lodge of Perfection; Further Instructions for a Lodge of Perfection; 4°, Secret Master; 5°, Perfect

Master; 6°, Intimate Secretary by Curiosity; 7°, Provost and Judge; 8°, Intendant of the Buildings; 9°, Master Elected of Nine; 10°, Illustrious Elected of Fifteen; 11°, Sublime Knights Elected; 12°, Grand Master Architect; 13°, Knights of the Royal Secret; 14°, Perfection; 15°, Knights of the East; 16°, Princes of Jerusalem; 17°, Knights of East and West; 18°, Knights of White Eagle or Pelican; 19°, Grand Pontif; 20°, Sovereign Prince of Masonry or Master ad Vitam; 21°, Prussian Knight or Noachite; 22°, Knights of the Royal Ax; 23°, Knights of the Sun; 24°, Knights of Kadoch & the Ne plus ultra of Masonry; 25°, The Royal Secret.; Form of submission to be signed by all those who are initiated.

This document is a reproduction of an invaluable Masonic manuscript—not an exposé—and is the single most important source of information on the early Scottish Rite rituals in existence.

The contents of this Book

		Transcript Page	Original Page
The 7 clahses of antient and Modern Masonry		2	1 . -
Laws and regulations for a Lodge of Perfection		5	4 . -
Statutes and regulations for D?		13	15 . -
Further Instructions for D?		24	28 . -
4th degree	of Secret Master	27	30 . -
5th ditto	of Perfect Master	37	40 . -
6th ditto	of Intimate Secretary, by Curiosity	48	52 . -
7th ditto	of Provost and Judge	55	60 . -
8th ditto	of Intendant of the Buildings	62	66 . -
9th ditto	of Master Elected of Nine	72	76 . -
10th ditto	of Illustrious Elected of 15	85	90 . -
11th ditto	of Sublime Knights Elected	92	96 . -
12th ditto	of Grand Mr Architect	105	108 . -
13th ditto	of Knights of the Royal Arch	121	124 . -
14th ditto	of <u>Perfection</u>. ultimate of Symbolic Masonry	140	142 . -
15th do.	Knights of the East	187	184 . -
16th do.	Princes of Jerusalem	197	198 . -
17th do.	Knights of East and West	205	208 . -
18th do.	Knights of White Eagle or Pelican	211	214 . -
19th do.	Scotch Masonry, by the name of Grand Pontif	219	224 . -
20th do.	Sovereign Prince of Masonry or Master ad Vitam	222	228 . -
21st	Pruhsian Knight or <u>Noachite</u>	230	234 . -
22nd do.	Knights of the Royal Axe	238	244 . -
23rd	Knights of the Sun princes adepts, Key of Masonry	240	248
24th	Knights of Kadoch and The Ne Plus Ultra of Masonry	258	276
25th	The Royal Secret	273	302
	Form of Submihsion to be Signed by all those who are initiated	278	309 . -

Copy of the Constitution for a Grand Chapter of Princes of the Royal Secret. .... Ne Plus Ultra

By the Glory of the G. A. of the Universe   Lux ex Tenebris

At the East where shines the Great Light and where reigns Silence Concord and peace the 5th day of the month called year 1770, of the creation 5531. Equal to 30th of April 1770.

Unitas Concordia Fratrum

To our worthy and venerable Brethren, Henry Andrew Francken, Deputy Inspector. William Adams Deputy Inspector. William Wynter. Gabriel Jones, John Prendergast, Edward Bowes, and Martin Matthias Princes of the R. S. - Greeting .... Whereas there is an absolute necehsity to form a grand chapter of Sublime Princes of the Royal Secret in the Island of Jamaica and territories thereon depending and by the power wherewith we are invested, We by these presents do appoint and constitute you the said H. A. Francken, W^m. Adams, W^m. Wynter, Gabriel Jones, John Prendergast, Edward Bowes, and Martin Matthias into a Grand Chapter of Princes of the R. S. and by these presents our Honorable Brother and Prince W^m. Wynter to be President and Grand Commander in all Grand Chapters, Grand Councils and Consistories, in his absence our worthy Brother and Prince Gabriel Jones and in the absence of him the most Ancient Prince present and that ye shall strictly behave yourselves to all the Statutes, rules and regulations of the nine Commihsioners named by the Grand Chapter of the Sublime Princes of the R.S. at the Grand East of France and Prussia consequent by the Deliberation dated the 7th Dec. 77/12 to be ratefied and observed by the aforesaid Grand Chapter of Prussia and France and by all the regular and particular Lodges, Councils, Grand Councils, Grand Chapters, Consistories etc. over the surface of the two Hemispheres to govern and regulate all Lodges, Ccuncils, Grand Councils Grand Chapters Consistories etc. from the Secret Master to the Royal Secret hereby impowering ye and your successors finally to determine all causes complaints etc. and no appeal shall be had or made from your sentences orders or decrees but the same shall be final and conclusive to all intents and purposes whatsoever.

To which we Stephen Morin have hereunto subscribed our name and affixed our seal of arms and also the Grand Seal of Princes of Masons in the place where the greatest of treasures are deposited the beholding of which fills us with Joy comfort and acknowledgement of all that's good and great near the B.B. in Kingston the day and year above written

        Signed S. Morin G. Insp. G.
        S. P. of M^s. etc. etc. etc.

Martin Matthias Grand I^r. General
Sovereign P. of M^s. etc. etc. etc.

 Copied by I. D. D. G. M. P.R.S. as the original in his pohsehsion is most defaced and may be destroyed or lost. date June 24th 1794

The Royal Art or Society of Free and accepted Masons is divided by order into Twentyfive degrees, ... and proved -

All these degrees are distributed into 7 clahses through which one must pahs without dispensation, and must follow exactly the order of time between each degree which are ranged by mysterious Numbers.

Clahs 1st consists of 3 degrees. vizt years

No.			years
1st	Entered apprentice	Must serve	3 . -
2nd	Fellow Craft	to serve	5 . -
3rd	Master. All three subject to the superior to become fellow craft and Master		7 . -
		– which is 3 times 5	15 years

Clahs 2nd consists of 5 degrees. vizt

4th	Secret Master,	must serve	3 . -
5th	Perfect Master	do.	3 . -
6th	Intimate Secretary	do.	3 . -
7th	Intendant of the buildings	do.	5 . -
8th	Provost and Judge	do.	7 . -
		which is 3 times 7 years	21 years

Clahs 3rd consists of three degrees. Viz.t   years

   9th degree, Elected of the Nine, serve - - - - - - - - - 3 . -
 10th do.   Knights elected of 15, do. - - - - - - - -   3 . -
 11th do.   Illustrious Elected chiefs of the 12 Tribes 1 . -
                                                                 which is 7 years

Clahs 4th consists of 3 degrees. Viz.t
 12th degree, Grand Mr Architect - - - - - - - - - - -   1 . -
 13th do.   Knights of the Royal Arch - - - - - - - - - 3 . -
 14th do.   Grand Elect, Perfect and Sublime Mason - - 1 . -
                                                        which makes 5 years

Clahs 5th consists of 5 degrees. Viz.t
 15th   Knights of the East or the Sword - - - - - 1 . -
 16th   Prince of Jerusalem - - - - - - - - - - - - 1 . -
 17th   Knights of East and West - - - - - - - - - 3 . -
 18th   Knights of the Rose Crohs - - - - - - - -   1 . -
 19th   Grand Pontif, Worshipful Master ad Vitam - 3 . -
                                            which makes 3 times 3 - 9 years

Clahs 6th consists of 3 degrees. Viz.t
 20th   Grand Patriarch - - - - - - - - - - - - -   3 . -
 21st   Grand Master of the Masonic Key - - - - -   3 . -
 22nd   Prince of Libanus, Knight of the Royal Ax - 3 . -
                                            which is 3 times 3 - 9 years

Clahs 7th consists of 3 degrees. Viz.t
 23rd   Sovereign Princes Adepts, Chiefs of the
               grand consistory - - - - - - - - - - - - - 5 . -
 24th   Illustrious Knights of Kadoch, Commanders
               of the white and black Eagle - - - - - -   5 . -
 25th   The Most Illustrious Sovereign Princes of
               Masonry, Grand Knights, Sublime Commanders
               of the Royal Secret - - - - - - - - - - -   5 . -
                                            which is 3 times 5 - 15 years

                                            which makes in all - 81 years

All these degrees in which they must militate, during a number of mysterious years to attain succehsfully to each following degree, form the Perfect number of 81 years.

8 and 1 makes 9, and 8 & 1 makes 81, - also 9 times 9 makes 81, all perfect numbers. Very different from 1 & 8 which is 9, also 1 & 8 makes 18, and twice 9 is 18. But these last numbers are imperfect numbers - and this combination is thorny and difficult. But a Free Mason who has fully compleated his time at length will gather

T h e   M a s o n i c   R o s e .

Laws and Regulations for the Government
of a Lodge of Perfection
Health, Stability and Power

Preamble

As all well regulated societies, have certain rules and regulations for their better support and government, and as Free and accepted Masons are bound in a more particular manner, to practice the social, and inforce the moral virtues, Especially in the Lodges of Perfection, constituted by the Right worshipfull and Thrice Puissant Henry Andrew Francken - Grand El^t. Perf^t. & Sublime Mason, Kn^t. of the East, Prince of Jerusalem & & & Patriarch Noachite, Sovereign Knight of the Sun and Kadoch, Illustrious Prince and Grand Commander of the Royal Secret & & &, Senior Dep^{ty} Grd. Inspector general over all Lodges, Chapters, councils and Gr^d. Councils of the Superior degrees of Antient and Modern Masonry in the West Indies and North america & and granted under our hand & seal at arms with the great seal of Masonry affixed there to bearing date of the vulgar aera the 20th day of December 1767 "By the Name of the Ineffable"; to be held in the city of Albany in the Province of New York.- The persons here after subscribed their names and members of said Lodge of Perfection called the Ineffable do assent to the following Laws and Regulations for their better government under the Penalties hereafter mentioned vizt.

- 6 -

1st

Constitution

That those members mentioned in the constitution shall meet by order of Brother N.N. the Master appointed when he shall open the Lodge of Perfection, and after saying Prayer, read himself the constitution, these Laws, and then appoint his officers, after which they shall agree by a majority when and where to meet, as shall be judged convenient.

2dly

Numbers of members by 27

but he may not to be elected

Juwel & order to be provided by the body

That the members of this lodge never Exceed the number of Twenty Seven including the Master, and that no person be raised in this lodge, unless he can be vouched to be a regular made Master Mason, and is a member of a Regular constituted lodge of the 3 first degrees; and is also or has been an officer in such lodge; - that such Mason desiring to be raised in this lodge and to become a member shall by petition be proposed by one of the members, when he is to be ballotted for, the next ensuing night, and if but one black Bead or nay shall appear in Ballotting said Petitioner can never be proposed again in said lodge - but if chosen by unanimous consent, he is to be raised the next ordinary lodge night, when on his reception, the lodge is to furnish the Juwel apron order etc. of said degree, the expenses of which the Initiated brother is to be acquainted with before hand, that he may come prepared to pay the same when the Ceremony is over.

3dly

Payments for each degree

That the Brethren who shall be admitted into this Body, shall pay for the Initiation of each degree of the first Nine from the Secret M^r to the Grand Mr Architect the sum of _____ . For the Initiation of the 13th degree or Royal Arch the sum of _____ and for the perfection or 14th degree the sum of _____ as also for the Juwels, aprons, orders etc. for every degree, as mentioned in the foregoing article.

4thly

That no member of this lodge can be raised higher, unless he has at least been two succeeding ordinary lodges present, and is very

Times of Raising

perfect in his former degrees, at least for the first 9 degrees and between the Gr^d. M^r. architect and the Royal Arch, at least 3 ordinary lodges - and if the candidate should be found dificient in the ceremonies requisite in the last degree, he is to be admitted by discretion of the Master, or remanded back to the studies of his former degrees. And in case such cand. should murmur against such proceedings of the Master, and not making proper atonement for his behaviour he shall be excluded as a member of said lodge; of w^h. a minute is to be kept in the lodge book. -

5thly

Secretary to ?p fair ??c^{ts}.

As soon as a candidate becomes a member of this Body, the secretary shall read these Laws (Standing) to which said member shall subscribe his name. - The Secretary is to keep fair and correct accounts, of all the monies he may receive and disburse, in a ledger, and to state the cash and personal accounts - the ledger to be posted, and the cash accounts ballanced once a quator, and paid over to the treasurer, who's receipts shall be a voucher for the Secretary - and whoever refuses, or wilfully neglects to pay his dues or fines when demanded will be excluded this lodge - The minute book is to contain the transactions of the lodge - and Entries of all Receipts and disbursements - the minutes of each lodge night, to be made, and read before the lodge is to be closed.

6thly

Visiting Brothers

A visiting brother who produces a certificate from the constitutor of this lodge, or from a regular constituted lodge of perfection, shall be permitted their first visit, gratis, for each succeeding night pay _____ shillings towards the contingent fund, and his proportion of the Expenses of the night. - There are particular times of business when no visiting brother can be admitted - but, in case a visiting, a knight of the East, Prince of Jerusalem etc. shall visit this lodge, and by producing a proper certificate of his highest degrees, he is to be received according to his rank and

Visiting & ? dignity, on the same terms as mentioned in the beginning of this article.

7th

Quaterly payments

Each member of this body is to contribute towards its support the sum of _____ per annum, by four equal payments vizt. on the Feast of S^t.John the Baptist - the 24th of September, the Feast of S^t. John the Evangelist, and the 25th of March - the whole of each quarters due to be paiable from the first day of the quarter - so that if a member should remove from the society any time after the commencement of a quater, he is to pay the whole there of; and a new member is to pay the due of that quarter in which he joins - each member in case of absence or sickness, on the above mentioned quarter days, shall appoint a person to pay for him, under the penalty of _____ for each neglect, or excluded this lodge - the quarter days to be deemed stated meetings and remembered accordingly.

8thly

M^r. or officers refusing to do their duty

If the Master, or any other officer of this lodge shall misbehave, or render himself of the lodges (worthy's?) and submission, he shall at the elction of the members be duly tried and treated according to the nature of the crime,- and if the M^r. shall neglect or refuse to fine delinquents agreeable to these Laws, he shall at the election of the members present, pay the fines so neglected himself, provided that the Body is to judge whether the fines are justly incurred.

9thly

Raising brothers clandestinely

Any member of this lodge that shall be present aiding or assisting at the raising of a Mason in any of the superior degrees clandistinely, shall be expelled this lodge for ever, and never be permitted to become a member of any lodge of perfection and an entry there of to be made in the minutes.

10th

If drunk in the lodge

If any member of this lodge shall forget himself so far, as to come drunk into the lodge, get drunk during the lodge hours, make any disturbance or uproar therein, shall be Expelled for that evening, and afterwards dealt with, as the present members think proper.

11th

A member addrehsing the chair, must do it standing, and only one person to speak at a time, and only once on the same subject, unlehs called upon by the chair - and whoever shall presume to swear or curse and blaspheme during lodge hours, shall be fined for each such offence the sum of _____ for the use hereafter mentioned - and he that refuses Silence after the third Stroke of the Master's Mallet, shall forfeit the like Sum.

12th

1. not attending lodges

Any member, who shall not duly attend the lodge agreeable to the Masters orders, shall pay the sum of _____ for the neglect of each state & lodge, and the sum of _____ for each Extraordinary lodge he neglects, and no Excuses whatever to be taken except lameness sickness or absence from Town.

13th

The Keys of the chest to be kept

The Keys of the chest is to be kept by the Master Senior Warden and grand Treasurer, one key each, and in case any of them should be from home or absent from town, they are to leave their respective keys so, that they may be easily had, whenever the lodge may have occasion to assemble, under the penalty of _____ for each neglect, besides repairing the chest, in case that lock should be broke open. The chest never to be opened, but in the presence of the Body, and no monies disposed of, out of it, without the consent of the Majority of the Members present.

14th

Raising or emergencies

That in case if any of the Members is desirous of being raised higher (without waiting the limited time, mentioned in the 4th article, and being well versed and skilled in his former degrees, or in case of departing this province Island etc.) shall by the unanimous consent of the M^r officers and the Gr^d El^t & Sublime members of this lodge be raised and even receive one, two or three degrees at an ordinary lodge night, paying over and above the stated sums of initiation of each degree the sum of _____ as far as the Gr^d.M^r. architect, for the degree of Royal Arch over and above the stated sum of _____ . And in case such member on an Emergency should desire an Extraordinary lodge to be called for that purpose, he is to defray the whole nights Expenses, and the Tiler his fees - Every member that takes out a Certificate of his degrees shall pay for the same the sum of _____ to the Secretary for the use of the box.

Certificates

15th

absence of the Master

In case of Absence or Sickness of the Master, the first officer shall officiate pro tempore, and the other officers ad Rato.

16th

Raising to the Perfection, all the members to give their votes

When a Cand^{te} is proposed to the Perfection, all the members of that degree are to have notice there of, and if they can not be present, they are to send their votes, for or against, sealed to the Master - Likewise all the members of said body shall be acquainted when any Cand^{te} is to be admitted for a member.

17th

appointment of M^r and Officers

Upon the feast of St John the Baptist, each year a Master shall be appointed by the constitutor of this lodge - however it shall be permitted the members by petition to propose a Master for the ensuing year, which is approved of, shall be sent under said Founders hand & Seal, or under the hands & Seal of a grand Council (if any established) and such Master so appointed shall on said Feast day appoint his officers.

18th

appropriations of the monies

All the monies that shall arise from the quarterages, Initiations, fines etc. shall be appropriated for the Decorations of this lodge and such other uses, as the Body shall judge proper.

19th

That a brother who has been made regular an <u>Arch Mason</u> in a regular lodge of that degree, but knowing nothing of the foregoing degrees preceeding the R:A. and being desirous of joining

R.A.Mason desirous of becoming member	this lodge, must go through the various degrees, but is to pay nothing for the 13th Degree, Except for the Juwel order etc. suitable, which he will be presented with.

20th

Juwels etc. provided by the body	That the Juwels, aprons, orders gloves etc. for the cand^{tes} of every degree shall be provided by the Body, and always in readyness; which are to be paid for as mentioned in the 2^d article.

21st

Temporary orders	That all temporary orders and regulations consistent with these laws, shall be unanimously agreed to in this lodge, and minuted; such minutes sent to the constitutor or Founder of this lodge, quaterly, or to the gr^d council if any established; and if disapproved of, disannulled, and if approved, to be of the same force as these laws.

22d

Tilers salary and duties	That a worthy M^r. Mason shall be made choice of and the degrees as far as perfection conferred on him gratis to serve the body in quality of <u>Tiler</u>, for which the Body shall allow him the sum of _____ from each brother who shall obtain the ultimate degree of Perfection therein. - Said Tiler shall be obliged to carry all summonses from the M^r to the respective members - but is to bear no Expenses attending the lodge.

23d

any matters reported out of lodge - -	If any member of this Body, shall report any of the transactions (requested to be secret) though not immediately relative to the craft, shall on the evidence of two members be expelled this lodge.

24th

o matters to be disclosed out of lodge -	If any mason, whether a member or not, shall be convicted of mentioning anything relative to the craft, shall never be permitted on any pretence within the doors of this lodge, but shall be dispised and treated with the utmost contempt by all the brethren.

25th

no monies to be paid out the fund after lodge

That, as this lodge is intirely constituted for the good and propagation of the Royal craft, it is therefore especially agreed and ordered, that any expenses which may be made after lodge hours, shall not be paid out of the Fund. - And if any of the members chuse to stay, soup etc. shall defray such Expenses out of their private pockets.

26th

The founder visiting the lodge -

Whenever the constitutor or Founder of this Lodge shall visit the same, he is to have the chair offered him; all the transactions to be laid before him and finally to judge in any complaints that is to be laid before him, and free of all Expenses.

27th

Regulations for a procehsion

Whenever a Procehsion is concluded on, all the members of this lodge who are able to walk, shall be decorated to the Decision of the Master, with as many decorations of their degrees as with Decency can be displayed.- And every member (if not absent from town) who shall not join in the procehsion shall be fined _____ for the use of fund. The expenses of the Festival shall be paid by every member his share, till the Lodge is furnished with all its Decorations - But afterwards shall be defrayed out of the General Fund.

28th

No expelled member to be admitted in any lodge -

If any member shall so far misbehave to be Expelled this lodge; an account there of made in the Minutes shall be forthwith sent to the constitutor of this lodge, or the grand council (if any established) who shall givt notice there of to all regular constituted lodges of Perfection, and such expelled member shall never be permitted to enter this or any other lodges, on the same Establishment, nor even as a Visitor, nor never permitted to join in a procehsion.

Lastly

In case the constitutor or founder should depart this continent, and no council of Princes etc. Established the Body of this lodge shall have Power within themselves to Elect their Master every year by a Majority, and make such further by laws, as shall be found most Beneficial, for said Lodge. Amen.

Finis

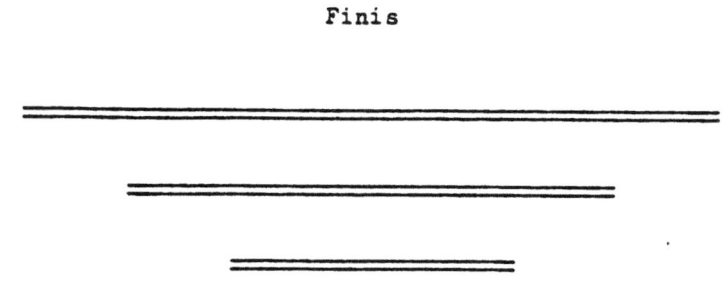

For the government of all regular Lodges of Perfection, as transmitted from the Royal Council of the Sublime Princes of the Royal Secret at Berlin, and observed by all lodges of Perfection, To our Most Respectable and Thrice Puihsant Brother Stephen Morin, Gr^d. $Insp^r$. of all Lodges etc. in the New World, and to his Lawful Deputies. Viz^t.

Artcles 1st

No lodge of Gr^d. El^t. $Perf^t$. and Sublime M^{ns}., can proceed to any Masonic work, either by election or reception, unlehs it is furnished with a constitution from a Prince Sublime of the Royal Secret and Gr^d. Inspector of the order or his Deputy, Duly Signed and Sealed, and in default of such a constitution and power it shall be reputed irregular and all the work declared null and void.

2^d

No lodge of Gr^d. El^t. $Perf^t$. and Sublime M^{ns}. can carry on any correspondence with any other G. E. P M G S. Lodge, except those which shall be sent by the Secretary general of the Gr^d. Council, to the Gr^d. $Insp^r$. or his deputy, and communicated by them. -

3d

When a lodge of G. E. P. M & Sub^me shall have any knowledge or discover a lodge of G. E. P. M & S. which shall not be comprehended in the Lyst's delivered by the Gr^d. Insp^r. or his Dep^ty it is indispensably necehsary to give the most early notice thereof with all the particulars pohsible relative thereto, to the Gr^d. Inspect^r or his Dep^ty in order to communicate the same to the Gr^d. Council.

4th

If any bretheren should irregular meet in order to initiate any one into these degrees, they shall be admonished and advised to desist therefrom; and no member of a regular lodge shall own help or visit them in any manner whatsoever, under such penalties as the particular Private Laws of the Gr^d. E. P. & S. M^n's Lodge shall provide. -

5th

If a Regular lodge of G. E. P. & S. M. on account of any misdemeaners shall exclude any of its members, they shall immediatly give advice thereof to the Gr^d. Insp^r. or his Dep^ty, in order, that he may transmit the same to all regular lodges, and warn them of the matter, and also communicate the same to the G^d. Council. - If a Royal Lodge should have infringed the laws that have been imposed by the solemn Engagements of our secret constitutions, and should refuse to submit and beg pardon in the most submihsive manner, by a petition Sign'd by all members thereof, confehsing their faults, and shall give sufficient proof that they have ceased their works, untill it pleases the Gr^d. Council of the Sublime princes to releive their Interdiction, and suffer them to enter again in favor and obtain forgivenehs; such Royal lodge shall incur the same penalties as mentioned in the preceeding articles - The Sovereign Gr^d. Architect of the universe (who always presides at our work) support and maintain us in uprightnehs and Equity

6th

thing new relative to these degrees or the order in general, must immediatly give notice thereof to the Grand Insp^r. or his Deputy -

7th

These present Statutes and regulations, must be read to each Brother when he arrives to the degree of Knight of the Royal Arch, when he must promise to follow them exactly, and also acknowledge at all times the Kn^{ts} of the East, Princes of Jerusalem, Kn^{ts} of East & West, Kn^{ts} of the white Eagle and Rose crohs, Patriarchs of the Royal axe, the Gr^d. pontif chiefs of the Masonic key, Knights and Princes adepts, Kn^{ts} of white and black Eagle, and the Sublime Sovereign princes of the Royal Secret & with the Gr^d. Insp^r. and his Deputies for their worthy chiefs - They must promise to pay respect to and obey their councils in what shall be perscribed by them; and must also promise to improve their Zeal fervor and constancy for the order, that they may one day arrive to the degree of Gr^d El^t. Perf^t. and Sub^{me} M^n, in short to bear submihsion and all obedience to the Statutes and regulations that shall now or hereafter be made by Princes Sovereign chiefs of the Masonic order, and shall render them all the Honors due to them in such form as shall be perscribed to them. And also sign the submihsion in Form to render the same more obligatory -

8th

All the Lodges of Gr^d. El^t. perf^t M & Sub^{me} ought to be composed of 9 gr^d. officers, and a number of fixed brethren not Exceeding 27 in all. (See the draft)

1st The thrice puihsant in the East representing Solomon, on his right hand a brother representing Hiram king of Tyre, in the absence of the gr^d. Inspector or his deputy - - - - - N° 1 -

2^d On the left hand of the Th^r puihs^t. is the grand keeper of the Seals representing <u>Galaad</u> the son of <u>Sophonia</u>, Chief of the Levites - N° 4 .

3^d Before the Table of shewn bread, is the grand Treasurer, representing <u>Guibelum</u>, Solomons confidant and his gr^d. Treasurer - N° 5 .

4th Near the Table of prefumes must be the grand Orator, representing Abdemon who was the brother that Explained several Enigmas which Solomon proposed to him, and also in the fullest manner the charakters on the broken pieces of the columns that were found in the antient Ruins of Enoch on Mount Acheldama - N°. 7.

5th In the South before the Table of perfumes is placed the gr^d. Secretary, representing Joabert, a favorite of the 2 allies - N°. 6.

6th In the North, sits the gr^d. M^r. of Ceremonies, who represents Stolkin, a zealous M^r. & favorite of Solomon - - - - N°. 8.

7th In the West is the Senr. Gr^d. Warden representing Adoniram the son of Abda, Prince Harodim of Libanon. before the death of H. Abif he had the inspection of the workmen in Libanus and was the first of the 7 Secret Masters - - - - - N°. 2.

8th On the left of the Senior Warden, is the Junr. Warden representing Mohabon, the most zealous Master of his time, and a great friend of Hiram Abif - - - - - - - - - - - - - - N°. 3.

9th A little behind the Warden in the center of the west is the captain of the guards, who represents Benaja or Zerbal, who acted as such when the alliance was found by the 2 kings - N°. 9.

There ought to be 2 Tilers, to Tile without and within

9th

A Royal lodge of Perfection must proceed once in every year, to the Election of a gr^d. M^r and new Gr^d officers, if no gr^d. Inspector or his dep^{ty}. is on the spot and no member can be Elected gr^d. M^r. unlehs he is at least a prince of Jerusalem. The proper day for said Election ought to be on the 3^d day of the 6th month called adar, equal to the 21st February, a memorable day of the year 2995, when the precious Treasure of the antient Masters was found by the 3 Zealous Masters in the antient Ruins of our antient Patriarch - when the M^r and officers are chosen they shall take an Ob^n Either before the gr^d. Insp^r., his Dep^{ty}. or the members of the body, to fill their offices with Zeal fervor and constancy

10th

All party affairs is Exprehsely forbid at an Election of officers, on the penalty of being excluded the lodge, and the name of such brother erazed out of the List.

11th

All the bretheren shall be adorned in lodge, according to their degrees, and such brother who shall enter the Lodge without his ornaments, or the Ensigns of a Superior degree, shall be deprived of his vote for that night, and shall pay to the Treasurer such sum, as the Lodge shall inflict.

12th

If a gr^d. Insp^r. or his dep^{ty}. shall think proper to visit in any part of the two Hemispheres, Either a gr^d. Council, council, or a lodge of Perfection, being furnished with an authentic patent, and presents himself at the door, of such gr^d. Council etc. he shall be received with all the Honors that are due to him, and shall enjoy all the priviledges and prerogatives etc. etc. etc. that is to say - when he visits a lodge of Perfection, or any other whatsoever; the most powerful Gr^d. M^r. shall send 5 bretheren, two of which are to be officers, & Introduce him with all the honors due to him.

13th

The Royal lodges of Perfection must be kept on such days and hours as shall be appointed, of w^h. the bretheren of that lodge shall have timely Notice from the Secretary in reasonable time. And in case any of the bretheren should be prevented giving their attendance by businehs of Consequence, they shall send notice there of to the gr^d. Secretary with the cause of their detention, the morning preceeding the lodge at farthest, under such penalties as the T: P: M^r. and the lodge shall think proper.

14th

All lodges of Perfection must visit each other by Deputation or Correspondence, as often as pohsible, as they ought reciprocally to procure each other all the light they can acquire.

Any brother going to travel, on his request the gr^d. Secretary shall deliver him a Certificate, which must be signed by the Th: Puihs^t. Master, the wardens, and the gr^d. Keeper of the Seals who shall affix the Seal of the lodge there to, and the gr^d. Secretary is to countersign it. And the brother who receives the same must put his name in the margin (Ne varictur)

16th

The G: E: P M & S may pahs bretheren found worthy, and have been dignified in a blue Lodge, into all degrees preceeding perfection vizt. Sec^t M^r., Perf^t M^r, Initmate Secretary, Prev^t. & Judge, Intend^t of the buildings, Elected of 9, Kn^ts. El^d of 15, Illus^s. Kn^ts., Gr^d. M^r. Arch^t., and Knight of the R---- Arch - The Thr: Puihs^t may give one, two or 3 degrees at a time, if necehsity requires it, and the broth^r by his zeal is deserving of it. And the last degree of perfection when the Cand^te is capable and fit to receive it.

17th

Besides the feasts of 24th of June, & 27th December the G. E. P. M & S^mes are to celebrate every year the Dedication of the Temple of the Gr^d. Arch^t. of the universe, on the 5th of October - The Senr Prince and highest in degree, shall that day preside, and the 2 next Masons of the high degrees, shall officiate as wardens, with the rest of the officers as appointed by the President.

18th

A brother being Initiated in the 4th degree of the Body of the Lodge of Gr^d. E^t etc. shall give notice thereof to the Founder, or Gr^d. Insp^r. or his Dep^ty. with his name and occupation that it may be communicated to the Gr^d. council.

19th

All motions whatever to be made must be by a member who is in the 14th degree, and when made the younger Bretheren may give their sentiments thereon.- And when a Cand^te shall be proposed in lodge, it must appear that he has an affection for his Religion and State;

to be a man of truth probity & discretion, who has given proofs of his zeal, fervor and constnacy for the Craft of the first 3 degrees, and his bretheren.

20th

The gr^d. wardens after having received Notice from the Thr: Puihs^t, that he intends to call a Lodge, are to give their attendance and to ahsist him; and contribute all in their power towards the welfare of the Lodge; and upon these occasions the Gr^d. M^r. of Ceremonies shall have previous notice to prepare the said Lodge.

21st

The gr^d. Keeper of the Seals, is to have pohsehsion of the archives of the lodge, to prepare for any reception, to have all things in order; he is to put the Seals to all Certificates, or other papers signed by the officers of the Lodge

22d

The gr^d. orator, is to deliver orations at every reception, and at times discourses on the Excellence of the order; he is to Instruct new made brothers, and explain the mysteries to them, exhort them to continue their Zeal fervor and constancy, in order that one day they may arrive to be a gr^d. E^t. P M & Sub^{me}. If he observes any Indiscretion in the bretheren, or knows of any disputes, he is to acquaint the lodge there of, that matters may be reconciled and made easy.

23d

The gr^d. Treasurer must have in keeping all the fund of Charity arizing from receptions &, he must keep a fair book of accounts to be ready at all times for Inspection of the Lodge. And as charity is an Indispensable duty among Masons, the bretheren are to add to that fund by voluntary Contributions according to their Circumstances and abilities.

24th

The gr^d. Secretary ought to keep a register of all the transactions, fairly written in a book to be ready for the inspection of the lodge etc. The gr^d. Insp^r. or his deputy he must ihsue notices according to the Th. Puihs^{ts} orders in time, that they may with Certainty be delivered; he must also make out what is requisite to transmit from the lodge, Either to the gr^d. Council, gr^d. Inspect^r or his deputy, as well as to foreign parts. He is to be constant in his attendance, and to have the care of the archives relative to his office.

25th

The gr^d. M^r. of Ceremonies, must be early at the Temple, to prepare every matter so, that the work be not retarded. He is always to be one of the Examiners of visitors, and he is to introduce them according to their dignities, and to be gr^d. preparer, therefore the Brother elected for that office ought to very expert in all the degrees, so as to be a credit to the Lodge.

26th

The Captain of the guards is to superintend the Tilers, as it is his duty to see the lodge well secured; he is to preceed all visitors, with his hatt on, and his sword in his hand, Except when the visitor is a Kn^t. or a Prince Mason, when he is to be uncovered. He is to advize the Thr: Puihs^t. of any visitors desiring admittance, and to attend at the Examination - He is also to preceed new made Brothers in the ceremonies of Initiation - and when the Captn. of the guards announces a Prince visitor, he is to be received with the following Honors vizt. All the bretheren are to form an arch with their swords, when the grand M^r. of Ceremonies conducts the prince visitor under the arch till he arrives at the foot of the Throne; after which, the T: P. conducts him to the Seat of eminence -

27th

If at any time a lodge of perfection should deserve to be dihsolved or interdicted for any time; the officers are indispensably obliged to deposit into the hands of the gr^d. Council, if there is any, and in default thereof to the grand inspector or his Dep^{ty}. Their constitution, Statutes Laws and regulations, with all their papers etc. in order that the whole may be deposited at the fountain head, and remain there until that lodge is admitted to grace again.- And the members of such lodge remaining obstinate to the decrees of said gr^d. council etc., their names degrees & civil qualities shall be transmitted in writing to all the corners of the earth, in order that they may incur the scorn of all Masons. - We pray the great architect of the universe to prevent such an event, and inspire us in the choice of good brothers, for the perfection of the order.

28th

If any member of a lodge which has been dihsolved by the gr^d. Council etc. shall in a Petition to said gr^d. Council etc. prove that he was innocent in the matter, he sahll be received to grace and joined to any other Lodge, that shall be constituted in its room.

29th

No transactions done in the lodges, ought on any account whatsoever to be revealed when out of the same, to any but members of that lodge, under such penalty, as the lodge shall think proper to inflict.

30th

No visitor shall be admitted till the lodge is open'd, and first well examined, and repeat the Ob^n. Except any member can vouch that he has seen the visiting Brother in a regular constituted lodge of that Degree.

31st

Every lodge may receive 2 Tilers; their lives ought to be irreproachable and known, and their Decorations is to be defrayed at the expences of the lodge; thea are to carry the attribute to the 3^d button hole of their coats.

32d

The Knights and princes Masons being the gr^d. lights of the lodge; any complaints against any of the members being reduced into writing; and shall be delivered them the next lodge night, which they

shall hear and determine and in case any party shall think himself
agrieved by such determination, he shall have liberty to appeal
to the gr^d. Council if any established, or to the gr^d. Insp^r. or
his deputy, whose determination shall be final and Decisive. -

33^d

Secrecy in all our mysteries, being one of the most indispensable
obligations, The T: P. gr^d. M^r. shall before the closing of every
lodge recommend that duty to the bretheren, according to the usual
manner and form. -

34th

If a brother should happen to be sick, any member knowing it, shall
give the earliest advice there of to the T: P. in order that he may
receive ahsistance if he should want it; and a brother appointed by
the name of Hospitable brother is to have the care of him to see
him properly attended.

35th

If any member should die, all the bretheren are obliged to attend
his funeral in the usual manner. -

36th

If any brother or worthy member should be under misfortunes, it is
the duty of every Individual in the lodge to endeavour to soften
them. -

37th

If the T: P: should not be present in the lodge, an hour after the
stated time of meeting, and there should be 5 bretheren present,
the Senior officer shall immediatly fill the Throne and proceed
with regularity to the businehs of the night, provided there is
no gr^d. Insp^r. or his dep^{ty}. present, in which case the gr^d. Insp^r.
or his dep^{ty} shall be desired to fill the Throne. -

38th

To establish regularity in the lodges of G. E. P M & Sub^{mes}, the
gr^d. Insp^r. or his dep^{ty} must yearly be furnished with a lyst of

the members of the lodges, their different degrees, civil qualities etc. that he may lay them in order before the gr^d. council and transmit copies to all regular lodges; the said lodges shall also acquaint the gr^d. Insp^r. or his dep^{ty}., of any new matter w^h shall be communicated to the said lodge - .

39th

If the members of such a Lodge think it necehsary to make any alterations' or additions to the present constitution and regulations, they shall not do it but by motion in writing previously the lodge next before the annual Feast, and when the members have seriously considered the matter in question (which must not be contrary to the established Statutes) the writing shall be communicated to the gr^d. council of the princes, and if they approve of it, they shall send it to the gr^d. Inspector or his deputy, who shall decide the matter proposed without altering any thing of our antient customs Ob^s or Ceremonies, or deminishing the strength of the present constitution, Statutes and regulations, under the penalty of Interdiction. -

Thus all lodges of the Grand Elect perfect Master, and Sublime, shall direct and govern themselves regularly Established under our protection in the future in all places of the Earth, where the order shall be in this manner established, and shall be always directed by the gr^d. Insp^r. or his Deputy or prince of Masons, either in particular or in gr^d. council if any Established, and to be able to attain it, and to give the first form and existance.

We have resolved to name and Create Inspect^{rs}. and deputies, to travel by sea and by land, to notihse & observe the regulations in all the lodges regular constituted; copies of which laws and regulations, shall be delivered by our said commihsaries, Inspectors and Deputies with authentic Titles and powers in form, to be known and authorized in their function. -

In this manner our chiefs and protectors worthy of the Royal Art, have decreed when ahsembled lawfully in their true Sciences with full power, they being representatives for the sovereign of Sovereigns.

Done at the great East of Berlin & Paris in a Holy and secret place under the C C, near the B. B. the 25th of the 7th month of the year 7762, and transmitted to the most Respble and most Excellent Brother Stephen Morin, Grand Inspector of all Lodges etc. regularly constituted in the new world.

Finis -

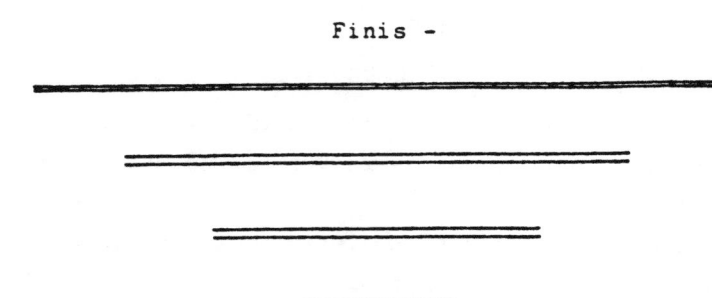

Further Instructions for the regulating lodges of Perfection

1st

No Lodge of perfection can proceed to any Masonic work either by election or reception, unlehs it is furnished with a constitution from a Brother at least a Knt. of the Sun, being a grd. or Depty. Inspector of all the orders duly Executed without which it shall be Irregular, and their works null and void.

2dly

All matters of Correspondence shall be directed to the grd Inspr. of the place, where such is to be sent, and in default of such, to his Depty., which will be communicated to the Respble lodges and chapters.

3dly

On a discovery of an Illicit lodge, notice shall be given to every Lodge of the higher order, with a discription of the persons, appearance, occupation etc. and when any matter shall be discovered that may concern the Superior degrees, notice shall be sent to the grd. Inspr. or his Deputy. -

4thly

These laws shall be read to each brother when he attains the degree of perfection; who must promihs solemnly to follow at all times these precepts; and acknowledge the Kn[ts] of the East, Princes of Jerusalem, Kn[ts]. of E[t] & W[t]. Kn[ts]. of the Sun, Kn[ts]. of K---h, and Pr[es] of the R. Secret. for their worthy chiefs, to bear them respect and obey them in all that shall be perscribed by those respectable valiant chiefs, to improve their Zeal fervor and constancy for the order in general - To submit to all the Statutes made, or to be made by them; and shall render them y[e]. Honors that are due to them in such a manner as shall be perscribed to them. And sign a submehsion in writing -

5thly

The lodges of G. E. P. M & Sub[me] (id est) lodges of perfection must be composed of 9 officers, and the members thereof never Exceed 27 bretheren, M[r]. & officers included on the spot, except any should remove, in which case, any vacancy may be filled up - any one of the 5 officers of a blue, or symbolical lodge of the 3 first degrees, can be brought to these degrees, but no M[r]. Mason, unlehs he is an officer of a regular blue Lodge or has been an officer in such lodge - Neither can a lodge of these higher degrees be constituted within the distance of 25 leagues of one already constituted. Which said lodges are to correspond with the grand or Dep[ty]. Insp[r]. at least once a years, and give an account of their works, with the nanes of the persons that belong to them, and their dignities - and this can not be disposed with - The 9 officers represent as follows viz[t].

1st A mighty powerful gr[d]. M[r]. represents Solomon, who must be at least a Kn[t] of the Sun - In the East under a canopy.

2[d] The Sen[r]. gr[d]. Warden represt[s] Adoniram the son of Abda - pr[e]. of Jerusalem - In the West - .

3[d] The Jun[r]. gr[d]. Warden - represt[s]. Mohabon, a prince of Jerusalem at the left of the Sen[r]. gr[d] Warden.

4th The gr[d]. Keeper of the Seals represt[s] Galaad, a pr[e]. of Jerusalem at the left side of Solomon - is also gr[d]. orator -

5th   The gr^d. Treasurer - <u>Guibelum</u> - a pr^ce of Jerusalem

6th   The gr^d. Secretary - <u>Ioabert</u> - - pr^ce of Jerusalem

7th   The gr^d. Orator   - <u>Abdemon</u> - - pr^ce of Jerusalem

8th   gr^d. M^r. of Ceremonies - <u>Stolkin</u> - - - - D^o -

9th   Cap^tn of the guards - <u>Zerbal</u> - - - - - - D^o.

NB, at the Right hand of Solomon, under a canopy sits King Hiram of Tyre - Every officer to be decorated properly.

6th

There must be every year an election of officers in full Council of princes, which must be on the 3^d day of the 6th month, the memorable day of the year 2995, as set forth in the 13th degree. There must be no Ballotting, but the votes must be taken openly and free. The officers then chosen must take an Ob^n. to fill their offices to the best of their power, with honor to the craft, and then are lead to the lodge and Installed by the gr^d. Insp^r. or his Deputy.

7th

Every brother must appear in any lodge with his badge of his order, under such fine as the lodge he belongs to may inflict.

Lastly

Besides the Holy days of 24th June & 27th of December the Gr^d. Elected, perf^t and Sub^me must Celebrate every year the Dedication of the 1st Temple, on the 5th of October.

Finis

Secret Master - 4th Degree.

The lodge of Secret M^r ought to be hung with black and strewed with Tears -

The M^r represents Solomon, is stiled Thrice puihsant, who comes to the Temple to appoint 7 skilful masters to represent, and in the Room of Hiram Abif.

There is only one warden, who is called Adoniram. He had the inspection & management of the labourers and workmanship at Mount Libanus - and after the death of H. A. he was the first of the 7 Secret Masters to represent him

Preparatory, to open the Lodge.

Solomon holds a Scepter in his hand, in a black Cloack lined with Ermin, is placed in the East, a Triangular table before him, on which is a crown of Laurel and olive branches interwoven - He wears no apron.

Adoniram in the West, acts as Inspector.

No use is made of any hammer or mallet in this degree, the works of the Temple being suspended by the mournful fate of H. A.

Solomon is decorated with a broad blue ribbon from the right shoulder to the left hip, a Triangle suspended thereto. -

Adoniram, must be decorated with a broad white ribbon bordered with black like a collar, an Ivory Key suspended thereto, with the letter Z in the wart. -

All the bretheren are to be decorated as Adoniram, with aprons and gloves, black strings to the aprons. The white is the candour and innocense of the masters, and the black denotes the mourning of their deceased chief - The flap of the apron blue and a fixed Eye painted or Embroidered thereon. -

The lodge should be Illuminated with 81 lights in 9 Branches, but is generally dispensed with, and use 3 branches of 3 each.

To open the Lodge.

Q. Brother Adoniram, are you a Secret M^r.?

A. Thr: Puihs^t, I have pahsed from the Square to the Compas, I have seen the Tomb of our Resp^{ble} M^r. H. A. and have shed my tears thereat, with my bretheren, and the wisest and most powerful King.

Q. What is it o'clock?

A. The Morning Star has dispelled the shades of night, and the great light begins to gladden our lodge.

Then Solomon says: as the morning is the forerunner of this great light which begins to shine, and as we are all Secret Masters, 'T is time to begin our work. therefore this Lodge is open - on which the Th: P. and all the bretheren shall strike 7 times with their hands, and then the T. P. makes the Sign of Silence by putting the 2 first fingers of his right hand on his lips, w^h. is answer'd by Adoniram and all the bretheren with 2 fingers of their left hand, and so alternatly this being done, all the bretheren salute the T. P. by laying their right hands on their hearts, then salute the Insp^r. and each other.

Form of a Reception

The cand^{te} or blue M^r. must be well recommended & Examined in his 3 first degrees by an expert brother, previous to his Introduction, and when found qualified the Examiner knocks 7 on the door, Enters and reports to Adoniram that a blue M^r desires the degree of Secret M^r., which he merits by his knowledge and abilities in Masonry w^h. Adoniram reports to the T: P: and that he will be answerable for his zeal Fervor and constancy. Then the T:P: orders the cand^{te} to be introduced and Adoniram instructs him to make the 3 first signs to the T: P: that of Ent^d appr^{tice}: F. Cr^t. & M^r. Then Adoniram conducts him to the altar befcre which he kneels on his right knee, his head a little inclined, as tho' his Eyes were dazzled by the brightnehs of the great light with his right hand forming a Square on his forehead, when the T: P: addrehses him as follows vizt. You have as yet my brother only seen the thick veil, which conceiled the Holy of Holy's of the Temple; your fidelity zeal and constancy have procured you favor, I intend you. I will show you our Treasure and deposits of this sacred place, come to me as a M^r. Mason, and contract your new Ob^n - "I A, B, do in the presence of the great architect of the universe, and of this Resp^{ble} Lodge of Secret M$^{r's}$ sincerely promise and swear, that I will not reveal or make known to any person whatever below this degree the least part of it.

"I do also promise never to reveal any of the Laws transactions or anything done in this lodge or any other lodge, when out of it, unlehs to a known brother, but strictly conform myself to all the laws, rules and regulations, which shall now or hereafter be communicated to me.

"I do further promise a due obedience to the gr^d. Insp^r. or his dep^{ty}., as they are the Supreme heads of all Masonry.

"I also promise an entire obedience to the precepts & commands of the lodge of G: E. P & Sub^{me} and submit to them in every matter, they shall dictate.

"I further promise never to be aiding, consenting or ahsisting in raising any body in this degree, but in this Royal lodge, nor to hold conversation on the craft with any person, but such as shall convince me that he has been regular made - all this I promise under the penalties of my former Ob^{ns}, and I pray the great Arch^t of the universe to strengthen me in uprightnehs Justice and Truth. Then the T: P: decends a step and puts the crown of Laurel and olive on his head, then being raised the T:P: addrehses him thus: My dear brother, I receive you Secret Master and give you rank among the Levites, I place this crown on your head in which the Laurel is an emblem of the victory w^h you ought to gain over your pahsions; the olive, of that peace and unanimity w^h. should ever subsist amongst bretheren; it will be your own fault if you do not obtain the favor, w^h God alone can bestow, of arriving in time at the sacred place, where you may contemplate wrapt in divine joy and Extasy, <u>The Pillar of Beauty</u> -

I decorate you with this Ivory Key, suspended by a white ribbon border'd with black, as an emblem of y^r fidelity Innocence & discretion; the white apron and gloves bound with black denotes the candour of the Secr^t. Mast^{rs}, into whose numbers your merit has gain'd you admihsion. The black denotes your grieve for the lohs of H. A. - My dear brother, by the rank you now have among the Levites, in quality of Sec^t. M^r., you are become the faithful guardian of the Sanctum Sanct^m, and one of the 7 to replace the lohs of our dear M^r. H. A. to conduct the works, which we are to raise to the divinity. I must earnestly recommend to you the necehsary watchfulnehs over your workmen, which the Eye display'd on your apron is an Emblem.

Your pahsword, is <u>Zizon</u>, a hebrew word signifying <u>Balustrade</u>. Your Sign is, that of Silence, by putting the two first fingers of each hand alternatly on your lips; but you must observe to answer with the opposite hand to that with w^h. the Sign is made. Your Token is to gripe each others hand with masters gripe, and each others elbow with the left hand, and Ballance horisontally 7 times each other, crohsing your legs during Ballancing. The Sacred words are <u>Job</u>, <u>Adonai</u>, & <u>Jua</u>, these are the names by which it pleased God to distinguish himself, when he appear'd first to <u>Moses</u> on Mount <u>Sinai</u>, the Initials of which you see on the Triangle in the draft.

There is moreover my brother a gr^d. word which belongs to the Sec^t. M^r., the word which <u>Moses</u> himself engraved on a golden Triangle plate in hebrew charakters, the 3^d time he spoke to <u>God</u> on s^d mount. This sacred and mysterious word, my brother you must wait the will of <u>God</u> to discover it to you; for he forbad <u>Moses</u> ever to pronounce it; which Alec, <u>Aaron</u> & Solomon had afterwards only the power of spelling it by single letters, with Holy awe and reverence.

From this sacred word proceeds the 9 names by which <u>God</u> pleased to distinguish himself, and every one of these 9 names have a refference to 8 attributes of the Divinity by 9 vowels, joyn'd together they form the number of 72, and these same names contain 888 letters. Cabalistically comprehended in the 9 vowels before mentioned - these 9 names are "<u>Eloah</u>, <u>Adonaii</u>, <u>Jehevah</u>, <u>Javhe</u>, <u>Job</u>, <u>Aloin</u>, <u>Achab</u>, <u>Osem</u> and <u>Jesoiis</u>. -

Having thus initiated you in our mysteries my brother, go and give the pahsword, the Sign and Token and word to all the bretheren and having so done, come and take your seat, and attend to our Lecture.

The Secret Masters Lecture

Q. Are you a Secret Master?

A. I am, and glory int.

Q. How were you received?

A. I pahsed from the square to the compahs.

Q. Where was you made a Sec^t. Master?

A. Under the Laurel and olive.

Q. In what place were you received?

A. In the Sanct^m Sanctorum.

Q. Who made you Secret M^r.?

A. Solomon, ahsisted by the Noble Adoniram, Insp^r. of the works of the Temple.

Q. What did you perceive on entering the S^m S^{rum} ?

A. Evident marks of the Divine Presence.

Q. Did you perceive any particularly?

A. I perceived the great Circle, the Triangle in the Middle & its contents, together with the Blazing Star in the Center of all, which dazzling my Eyes, struck me with Holy awe and reverence.

Q. What did the charakters in the Triangle seem to Signifie?

A. Things beyond the reach of dimsighted mortals, and which I dare not name.

Q. We are now in Lodge, and dispence with the restraint.

A. I saw the great light, but comprehended it not.

Q. What did you perceive in the middle thereof?

A. The Ineffable name of the great arch^t of the universe. From him <u>Moses</u> alone had learned the first pronounciation of it, which from thence forward he forbad others to use, in so much that the true pronunciation is now lost; and we are even uncertain of the number of Syllables it contains, but I hope one day to arrive at the knowledge of that Ineffable word.

Q. What did you perceive more?

A. Nine order words in Hebraic charakters.

Q. Where were they placed?

A. In the 9 Luminous beams, which shot forth from the Flaming Triangle.

Q. What is the Signification of these 9 names?

A. These are the 9 names whereby <u>God</u> distinguished himself when he spoke to <u>Moses</u> on Mount Sinai, giving him hope that one day his true name should be revealed to his desendents.

Q. Give me the 9 names and their signification?

A. Eloah, Adonaii, Ichevah, Javhe, Job, aloin, achab, osem & Jesoiis. Each of these names comprehend 8 attributes of the Divinity, which in all composed of 888 letters forming 72 names, which are accepted as the name of the Divinity, according to the alphabet of the Angels and the cabalistical Tree.

Q. What means the Circle surrounding the Triangle?

A. It represents the immensity of the power of God, which hath neither beginning nur Ending.

Q. What does the Blazing Star represent?

A. It is a luminous guide to our contemplation of the Divinity.

Q. What does the Let G, in the center imply?

A. Glory, Grandeur & Gomes.

Q. What do you mean by these 3 names?

A. By glory, I mean God, who is necehsarily most glorious by grandeur, I mean the man, who by the nearest approaches to perfection becomes the greatest - By Gomes, I mean that word the first pronounced by our common Father, starting from sleep & signifying his gratitude to <u>God</u> for his benign Exertion of almighty power, in forming his fair ahsociate <u>Eve</u>. Gomes, thanks

Q. What signifies the 5 points of the Blazing Star?

A. The 5 orders of architecture, which were used at the construction and Decoration of Solomons Temple, they are also emblems of the 5 senses, which are absolutely requisite to the perfection of all rational beings.

Q. What more did you see in the S^m S^rum ?

A. The ark of alliance, the Golden candle stick with 7 branches and the Table with Shew bread.

Q. Where was the ark of alliance placed?

A. In the middle of the S. S^rum under the Blazing Star.

Q. What doth the ark under the blazing Star allude to?

A. As the ark was the Emblem of alliance, which <u>God</u> had made with his people and was covered by the wings of Cherubims, in the like manner is the Circle which inloses the Triangle in the blazing Star, Emblematically the new alliance of the bretheren masons.

Q. What was the form of the ark of alliance?

A. An oblong Square.

Q. Of what was it made?

A. Of Shettim or Cedar wood, covered without and lined within with gold, Topt with a Crown of gold, and supported by 2 golden cherubims.

Q. What was the cover of the Ark Called?

A. The propitiary, or place that served to appease Gods anger.

Q. What did the Ark contain?

A. The Testimony, w^h <u>God</u> gave to <u>Moses</u>, and the 2 Tables of the <u>Law</u>.

Q. What did the 2 Tables contain, and what were they made of?

A. They were made of white Marble, and contained the Ten commandments in Hebrew, as dictated by God to Moses, and thus divided: the 4 first respecting our duty to God, on the 1st Table, the 6 last on the 2^d Table, respecting our duty to man.

Q. Of what use was the Table you saw in the S. S^rum ?

A. To place the 12 loaves of the Shew bread on, which by the command of God were always to be kept in his presence.

Q. Of what were they made?

A. Of the finest flower.

Q. How placed?

A. Six on the right, and six on the left, forming to heaps.

Q. What did they put above?

A. The best and purest Incence.

Q. Why?

A. As a memorial of the oblations to God.

Q. What was the Hebrew name of the S^m S^{rum} ?

A. <u>Dabir</u>.

Q. What does it mean?

A. Speech.

Q. Why was it so called?

A. because there the divinity resided, and from then deliver'd his oracles.

Q. Who constructed the Ark?

A. When Moses had received orders from God to construct the Ark, he made choice of Bezeleel the son of Uri of the Tribe of Juda, and of <u>Mary</u>, sister to Moses; he likewise choose Aholia son of Ahisamach of the Tribe of <u>Dan</u>, two able workmen, for that purpose, and on this occasion the people of Israel, shewed so much regard ardor and Zeal, and so chearfully offered up their labor & wealth, that Moses by the advice of those who the direction of the work, was obliged by Sound of Trumpet to make it known, that he had no further occasion for their generous ahsistance - the work was then began according to the plan which was revealed to Moses, who likewise had particular directions as to the number of the vehsels which were to be lodged in the Tabernacle for the use of the sacrifies.

Q. how comes the candlestick to be confined to 7 branches?

A. As the number 7 represents the 7 planets.

Q. What was the top of each of the 7 branches?

A. There was a lamp, and each of them pointed East & West.

Q. of how many parts did this candlestick consist?

A. of 70. -

Q. What does this number of parts represent?

A. It is figurative of the 12 Signs of the Zodiac, through which the planets move.

Q. What does the fixt Eye, always drawn in our lodge represent?

A. One only light w^h dispells darknehs from us.

Q. How did they go up to the gallerys of the Temple?

A. By a Staircase in the form of a Screw, contrived in the north wall of the Temple, by which they ahsended by 3, 5 and 7 Steps, and was called a shell or cochell, on account of its screwlike shape.

Q. How many doors were there, to the S^m S^{rum} ?

A. Only one to the East, which was called Lara, and which was covered with a cloth of purple, hyacinth, gold and azure.

Q. What do these colours represent?

A. The four Elements.

Q. How old are you?

A. 3 times 27, accomplished 81.

Q. What is your pahsword?

A. Zizon, which signifies Balustrade.

End of the Lecture.

To close the Lodge of Secret Master.

Q. Brother Inspector, what o'clock is it?

A. The close of day.

Q. What remains to be done?

A. To practice virtue, shun vice, and remain in Silence.

Then the Thr. puihs^ت addrehses himself to the bretheren, and says: As nothing is left undone, but to practice virtue and shun vice, let us be silent, and let the will of the Lord be done, - 't is time to rest, - . Brother Inspector give notice to the Bretheren that I am going to close the lodge by the mysterious numbers. -

The brother Adoniram repeats the same to the bretheren; on which the T: P: Claps his hands 7 times, and then all the bretheren together - after which, the Th. P. makes the Sign of Silence, which is answered by the bretheren properly, and the Lodge is closed.

E n d

Perfect Master. 5th Degree.

The Perfect Masters lodge, should be hung with green and ornamented with 4 white columns, Erected at equal distance on each side, and must be Illuminated by 16 lights, at each angle of the 4 Cardinal points

In the East a Red Canopy, a table before it covered with black & strewed with Tears.

Preparations for the opening of the Lodge.

1st - The Thrice Resp^ble M^r represents the Noble Adoniram the son of Abda, of the Tribe of Dan, who conducted the works of the Temple before the arrival of H. A. at Jerusalem - after w^h he was sent to Mount Libanus, to inspect the works there carried on for the use of the Temple. He was recalled on the death of H. A. and had the honor of being the first of the 7 substituted in his stead. He is decorated with the ornaments of the perfection and those of Prince of Jerusalem. He sits in Solomons Chair under a canopy holding a mallet.

2d - There is only one Warden who represents Stolkin; he is decorated with the Jewels of perfection etc. and sits in the West, holding a Mallet, and does the duty of an Inspector.

3d - The Introducing Brother represents Zerbal or Banaia, captain of the Kings Guard. He must wear a green Ribbon round his neck in the form of a collar, to which is to hang a compahs, whose points form an angle of 45 degrees, which is the Jewel of this degree. His apron white lined with green, and always carries a naked sword.

4th - All the bretheren, are to be decorated in the same manner, as the Introducing brother, the same collar & Jewel & apron, the flap down, the Jewel embroider'd there on, and on the area of the apron must be painted or Embroider'd 4 Circles, and in the center of the innerone a Square Stone with the letter I there on.

To open the Lodge.

Q. Broth:r Insp:r are we Tiled, and all perf:t Masters?

A. Thr: Resp:ble Master; the lodge is Tiled, and we are all perf:t Masters.

Q. If so, give notice to the bretheren, that am going to open the Lodge of perf:t Master.

A. Resp:ble bretheren, the Th: Resp:ble M:r gives you notice that he is going to open the lodge of perf:t M:r. To order my bretheren. Then first the resp:ble M:r. knocks 4 times, 2:dly the broth:r Insp:r knock 4, 3:dly a brother in the south 4, and then a brother in the North 4.

Then the Thr: Resp:ble M:r and all the bretheren make the Sign of admiration: their eyes up to Heaven, their arms Extended, and then look down, Crohsing their arms on their bellies, and then all cry out <u>Consumatum est</u>

Q. Broth:r Stolkin what's the clock?

A. T: Resp: it is 4.

Q. as it is 4 o'clock, 't is time for the workmen to begin their labour. Give notice to the bretheren that the lodge of perf:t M:r is open.

Directions for the reception of a Cand:te

The Cand:te being in the preparing room, decorated with the Regalia of Sec:t M:r in readinehs - When the lodge is opened, the Introducing brother moves from his seat in Solemn Silence, & striking the Insp:r 4 times on his right shoulder, thus addrehses him: Ven:ble B:r Insp:r Brother N. N. a Secret M:r is in the antichamber and solicits the favor of being admitted to the degree of P:t M:r - The B:r Insp:r Informs the chair of this Request, on which the T.R.M:r asks the following questions:

Q. Is he deserving of this trust, will you ans:r for his Zeal fervor & const:cy ?

A. Th: Resp:ble I do. - on which the T. R. Mr. orders him to be introduced in the usual manner. Then the Insp^r orders the introducing brother to go and receive the cand^{te} who goes out, and asking him some questions in regard of his former degrees, he takes away his sword and every other offensive wapon, then throws a string of green silk about his neck, both ends of which he holds in his left hand, and a naked sword in his right, and thus leads him to the lodge door, on which he knocks 4 great strokes; the brother Insp^r first repeats the same, and then informs the chair, that somebody knocks as a perf^t M^r. The Th.R: orders the Insp^r to enquire who it is. The Br^r Insp^r orders the Tiler (who is within the door) to open the door cautiously, and enquire who knocks. The Tiler obeys, and is ans^d by brother Zerbal that Brother N. N: a Secret M^r is desirous of the Honor of being admitted into the degree of P^t M^r. The Tiler shuts the door and reports the cand^{tes} request to the Insp^r who communicates the same to the chair, on which T. R. M^r orders him to be introduced, when the lodge is opend and the cand^{te} is lead to the South side near the Tomb, having the Sign of the Secr^t M^r on him. The Th. R: M^r. seeing him thus arrayed and in this attitude and addrehses him thus:

Q. What do you require brother?

A. The favor of being Rec^d. Perf^t M^r. (being prompted).

Then the T. Resp^{ble} M^r. says Brother Insp^r. let this Brother Travel. then the broth^r Insp^r leads him by the string from the South pahsing by the West and thus 4 times round the Lodge, and at each angle he kneels, and does the same every time he pahses the T.R:M^r after which he is carried to the Tomb, and is oblig'd to walk crohsways by the ends of the columns, which are laid acrohs forming a St Andrews Crohs - then he comes before the altar with his right knee a little bent, having still the Sign of Sec^t M^r on him. The T. P: M^r after a little pause tells him to kneel, and lay his hand on the Bible when he contracts the foll^g. Ob^n

"I A.B. do promise in the presence of the great arch^t of the universe on this Holy Bible and before this Resp^{ble} Lodge Inviolably to keep all such secrets as I shall be entrusted with, & never communicate them either directly or indirectly to any person whatsoever, except in the presence of this lodge under any pretext, and never to converse about them with any unlehs brothers to be known such and those lawfully made in a regular constituted Lodge, and this on the penalty of being dishonor'd and suffering such punishments, as I voluntary imposed on myself in my former oblig^s. So may God keep me in righteousnehs & Equity. Amen, Amen, Amen."

After this the T. R: M^r. takes off from his neck the string saying, My dear brother, Thus I remove the fetters by which vice enslaved you; and by the virtue of the power which I received from the most powerful of Kings, I raise you to the degree of Perf^t Mast^r on condition that you will faithfully observe every thing perscribed by our Laws.

1st The sign by which you will yourself known a perf^t M^r is that of admiration; your arms extended, the palms of your hands open looking up to Heaven; then let fall your hands and crohs them on your belly as low as you can, and cast your eyes mournfull downwards.

2dly The Token is to advance with the Toes of the right foot reciprocally towards one another, he answers the motion in the same manner until the Toes of each other touch, then bend both knees that they also touch; w^h. is called point to point; then both put the right hands on the breast, draw them acrohs making a square by 2^d motion.

The Second Token is pretty much like the blue masters, with this addition that your left hand on each others back and prehs with the fingers as if you would make them enter 4 times; you say Mahabon, then enterlace the 4 fingers of your right hands, and raise both thumbs against each other forming a Triangle.

NB. Mahabon was intendant of Solomons household and a great friend of Hiram abif -

The pahsword is accahsia, and the Sacred word Jeva.

After this, the following Historical account is given -

Solomon having been informed that the body of H. a. had been found, and already deposited at the lower end of the Temple on the north side near the well (in which his Masters Jewel had been found) was happy in having even the poor consolation of finding the precious remains of so great a man; therefore gave orders and strict charge to his gr^d Insp^r. the Noble Adoniram, that his funeral obsequies should be as pompous & magnificent as if they were prepared for the king himself, he likewise ordered that all the bretheren should attend with white aprons and gloves; and strictly forbad that the bloody stains (which still remain'd in the Temple) should be washed away until he had wreaked his revenge on the perpetrators of that horrid deed.

The Noble <u>Adoniram</u>, chief of the works of the Temple soon furnished a plan of a noble monument, w^h was executed and perfectly finished in the space of 9 days; and was built of black and white marble. - The Heart of H: abif was inclosed in an urn and was exposed for 9 days on the 3^d Step of the S^m S^{rum} and after that intended to be placed on the Top of a beautiful obelisk, w^h was built on the inside of the Temple at the West door, a little to the north in order to mark out the place where the murderers had first deposited him in a pit, before they removed him to the place where <u>Stolkin</u> found him under the Sprig of accahsia.

The heart of the Excellent H.A. was thus exposed to the public view in the urn, with a sword pierced through it, and there the bretheren came to exprehs their grief on the occasion, kneeling on the first Step of the S^m S^{rum}.

At the Expiration of the 9 days, the heart was embalmed and deposited in the obelisk, and with a Triangular Stone △ on which was engraved in hebrew the Letters IMB, the I being the Initial of the antient masters word, and M.B. the Initials of the new word, and a sprig of accahsia on the Top of the triangular stone.

<u>Solomon had after this all the Triangular medals taken from the masters; and it was then that the masters word was changed, as it is mentioned in the 3^d degree.</u>

The Body of the resp^{ble} H. A. was burried in the middle of a great chamber, separated from the Temple, with all ye honors due to so great a man. It was in this chamber where Solomon held his chapter, and used to confer with Hiram King of Tyre & H.A. on secret mysteries.

Three days after the ceremony was over, Solomon surrounded by all his court went to the Temple, where all the workmen were placed in the same order as on the day of the funeral -· the king offered a prayer to the almighty; then examin'd the Tomb, the canopy the repeated Triangle, with the letters on it, likewise y^e. pyramid and when finding every thing properly executed, he cried out in Extasy Looking towards heaven, <u>Consumatum est</u>. All the bretheren answ^d by the Sign of admiration, and cried, amen, amen, amen.

Lecture of the Perf^t Master.

Q. Are you a perfect Master?

A. I have seen the Circles and the squares, that enclosed the two columns, which laid acrohs one another.

Q. where were they placed?

In the place, where the body of our resp^{ble} Mr H.A. was deposited.

Q. What do the columns represent?

A. The columns of J & B through w^h I must have pahsed to arrive at the degree of perf^t Master.

Q. For what reason did Solomon establish the degree of perf^t M^r?

A. He did it in honor of the deceased, in order to imprint in the minds of the bretheren an unaffected love & respect to his memory, and at the same time to excite in them a laudable and generous resolution of using every pohsible method to find out the perpetrators of this horrid deed, for at this time it was not known, whether they had not the andaciousnehs to mix with the bretheren and joyning in the general consternation and grief, in order to conceal their guilt and prevent Suspicion.

Solomon, to ahsertain this matter, ordered a general muster of all the workmen, and found they all answered to their names, Except the 3 Ruffians who had committed the crime and had absented themselves.

Solomon, afterwards ordered the Noble <u>Adoniram</u> to build an Elegant Monument for him, at the W.S.W^t. part of the Temple, and that the body should there be privatly deposited, and no brother admitted to the knowledge of it, that was not a Secret Master. Said body was also secretly embalmed, and sometime afterwards it was removed to an other apartment Separate from the Temple, where the King held his chapter.

The heart of this great man, after having been Exposed for 9 days on the 3ᵈ Step of the Sᵐ Sʳᵘᵐ and having Recᵈ the homage of the bretheren, by kneeling on the 1ˢᵗ Step, was then shut up in an urn and fixed on the Top of the obelisk with a sword pierced though it, implying that an attrocious deed cried out for public vengeance.

Q. What instructions have you received from yᵉ. different Degrees through which you have pahsed?

A. By them I learnt to regulate my morals, to cleanse my heart from all Stains, in order to qualifie myself for the high Degree of perfection which I live in hopes, that I shall arrive at.

Q. What does the square stone in the center of the circle mean?

A. It teacheth us, that the foundation of our building must be laid on a living rock, of which we are originally formed.

Q. What are the 3 circles for?

A. They are an Emblem of the Divinity, which had neither beginning nor End.

Q. And what do they all together represent?

A. The creation of the universe, which was accomplished by yᵉ will of God, and the powers he gave to the primitive qualities.

Q. What do you mean by that?

A. I mean by it, heat, cold and moisture, from the combination of which the 4 Elements spring.

Q. how come they to be mentioned here?

A. In order ever to remind us that God is every where, & that without his divine ahsistance, no solid building can be raised.

Q. What does the letter J, in the middle of the Square stone signify?

A. It is the Initial of the perfect masters word.

Q. Will you pronounce it?

A. J .... E .... V .... A.

Q. What does it mean?

A. It is the name by which I know the great archᵗ of the universe.

Q. how have you been received perf^t master?

A. A point to my heart, and a Rope round my neck.

Q. Why a point to your heart?

A. In memory that I have consented, that my heart should be pluckt out if I broke through my oblig^s and divulge the Secrets of Masonry.

Q. Why had you a Rope round your neck?

A. To teach me by this humiliating posture, that I must not pride myself in the progreſs I make in Masonry and virtue.

Q. how many signs have you?

A. one, by five.

Q. Why one by 5?

A. To call to my remembrance the degrees I have paſsed.

Q. Have you an Tokens?

A. Yes Illust^s M^r.

Q. How many have you?

A. One by 5. to remind me of the 5 points of my Entrance.

Q. What are they?

A. The 4 rounds about the Temple and the 5th the Sign of admiration.

Q. What does the Tomb represent, which you perceived at y^r entiring the Lodge?

A. It represents the Burial of our resp^ble M^r. H. A. in the valley.

Q. Why is it placed at the north west of the Sanctuary?

A. In order to teach us, that a man must divest himself of all worldly care, to be qualified to Enter the S^m. S^rum.

Q. What is the meaning of the rope that comes from the coffin in the north, and reaches by the obelisk in the south, where it binds the 2 columns together, w^h. lay croſsways?

A. It represents that Rope which the bretheren made use of, to draw the body up, and afterwards to let the coffin down, which said rope was made of with 's.

Q. Does that rope signifie anything Else?

A. It signifies that we have broke the Shackels of Sin.

Q. What have you done in entering the Lodge?

A. I came to the altar walking as an Ent^d appr^{ce}. F. craft and master, to crohs the 2 columns.

Q. Why so?

A. It serves to remind me that I was by means of pahsing through these degrees, to obtain the Honor of being made a perf^t Master.

Q. Is there no mystery couched under this Explanation?

A. It teaches us that we cannot arrive at the S. S^{rum} by any other method than by a purity of Morals, a rectitude of intention and Secrecy, which are to be learnt in the first degrees.

Q. Why did you enter the Sanctuary by the Side?

A. In order, to learn by that, how I must avoid the common ways of mankind.

Q. What is your colour?

A. Green.

Q. for what reason?

A. To imprint in my mind, that being dead to sin, I expect to gain new life by the practice of virtue, and to make a progrehs by this means in the sublime sciences, which I hope one day to be acquainte: with by arriving to the higher degrees.

Q. Who can communicate them to you?

A. God alone, whose knowledge is infinite.

Q. What do the 2 pyramids in the draft represent, the one being in the south, and the other in the north? and what signifies the figures on them?

A. Those pyramids represent Egypt, where the sciences were much cultivated, and some of them had their origin - on the south pyramid is drawn the meteor which guided the masters in their search for the Body of our Resp^{ble} M^r. H. Abif, and on the north pyramid is the perf^t Masters Jewel represented.

Q. What does the P^t. M^r. Jewel represent?

A. To remind us that a perf^t M^r. should act accordingly to ye strictest rules of Propriety caution and attention, in the whole Tenor of his proceedings through life.

Q. What was the name of the M^r. of the Ent^d apprentices?

A. His name was <u>Jachin</u>, and to him Solomon did the Honor of calling the column on the right hand side of the Porch by his name.

Q. How was the master of the fellow Crafts, called?

A. His name was Boaz. He was of the Tribe of Juda, and family of David, a man much esteemed and respected by Solomon who for that reason dedicated to him and called by his name the column at the left side, where the F. Cr^{ts} met & Rec^d their wages.

Q. And what was the name of the M^r. of masters masons?

A. His name was <u>Mahabon</u>, a virtuous man, held in high esteem by Solomon, one of the principal intendants of his buildings; he was an Intimate friend of H. A. which induced that king to send him in search of that body of his dear friend Deceased when every former attempt to find it had proved abortive. Solomon ordered him to go, and required 3 things of him, the first was, that he should bring that respectable masters Jewel; the 2^d was, that he should bring that great and ever respected and lamented man dead or alive, and the 3^d was, that he should discover the perpetrators of that horrid deed.

Q. Did Mahabon comply with these orders?

A. No, not intirely, but did with the 2 first articles of it.

Q. Give me an account of this matter.

A. Mahabon on company with the 15 masters that were chosen to attend him in this search, first went to the Temple, where seeing that blood had been spilt in many places of it, he at last traced it to the well, in the north part of the Temple, when he immediatly concluded that H.A. had been killed there, & perhaps flung in the well. thus prompted and further encouraged by the appearance of a Luminous light or meteor standing over the well, he determin'd to have it drawn dry; this being done, he went down in it, but found not the body, as he expected but was lucky to find the masters Jewel, which was the same with the other masters. It seems and appears very reasonable, when attacked by the Ruffians, he certainly must have pluck'd off his Jewel, and threw it in the well (near y^e. great Staircase) for fear that it should fall into the hands of those villains. Mohabon, blehsed Heaven and Jointly with his ahsociates offerd a prayer of thanksgiving for their signal succehs.

After this they went on in order to comply with the other part of their orders, being still miraculous preceded by the meteor; at length it Stopt on a small hill between Lyda and Joppa to rest a while, and there it was that Br^r Stolkin found the Body etc., as it is mentioned in the 3^d Degree.

End of the Lecture.

To close the Lodge of Perf^t Master.

Q. What's the clock Brother Stolkin?

A. T: R: Adoniram it is 5 of the clock.

Q. Since it is 5, and the work ended, 't is time to refresh ourselves. give notice, I am going to close the Lodge.

A. Take notice Bretheren, this Lodge is going to be closed - Then Adoniram knocks 4, then Stolkin 4, then a brother in the south 4, and then another in the North 4, after which all of them make the sign of admiration and consternation, admire the Tomb and close.

End of the 5th degree

Perfect M^r. by Curiosity. 6th Degree.
or
Intimate Secretary
===

This Lodge ought to be lighted with 27 lights in 3 branches of 9 each, placed in the same manner as the 3 lights in a symbolic Lodge, East West and South, hung with black, strewed with Tears.

When a reception, there remains only 2 bretheren in the lodge after it is open'd, who represent Solomon & Hiram King of Tyre, and are drehsed in blue cloaks lined with Ermin, crowns on their heads, and each a Szepter in their hands, a Table between them on which are 2 swords acrohs and a Roll of parchment. -

The room where this lodge is held represents Solomons hall of audience for the Masons.

This lodge is opened & closed by 27 knocks of a mallet, by 9 at a time, a little distance between the 8th & 9th

To open this Lodge.

Solomon strikes 3 times 9, King Hiram the same, after which all the bretheren bend their right knees, crohs their hands and raise them so that the 2 thumbs touch the forehead, and altogether say in a low voice, <u>Jeova</u>, <u>Jeova</u>, <u>Jeova</u>, after which they draw their swords and retire; Solomon having previously appointed them his guards, and chose a captain and lieutenant among them, whose businehs it is to see that the others behave with Decency, to keep the lodge well Tiled and ever drive away bretheren who would come near it - thus there remains only the 2 Kings. - NB. the bretheren in this lodge are called perf^t masters, and are to wear white aprons, lined bordered and trimmed with a firy colour'd silk; round their neck a ribbon of the same colour, to which hangs a plain Triangle - the same triangle to be painted on the flap of the apron - they should all wear white gloves bordered with read.

Form of a Reception

The cand^{te} being in the antichamber, the capⁿ of the guards orders one of his people to take away his hatt, sword, gloves, Jewel & apron of perf^t Master, they places him at the lodge door, which is on purpose left on a Jarr, that he can put his head in and peep in the Lodge, when the guards make a little noise at the door, which being heard by King Hiram, he looks about and seeing a man peep lifts his hands to heaven & cries in a rage "O heavens we are overheard" on which Solomon says: "That cannot be as my guards are at the door". King Hiram without any reply, runs to the door seizes the peeper by the hand drags him in to the presence of Solomon and says: here he is. Solomon says: What shall we do with him? We must kill him replies Hiram and puts his hand on his sword, on w^h. Solomon quits his place runs to King Hiram and puts his hand on King Hirams sword. Says: Stop my brother, strikes at the same time a hard stroke on the Table, on which the capt^n & the guards enter and salute the king by drawing their right hand from the left shoulder to the right hip - Solomon then says: Let that guilty man come forth when wanted, you'll answer for him. on which the guards depart with the prisoner, and Solomon and Hiram remain alone for some time as in deep conversation but talking very low. Then Solomon strikes another great stroke, on which the captain and the guards enter leading in the cand^{us} and remain with him in y^e. west till by a sign of Solomon they bring him before the Throne, and they taking their seats, when Solomon thus adrehses the Candidate.

By my entreaties and sollicitations I have so far prevailed on my worthy ally the King of Tyre (whom you by your curiosity had offended) so as to pronounce sentence of death against you) I say I have so far prevailed with him as not only to procure pardon for your offence, but even obtained his consent to receive you master and even Intimate Secretary to the articles of our new alliance. Do you think you can Inviolably keep secret what we are going to communicate to you, and will you bind yourself by an Inviolable oblig^n. in the most solemn manner of your fidelity? he ans^{rs} in the affirmative, he then kneels puts his hand on the Bible and Contracts the foll^g oblig^n.

"I A. B. do promise and swear in the presence of the great archit^t of the universe, and this resp^{ble} lodge that I do solemnly bind myself By this oath, never to reveal to any person directly or indirectly, what is at present to be communicated to me, especially to brothers of lower degrees - and that I shall attend the summonses of this lodge, and conform myself to the laws and regulations of it.

"And all this I promise under no lehs penalty, than to have my body opened, my Entrals pluckt out, my heart torn to pieces, and the whole to be thrown to the wild beasts to be devoured. So help me God and keep me stedfast to my obligations A. A. A."

After this obligation is taken, Solomon shows the Draft of the Lodge to the Cand^{us} and Explains to him: vizt.

The window represented in the cloud is an emblem of the Dome of the Temple, you see in the glahs of it the letter J which is the Initial of the name of the g^t arch^t of the universe <u>Jeova</u>, the building at a distance represents the palace of Solomon with the door and gate to go in by. the mausoleum and tears mark'd out, is the masons chamber of audience, hung with black, where Solomon (when he could spare a minute from businehs) was used to shut himself up, to lament the unhappi Fate of H. A. It was in this chamber that Hiram of Tyre found Solomon in deep meditation, when he came to visit him.

The letter A signifies alliance, the first P. which is to the right of the mausoleum signifies Promise, and the 2^d P. on the left and the same line signifies Perfection.

Then Solomon orders the cand^{us} to advance and receives him Intimate Secretary saying, "I receive you Intimate Secretary, on condition that you will as faithfully fulfil your duty, and be as much attached to this order, as the person was, whom you have the honor to succeed in office.

The colour of the ribbon with which I decorate you, must ever bring to your recollection, the wounds w^h. that great man did receive from the traitors who so inhumanly mahsacred him; and likewise of the blood which he rather chose to spill every drop of, than to reveal the secret w^h I am going to entrust you with - We Expect my respectable brother that your fidelity will be proof against all temptation and danger, and that this sword with which I girt you, will serve to protect you against any villain who would dare attempt to surprize you into a confehsion of our mysteries.

Sign 1ˢᵗ   The first sign is to draw your right hand from your left shoulder to your right hip, bearing a refference or resemblance to your Obᵒⁿ

Dᵒ 2ᵈ   The Second Sign is, to crohs both your hands, let them fall by yʳ sword, at the same time lifting your Eyes to heaven.

Token   The Token is, take each others right hand in the usual manner of saluting, the one turns the others hand and says Berith, (alliance) the second then turns the first's hand, and says Neder (promise) then the first turns the 2ᵈˢ hand again and says Selemouth (perfection)

P. Wᵈ   the pahsword is Joabert, which is the name of Solomons favorite that peeped at the door) To this pahsword is answer'd Zerbal, wʰ is the name of Solomons confidant and Captⁿ of the guards.

S. W.   The Sacred Word is Jeova.

The History of this degree

Solomon in consequence of the Treaty established with Hiram King of Tyre, and his ambahsador having solemnly covenanted to furnish him with a certain number of measures of oyl and Honey, and Bushells of wheat, besides the grant of a province consisting of 30 governments, in lieu of Timbers hewn framed and drawn from the forest of Libanus by King Hiram's people as also for the hewn stones worked in the quarries of Tyre, ready made and fitted for immediate use.

This Treaty was to take place as soon as the Temple was completely finished - however a whole year elapsed without Solomon's paying any regard to this mutual agreement. During which time King Hiram visited these provinces, and had the mortification to find it a barren and sandy soil, inhabited by ferocious and uncultivated people, so that the pohsehsion of such a country was likely rather to be a burthen than of any advantage to him, upon which (and not hearing from Solomon he determin'd to go in person to Jerusalem and to expostulate with him for having neglected to comply with the terms of the Treaty. On his arrival he Entered the palace, went through the guard room, where Solomon's court was ahsembled and rushed into the king's apartment, where he happen'd to be alone bemoaning the Lohs of H. A. - King Hiram walked in so hasty and seemingly in so pahsionate a manner, as to give umbrage to and rouse the Zeal of one of Solomons greatest favorites Called <u>Joabert</u>, who was struck with a notion, that he came with some evil design against the person of his sovereign, which prompted him to follow King Hiram and go to the door to listen. King Hiram happening to look back or behind him espied him and Exclaimed oh Heavens we are overheard! and running to the door seized <u>Joabert</u> by the hand, & dragg'd him into Solomons presence, saying, <u>here he is.</u> - Solomon who could not doubt of his favorites trespahs, asked him, <u>what shall we do with him?</u> to which King Hiram replyd, <u>we must kill him.</u> Drawing his sword for that purpose, on w^h. Solomon coming from his Throne said, Stay my Brother and suspend your wrath for a while. he gave a great knock, on which the guards came in, when Solomon said to them, Seize that guilty man, and be answerable for his appearance when required - the guards being thus sent away, he thus addrehsed King Hiram: "This man Sire is the only person amongst my favorites and Lords of my court, who has a real and affectionate attachment to my person; I know him sufficiently to be convinced that the indiscretion he has been guilty of, is lehs to be attributed to an Impertinent Curiosity, than to his apprehensions of any dangerous accident befalling me. Your looks, change of countenance and hasty manner in pahsing through the room were, what Exited his curiosity and alarm for my safety - I therefore entreat you to recal the sentence of death, which you have pronounced against him, and I will be answerable for his Zeal, and discretion." The King of Tyre knowing how agreeable it would be to King Solomon that his favorite should be pardoned, readily consented; and the two kings renewea their Treaty; which was to be perpetual, with different clauses, and promihses on both sides of eternal fidelity - To which Treaty <u>Joabert</u> was the Intimate Secretary - This my bretheren is, what is represented in your reception of perfect master by curiosity or Intimate secretary - or English Master.

End of the History of this Degree.

Lecture

Q. Are you an Intimate Secretary, or perfect English Master?

Q. How have you been received?

A. By my curiosity.

Q. Did you run any risk by it?

A. Yes, that of loosing my life.

Q. What was done after you was detected?

A. I was committed to the care of the guards, and expected to have sentence of death pronounced against me.

Q. Were they Intimate Secretaries, or perfect masters?

A. I was then ignorant of it, but have since found that my resolution perseverance and firmnehs hath procured me the favor of being the first Initiated in this degree.

Q. What are the pahswords?

A. Joabert, & Banachad or Zerbal.

Q. What do these names signifie?

A. Joabert, is the name of Solomons favorite that peeped at the door, and the others noblemen and capt^{ns} of the guards, and each commanded one of the 12 Tribes.

Q. What is the great name?

A. J. E. O. V. A. (mentioned by single letters)

Q. What was you before you was Initimate Secretary?

A. A favorite of Solomon.

Q. From what country did you come?

A. From Capule.

Q. Your sirname?

A. Capuliste.

Q. How many governments did Solomon give to King Hiram in return for the work done by his people for the Temple?

A. Thirty.

Q. Where was you received?

A. In Solomons Hall of audience hung with black and 27 lights.

Q. What signifies the J, which you see in the window?

A. J. E. O. V. A.

Q. What does that word signifie?

A. It is the 3d pronunciation of the name of the great architect of the universe, which in this degree signifies, <u>Let us return thanks to God, the work is compleat</u>.

Q. What signifies the A and the 2 Ps in the Triangle?

A. The A means alliance, the 1st P promise, and the 2d P - means perfection.

Q. Why is the Lodge lighted by 27 lights?

A. To represent the 2700 candlesticks, which Solomon ordered to be made for the Illumination of Gods Temple.

Q. What represents the door in the draft of the lodge?

A. The door of Solomons Palace.

Q. What means the Triangle, that hangs to your ribbon?

A. The 3 Theological virtues, <u>Faith</u>, <u>hope</u> and <u>Charity</u>. You may give it another explanation vizt <u>Solomon</u>, <u>Hiram</u> of Tyre, and Hiram abif. - End of the Lecture

The Lodge is closed, as opend, by 27 knocks, 3 times 9 - a little distance between the 8th & 9th.

End of the 6th Degree

7th Degree, called Provost & Judge, or Irish Master

The lodge of Provost & Judge, or Irish Master, must be hung with Red, also Illuminated with 5 great lights, one of which is to be in the Center, and the other 4, in the angles of the Lodge.

The M^r in the East under a blue canopy, spangled with golden Stars; His Title is that of Thrice puihs^t and Illustrious, as he represents <u>Tito</u> Prince Harodim, Dean of the Provosts and Judges, first Gr^d Warden and Insp^r of the 300 architects who drew plans for the work men of the Temple.

The 2 Senior Masters act as wardens, the rest of the bretheren are placed to the right and left, Except the Introducing brother who sits behind the wardens in the west.

To open the Lodge.

The Thr: Illus^s strikes 4 quick and one slow, w^h is repeated by the wardens, in the same manner; Then the T: Ill^s asks the foll^g questions vizt standing

Q. Illust^s Brothers wardens, are we Tiled?

A. Thr: Illust^s M^r., we are, and can begin our work.

Q. Where stands your Master?

A. Every where, T: Ill^s puihs^t Master.

Q. How so?

A. In order to supervize the conduct of the workmen; to attend the businehs done by them, and to render Impartial Justice to each of them.

Q. What is the clock?

A. It is break of day, 8 o'clock, 2 o'clock and 7 o'clock.

Then the T: Ill^s strikes 4 & 1, on the altar before him, which are repeated by the wardens, - He then says: as it is 8, 2 & 7 o'clock it is time that the workmen should begin their work. <u>This lodge is open</u>. Then all the bretheren Clap 4 & 1 with their hands, & take their places.

The Form of a Reception

The Thr: Ill^s M^r holds a scepter in his hand, and orders the Introducing Brother to go and prepare the cand^{us}; He obeys and soon brings him to the door, on which he knocks 5 as before described, which are repeated by the wardens, & by the T. Ill^s., who is informed by the wardens that somebody knocks at the door as a Provost & Judge, when the T: Ill^s. orders the wardens to send some body to see who it is that knocks at the door, who brings word that Broth^r N: N. stands at the lodge door and desires the favor of being admitted to the degree of Provost and Judge. Then the Thr. Ill^s orders, that he is first to be well Examined as to his qualifications and Introduced in the usual manner.

The M^r of Ceremonies then leads him in to the lodge and placing him between the wardens, takes his seat. Then the Senr warden takes the cand^{us} by the hand, makes him kneel in a masonic manner and to say <u>civi</u>, laying his naked sword at the same time on the cand^{tes} left shoulder. Thus he remains until the Thr: Ill^s says <u>Ky</u>, upon which the Junr warden raises him and leads him 7 times round the lodge. At the first round opposite the Thr: Ill^s he salutes him, and gives the S. T. & w^d of an Ent^d appr^{tice}, at the 2^d round he gives the same of a fellow craft with the pahsword, and so on till he comes to the 7th degree, being the present, - when he is ordered up to the footstool of the Throne before the Thr: Illus^s who addrehses him thus: Respect^{ble} Brother, it gives me Infinite satisfaction to have this opportunity of rewarding your zeal for masonry, and your attachment for the M^r. of Masters, and this I do, by appointing you Provost & Judge over all the workmen of this lodge; for as we are fully convinced of your discretion, we do not hesitate to confide in you, and to communicate our most important secrets to you, which will encourage you to do y^r. duty in this degree, as you have done in the former ones, w^h you had the Honor of being admitted into.

I Intrust you with the key of the place, where lies deposited the remains (that is the body and heart) of our resp^{ble} Father H. A. but you must bind yourself by a solemn ob^n that you never will divulge the secret - come kneel and contract, on which he kneels, his hand on the Bible and repeats vizt "I A. B. do promise and vow, in the presence of the great arch^t. of the universe, and of all the Ill^s bretheren here present, that I will not directly or Indirectly divulge any part of the mysteries of this degree of Provost and Judge. - That I will use all pohsible means to compremise all differences between bretheren; To whom as well as the whole world I promise to render strict & impartial Justice, as it seems, this is the province allotted to me, by this respect^{ble} Lodge - I do lastly bind myself under the penalties of all my former ob^{ns} to pay a Just and due obedience to y^e. regulations and orders of the council of princes of Jerusalem. So may God keep me in truth, Equity and Justice Amen. A. A. "

After this ob^n the Thr: Ill^s. & puihs^t M^r. orders the cand^{us} to rise and come to him, when he gives him a stroke on each shoulder with the scepter, and speaks to him thus: By the power to me given and with which I am invested I appoint you Provost and Judge over all the workmen of the Temple, and as such I invest you with this golden Key suspended to a red ribbon, which you are to wear as a collar; here is your apron lined with the same colour, as an emblem of the ardour and zeal of the masters; The pocket in your apron is intended to keep the key of the plans in -

Token   The token is, enterlace the little fingers of each others right hand, & strike 7 times with the middlefingers each others palms of the hand -

Sign   The Sign is, you put the 2 first fingers of your right hand to your nose - which the other answers by putting the forefinger of his right hand to his lips, the thumb under the chin, thus forming a square.

words   The words are seven fold, civi, Ky. Stolkin, Hiram, geometras, Architect, and Xinxee.

gr^t w^d The great word is Jackinai, M-B, signifies Mohabon, the master of masters.

NB. one the flap of the apron, a key must be painted, being the Jewel of the order of this degree.

Lecture of Provost and Judge

Q. Are you a Provost and Judge?

A. I distribute Justice impartially to all workmen.

Q. How did you get admittance to the Lodge of Provost and Judge?

A. By striking 4 strokes, and a 5th after a Little pause.

Q. What do them 4 knocks, and a 5th separate signifies?

A. The 4, are the Emblems of the 4 fronts of the Temple, and the 5th the unity of God, whose Temple it is, and to whom is due every homage from us -

Q. What did you meet with at your Entrance?

A. With a brother, who conducted me to the west part of the Lodge.

Q. What became of you then?

A. The Senior Warden made me kneel on my right knee, and made me pronounce the word civi, which signifies to kneel.

Q. What ans^r did the Th: Ill^s. make to you?

A. He pronounced the word Ky, which signifies to rise.

Q. What did the Thr: Illus^s do next?

A. He constituted me Provost & Judge, depending on the good account he had of my Zeal for the craft.

Q. What did he give you?

A. A golden Key, to distinguis the degree I received, and with this a Sign Token and word, by which I may be known as a Provost & Judge.

Q. What is the use of that Key?

A. To open a small Ebony box where all the plans required for the construction of the Temple were kept.

Q. What do you mean by this?

A. I mean that we are only entrusted with the Secret, to know, where ye heart of our Mast^r H. A. is deposited.

Q. What is your word?

A. <u>Tito</u>.

Q. What does it signifie?

A. It is the name of the 1ˢᵗ grᵈ warden; he was a prince Harodim, yᵉ. oldest of the Provosts & Judges, and Inspʳ. over the 300 architects of the Temple.

Q. What was Solomons Intention in creating this degree?

A. As ist was necehsary to Establish order and regularity among such number of workmen; Solomon created <u>Tito</u>, Prince Harodim. <u>Adoniram</u> was created chief of the Provost & Judges, and the kings great confidant and favorite <u>Joabert</u>, was then Initiated in the mysteries of this degree. To him the Key was given to open the Ebony box, that contained all the plans of yᵉ Building which box you have seen in the degree of Secᵗ Mʳ. This box was hung under a rich canopy in the S. Sʳᵘᵐ. <u>Joabert</u> was so struck with admiration at beholding these things, that he fell on his knees pronouncing the word <u>Civi</u>. Solomon seeing him in this attitude pronounced the word <u>Ky</u>, and then put the seals in his hands, by wʰ. his knowledge dayly encreased.

Q. What did you perceive in the Lodge?

A. A fringed Curtain, with a canopy, under which was suspended yᵉ. Ebony Box containing the plans.

Q. Have you seen nothing else?

A. I saw a Triangle, in wʰ were these 2 Letters   thus entangled.

Q. What do they signifie?

A. That God himself was the great archᵗ of the Temple, and had inspired David and Solomon with the plan of it.

Q. What have you seen in the lodge besides?

A. A pair of scales, wʰ are the Emblem of Rectitude, with wʰ. we should always Execute yᵉ. duties of this degree, as we are appointed Judges to decide all disputes that may occur.

Q. Where is the body of the Respᵇˡᵉ Hiram abif deposited?

A. Under the footstep of the Throne in the chapter room, wʰ. is separated from the Temple, to wʰ. you go by an arch'd way on the North side of the Temple.

Q. Where is his heart entered?

A. In a golden urn, which is shut up in the obelisk.

Q. What means the 2 letters X & J in the north side of the draft?

A. Xinxee and Jackinai: the 1st signifies the seat or quiet of the soul, wh. is the pahsword - and Jackinai is the grd word.

Q. What means the letters I H S, with the sprig of accahsia on the H?

A. The I, Ina, the H, Hiram, and the S, Stolkin, the last is the name of him who found the body of H. A. under that sprig, being the mark in order to find the place again

Q. What does MB mean?

A. Mohabon, who found the Jewel of our respble H. A. in the well.

Q. Where were you placed?

A. In the middle chamber.

Q. Have you done any remarkable work, since you became a Provost & Judge?

A. I have ornamented the Tomb of our dear Mr H. A.

Q. With what was you ornamented, upon being recd a Provost & Judge?

A. a white apron lined with red, a pocket therein, and white and red roses.

Q. What is the intention of the pocket?

A. The eldest provost and Judge, make use of it to put the plans in, wh. he communicates to the Masters, who drew them out on their trehsel board.

A. What do the white and red roses mean?

Q. the red, are the emblems of the blood spill'd by our respble Mr. H. A., and the white signifies the candor and fidelity of the Masters.

Q. How old are you?

A. 4 times 16 -

Q. from whence come you?

A. I come and go every where.

Q. What is it the clock?

A. break of day. 8, 2 and 7 o'clock.

Q. Why so?

A. Because a perf^t M^r provost & Judge, should be every where, and at all hours, ready to be at hand, in oder to administer Justice. -

Then the Lodge is closed in the same manner as open'd. The Thr: Ill^s striking 4 & 1, which being answ^d by the Wardens, and then by all the bretheren with their hands. The lodge is closed.

Alphabet, of the Illus^s Provosts & Judges -

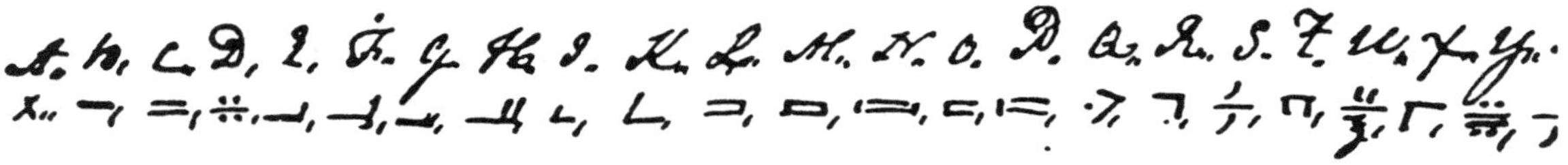

[handwritten cipher alphabet]

End of the 7th Degree.

8th Degree, Called Intindant of the buildings, or M^r. In Israel Many French Lodges, calld this degree, Scotch M^r of the three J.J.J.

The lodge of this degree, must be hung with red, and must be illuminated by 27 lights, distributed by 3 times 9 round the lodge, besides 5 other great lights, which are placed at the Foot of the altar opposite the Thr: Puihs^t Master, who in this degree represents Solomon.

The first senior warden, or Insp^r represents the Illus^s Brother <u>Tito</u>, prince Harodim. The 2^d or Jun^{or} warden, represents <u>Adoniram</u>, the son of <u>Abda</u>.

Solomon, stands in the East, the 2 wardens, in the West, at a distance from one another, so as to form a Triangle with the Thr: Puihs^t. The Junr. warden officiates as M^r of the Ceremonies on this occasion.

The Thr: Puihs^t M^r., as well as all the bretheren must wear a broad red Triangular ribbon round their necks, to w^h. a Triangle is suspended, on one side of w^h are to be engraved the Initials of 3 hebrew words, <u>Benehorim</u>, <u>achard</u>, & <u>Jackinai</u>, signifying, <u>one God, oh you Eternal</u>, on the reverse must be engraved in the angles of it, the Initials of Judea, Ky & iia, meaning, <u>Almighty God, God, God,</u> in the middle part of the Triangle on one side the letter G, and the other side the Letter A signifying Great Architect.

A white apron lined with red, and bordered with green, with a Star of 9 Rays embroidered on the middle of it, and above the Star a pair of scales, with a Sprig of accahsia on the top of the fulcrum thus, and on the flap of the apron a Triangle with the Initials B. A. I.

To open the Lodge.

The Thr: puihs^t holding a scepter, Interrogates Br^r. <u>Tito</u>

Q. Illus^s. Brother <u>Tito</u>, are we Tiled?

A. Th: puihs^t, we are safe and very secure here.

Q. What is it the clock?

A. It is break of day. Upon w^h the Thr: puihs^t strikes the altar

with his szepter 5 times, which are repeated by Brothers Tito
& Adoniram with their mallets; then the Thr: puihs^t says: as
it is break of day, 't is time to begin our work - My bretheren this lodge is open. then all the bretheren strike 5 times
with their hands, and make the Sign of Surprize and admiration,
which is to carry the right hand to the forehead, the fingers
a little Extended, as to prevent the light, then extend both
arms and hands looking up to heaven, then let fall your hands
on your Belly forming a Triangle with the thumbs and first
fingers.

Form of the Reception of a Cand^{te}

Note: the cand^{te} must be barefooted in this degree, when Introduced.

The Thr: Puihs^t Solomon addrehses the Senr. Warden, thus: -

T. P^t. . Brother Tito, how shall we repair the Immense Lohs we have
sustained on the Melancholly and treacherous murder of our never
to be forgotten Master H. A.? You know he alone was entrusted with
the decoration of the Secret chamber, where every thing the dearest
and most respectable to the Israelites was to be contained; there
the ark was to be deposited, and thereby was ye presence and the
protection of the almighty Ensured. Scarcely had this great man,
set about this important work, when he was snatched from us by the
most horrid and infamous plot. Most Illus^s Wardens, give me your
advice what to do on this occasion.

Tito - Most Illus^s. Thr: puihs^t. I am fully convinced of the lohs we
have sustained and of the difficulty to repair it; In my opinion
the only resource we have left is, to appoint a chief for each of
the 5 orders of architecture, and that we should all unite in
giving every ahsistance in our power toward the compleating this
3^d Secret chamber.

T: P^t. - Most Illus^s. prince and brother, your advice is too good to
be neglected, and to shew how much I am swayed by it, I now appoint
you brother Adoniram, and Abda your Father to inspect and conduct
the work - go to the middle chamber and see if there are any of
the chiefs of the 5 orders of architecture there.

The Junior warden goes to the adjoining room, and asks if there are any of them. The cand^us (Joabert) ans^rs. I am here, on w^h Adoniram, puts the foll^g. questions to him: "are you pohsehsed of Zeal enough to apply with a scrupulous attention to the works which the T:P: will commit to your care"? on which Joabert answers: "I look upon it as the greatest happinehs and advantage that I can be blehsed with, to have an opportunity of concurring with him, in the great and glorious object, w^h. he proposes, that of Erecting a Temple to the almighty worthy his glory". - Then Adoniram receives from him the S. T. & W^d of the 3 first degrees, & then knocks on the door 3, 5, & 7. and tells the brother who comes to the door that the brother he Introduces, is one who works in the middle chamber, on w^h the door is opend, and Adoniram takes the Cand^us with ye Masters gripe and leads him in the middle of the lodge, when the Cand^us kneels on a square flag stone opposite a Table, behind which Broth^r. Tito stands, who puts a sprig of accahsia or any other green sprig in his hand and in that posture he takes the following ob^n.

"I A: B. do in the presence of the great arch^t. of the universe and of these Thr: Illus: bretheren here present, promise, ever to keep Inviolable secret all the mysteries which shall be revealed to me and to observe all such rules as shall be perscribed to me by the gr^d. council of Princes of Jerusalem - and all this under the penalty of all my former Ob^s, besides that, of having my body cut in two and my Bowels torn out - So God maintain me in Equity and Justice Amen, A. A" -

Discourse

My dear and worshipful brother, King Solomon being willing and desirous of carrying on to the highest degree of perfection pohsible the works commenced by H.A., thought proper for effecting this businehs, to employ the 5 chiefs of the 5 orders of architecture ahsisted by the 3 princes Harodim, Tito, Abda & Adoniram his son. He was well convinced of their Zeal and abilities, and hoped soon to see their work compleated in a masterly manner - we flatter ourselves brother, that you will contribute with all y^r might to this great End. - your once representing a dead man, now must be to you as an Emblem that in order to succeed in this great work and execute it with the same spirit as our resp^ble Mast^r H. A. would have done - you must also be pohsehsed moreover with the same spirit and resolution as he was, which is to prefer death rather than divulge the mysteries of the order - we hope you will follow his praizeworthy Example? I will now raise you, not as you was raised before, but as Hiram was raised by <u>Stolkin</u> under the sprig of accahsia - Then brother <u>Adoniram</u> takes the Cand^tes right elbow in his left hand, and with his right hand the masters gripe, and by 3 different pulls, lifts him up from the stool and throws off the red veil, Then the Illus^s brother <u>Tito</u> gr^d Inspect^r gives him the foll^g. S. T. & word.

Sign the 1st is: that of amazement or surprize, which is to lift both your hands as high as the cheeks the thumbs to your ears the fingers extended perpendicular so as to form 2 squares, in walking you step as if astonished, and when standing you throw your body back.

Sign the 2^d is: by clapping your right hand to your forehead with your fingers and nails turned in on the Eyes, and say <u>Benchorin</u> - . The ans^w. to this is: to enterlace the fingers of both hands, and put the backpart of them to the left side of your belly, Look up to Heaven and say <u>Achard</u>.

Sign the 3^d is: That of grief figurative of the Fell^w Crafts sign; you carry your right hand to your heart, and at the same time the left hand down on the left side as if to struggle, then you move your elbows 3 times in a Circulatory manner from side to side and say Ky - to which the other replies <u>iia</u>, signifying God.

Token is: You touch each others heart reciprocally, then pahs and take each others middle arm, and with the left hand the elbow and pahs it 3 times.

words - One says, <u>Jackinai</u>, and the other ans^rs <u>Judea</u>.

Lecture of the 8th Degree.

Q. Are you an Intendant of the buildings or Master in Israel?

A. I have taken the 5 Steps of Exactitude, I have penetrated into the inner part of the Temple, I have seen the effects of the great and resplendit light in the middle of which I have seen in Hebrew charakters the 3 mysterious I. I. I. without knowing what they meant.

Q. How were you received Intent of the buildings or Mr in Israel?

A. By acknowledging my Ignorance.

Q. Where were you raised in that degree?

A. In order to dispel the darkneſs in wh. I was immersed and to get such light as would regulate my heart, and enlighten my understanding.

Q. Into what place were you Introduced?

A. In a place full of wonder & charms where virtue and sovereign wisdom resides - .

Q. What is the duty of an Intendt. of the Buildings?

A. His duty is, to keep the bretheren steady in the practice of virtue, by setting them good Example, and to correct their work.

Q. Why is it required in this degree before you are admitted, to show that you are acquainted with the 3 first degrees?

A. To shew that it is only gradually that we can arrive to the perfection.

Q. What do you learn from them 3 degrees?

A. The 1st or entd apprce teaches me moral virtue, the 2d or fellow Craft political virtue and the 3d or Master Heroic Virtue.

Q. Why have you been oblig'd to take steps backwards and forwards in your different degrees?

A. it was to shew that the progreſs towards virtue is slow and gradual, and that by humility we must curb that pride which is so natural to us, before we can presume to hope for perfection; and also that we must Judge so impartially of our actions, and so effectually govern our paſsions as not to leave any thing exceptionable in our conduct.

Q. Can you Explain the mysteries of our lodge?

A. I Shall endeavour in the best manner I can.

- 67 -

Q. What do the 3 mysterious letters in your Jewel signifie?

A. <u>Jackinai</u>, & <u>Jeevah</u>: Signifying <u>Divine wisdom</u>, & <u>Divine Beauty</u>. the 3ᵈ In the middle of the Triangle of the blazing Star is the Initial of the sacred and at present namelehs word.

Q. What does the Circle, in the Inside of the 3ᵈ Triangle imply?

A. The immensity of God, who has neither beginning nor ending.

Q. What do the 3 letters on the inside of the Circle mean?

A. oh you Eternal alone! pohsehs the attribute of the Divinity.

Q. What are the chief attributes of the Divinity

A.
	Letters		Lettʳˢ		Letters
Beauty	6.	omniscience	11.	Justice	7.
Wisdom	7.	Eternity	8.	compahsion	10.
Boundlehs Mercy	14.	perfection	10.	Creation	8.
	27.		29.		25.

These attributes together form the Number 81.

Q. Explain the Square of 9 to me, wʰ you did see in the tripple Triangle.

A. There are in the first 9   3 attributes - - - | 9 | 9 | 9 | 27. |
the same in the 2ᵈ.   9   3 ditto - - - - - | 9 | 9 | 9 | 27. |
and also in the 3ᵈ.   9   3 ditto - - - - - | 9 | 9 | 9 | 27. |
3 Columns, and added together form a square of - - - - - 81. -

Q. Why do you place Solomon in the Temple?

A. In memory of this being the first who consecrated a Temple to the Lord.

Q. Why do they place a brazen sea in the Temple?

A. To let us know that the Temple of God is holy, and that we must not enter it, before we have been purified from all uncleanehs.

Q. What does the Left side of the Temple signifie?

A. Masonry, under the Laws of Tipes and Ceremonies.

Q. What does the right side of the Temple Signifie?

A. True Masonry under the Law of grace and truth.

Q. Why do you place St John the Baptist, on the right side?

A. Because he was the forerunner of the true Temple, which the Lord had chosen to reside in.

Q. What is the meaning of the Tomb which is under the threshold of the door of the Sanctuary, in the degree of provost & Judge?

A. It is to us an emblem, that we must be purified by death, before we can enter the mansions of blihs.

Q. What does the candle stick with 7 branches signifie?

A. The presence of the Holy Spirit, in the hearts of those who observe faithfully the laws.

Q. Why are you barefooted at the time of your reception?

A. Because Moses was barefooted when he entered the Holy Land.

Q. What did you hear before you entered the Lodge?

A. 5 great strokes.

Q. What do they denote?

A. The 5 points of felicity.

Q. What happened in consequence of them, & what was done to you?

A. A Warden immediatly appear'd, who supported and Carried me round the Temple 5 times.

Q. What was his intention of his doing so?

A. That I might have an opportunity of admiring its beauty.

Q. What Ideas occured to you on this occasion?

A. Surprize, wonder and grief took pohsehsion of my mind at that time.

Q. Why was you thus affected?

A. I was thus affected, at the Sight of what I saw inclosed in the blazing Star —

Q. Pray what Could that be?

A. The Ineffable name of the great architect of the universe.

Q. Why had that Star only 5 Rays?

A. It was to show that in the Construction of the Temple the 5 orders of architecture were made use of - .
2dly to represent the 5 points of filicity.
3dly the 5 senses, without w^h. a man is imperfect.
4^{thly} the 5 lights of Masonry - and
5^{thly} The 5 Zones, Inhabited by Masons.

Q. Which are the 5 points of felicity?

A. To walk, and interceed for, to pray, love and ahsist your bretheren so as to be united with them in heart and mind.

Q. Why were you seized with wonder?

A. It was on seeing the beauties and ornaments of the Temple, where of I saw but a part.

Q. Why did you not see the whole?

A. A thick veil conceiled a part from my view, but I hope that the strong desire I have to improve, and my zeal for the Royal Art will disperse the cloud in time, w^h now obstructed my sight of them.

Q. Why was you seized with grieve?

A. As all the wonders I saw, brought to my remembrance the melancholly End of our resp^{ble} and dear M^r. H. A. -

Q. Did you find nature giving away, when you endulged your grief?

A. I must have sunk under the weight of my aflictions, if I had not been seasonable releived by those about me, whom I afterwards found to be my brothers.

Q. How did you discover that they were bretheren of you?

A. By their invoking the ineffable name, having previously pronounced Jackinai, w^h. I saw in the middle of the Blazing Star.

Q. did you promise to keep these matters secret, & under what penalty?

A. I did promihs the strictest secrecy, and that under the penalty of having my body Severed in two, and my bowels Torn out.

Q. How was you made to walk?

A. By the 5 points of exactitude.

Q. What do you mean by this?

A. I mean the 5 solemn steps I took in advancing to the foot of the Throne of the powerful king of Israel, when I took my ob^n in his presence.

Q. Why was you oblig'd to repres^t a dead man at your receptions and why then covered with a firy red cloth?

A. In order to denote to us that good Mas^s sh^d be dead to ye world and its vices -

Q. What do the Scales implie, w^h were put into your hand?

A. As it is an emblem of Justice, and given to me, to denote That I must do Justice by the bretheren, and conciliate all differences that may occur amongst them. And by the said scales I must also weigh my own actions and regulate my conduct in order to Justifie the good opinion conceived of me, by being appointed Master in Israel and Intend^t of the buildings

Q. Have you seen your Ill^s Thr. puihs^t M^r this day?

A. I have seen him.

Q. Where was he placed, and how clad?

A. He was placed in the east, under a rich Canopy, bespangl^d with brilliant Stars, and clad in azur & gold.

Q. Why was he clad thus?

A. Because, when the almighty appeared to Moses on mount <u>Sinai</u>, and delivered him the Tables of the Law, he seemed to be in a cloud of azur & Gold.

Q. Have you any remains of darknehs about you?

A. The Morning Star enlightens me, and the mysterious one guides me.

Q. Where was you thus conducted to?

A. I cannot tell you.

Q. How old are you?

A. 27.

Q. What numbers have you remark'd?

A. 5, 7, & 15.

Q. Where did you perceive them, and what do they mean?

A. I marked them in the arangement of the lights, and have already explained the 2 first numbers, the last represent ye 15 Masters who found the Body of H. A. under the Sprig of accahsia - w^h party was headed by Mohabon.

Q. Why do you wear green on your apron and ribbon?

A. To teach me that Virtue and Zeal in Masonry are the only roads to lead me to Virtue and Sublime knowledge.

Q. What does your Jewel represent?

A. The Tripple Ehsence of the Divinity. -

End of the Lecture

To close the Lodge

Q. What is the clock, Thr: Ill^s Warden?

A. T: Puihs^t the day is at an End.

T: P: speaks. Remember Thr: Ill^s Bretheren, and think of the 5 points of Felicity,'T is time to rest. He then strikes 5 w^h is repeated by the wardens, and then by all the bretheren with their hands by 5, 7, & 15. And thus the Lodge is closed - .

NB. Many lodges have the 27 lights, as 5, 7, & 15, and it seems proper to be so; and also the aprons to be lined with green, and bordered. And that the ribbon of this order should have a small knot made with a green ribbon and the End of it. - all this is conformable to our Instructions, and has been altered by those who call this degree, The Scotch M^r. of the 3 I. I. I. -

Finis

9th Degree
or
chapter of Master Elected of Nine

The chamber where this chapter is held, represents one of the apartments in Solomons Palace; the hangings red, with white columns intermixed with flames.

The M^r, represents Solomon in Royal Robes, and is stiled <u>The Most Sovereign</u>.

There is but one warden, who sits alone in the west; he represents <u>Stolkin</u>, and bears the Title of Inspector.

All the rest of the bretheren, must be in black, and all placed in the south, for in the north are to be the lights, 8 close together and one by itself.

When there is a reception, all the bretheren have their hatts flapt, the right leg over the left, their heads leaning on their Right hands, sitting as in doleful posture - their aprons to be lined and bordered with black, a broad black order from the left shoulder to the right hip, a poniard hanging there to with 9 red roses on said order near the poniard, 4 of each side and 1 at the bottom, having their poniards laying at their feet.

The draft of this chapter is an oblong square at the upper part of which to the right is drawn the city of Jerusalem, and on the other side is represented a Cave not far from the sea, and near <u>Joppa</u> Surrounded with Rocks, in which you discover a man, laying with his head on a Rock; you also see a burning lamp hanging in the cave, and a poniard at his feet, a running stream of water & a cup to drink out. - In the middle of the draft appears a bush as if on fire and burning by the reflection of a Rainbow above the cave you also see a brilliant star under the rainbow above the cave, which seems to stand fixt in order to point out the asylum the murderer had taken refuge in, to clude the vigilance of his pursuers. In said draft you likewise see a winding road, which leads from the City of Jerusalem to <u>Joppa</u>. - On this road near the cave you see a dog, which is the figure under w^h. the unknown guide is drawn, and one man following s^d dog closely; and at a Considerable distance behind them on the same road, you see 8 other men walking without order -

Near the room where this chapter is held, must be a small Room and an artificial Cave, and a large stone for the cand^e to sit on and a little Table before it, a lamp hanging, and under the lamp must be wrote with large Letters <u>Revenge</u>, a poniard on the Table; there must also be a spring, or a running spout, and a cup to drink out; and on the ground must be an Effigy of a man as if he was asleep, whose head is to be loose to the body, as the cand^e is to Cut it off and brings it in the chapter.

The Most Sov^n Sits under a Canopy in an Elevated chair of State in the chapter, covered with black, and before him a Table cover'd with a black and firy Colour'd Carpet, on w^h. is a Bible a Scepter and a poniard.

Solomon uses a Scepter instead of a mallet in this Degree and the Insp^r. strikes with his poniard instead of a mallet, which he constantly holds in his hand as a token of Revenge.

To open the chapter

Q. The M: S: asks: are you an Elected knight?

A. one cavern received me, one lamp lighted me, and a spring refreshed me.

Q. What was the clock?

A. break of day. - on which the Most Sov^n. knocks with his Scepter 8 quick, and 1 by itself, which is answ^d by the Insp^r. <u>Stolkin</u> in the same manner with his poniard, and then by all the bretheren with their hands - Then the Mt Sov^n. says this chapter is open then all the bretheren seat themselves in their proper attitudes.

Form of a Reception

The preparing Brother brings the cand^us to the door, & knocks very hard 8 & 1, which is repeated by the Most Sovereign on which the Insp^r. gets up and receives the cand^us, whom he carries in the middle of the chapter opposite the Mt Sov^n (all the bretheren sitting in their proper attitude) after a little Silence, the M. S. asks the cand^{us} viz:

Q. What do you want?

A. (the cand^{us}. being prompted) I come to ask the favor of being Initiated into the degree of M^r. Elected of 9.

Q. What motive could induce you to think that you deserve to have such a favor conferred on you?

A. My Zeal fervor and constancy, which I promihsed, and shall be doubled here after, has made me aspire to beg this favor.

Q. Learn my brother, that you ought impute your present admihsion into this degree and chapter, lehs, to a desire we may have of conferring this degree on you, then to an Inclination we had of making a Trial of your conduct and Courage and of your compliance with the ob^{ns} you have contracted in the different degrees you Recovered.

You may recollect that, when you was made a Mason after the light was shewn you, you did see all the bretheren armed; you know that it was in your defence, in case of your being exposed to any danger - you also know that them arms were intended for your distruction, and to be plunged into your heart to vindicate Masonry, if you should happen to be wicked enough to violate y^r solemn ob^{ns} and divulge the secrets of Masons and Masonry

Still notwithstanding the most sacred and Solemn obligations and the severe penalties which we submitted ourselves to Incur, in or swerving from them, there have been people vile enough to violate these Sacred Ties and to Expose themselves to all the Tortures which they had in such cases denounced against themselves - know, my Brother that at this present hour we have in our power one of the perpetrators and murderers of our Resp^{ble} M^r. Hiram abif, who groans under the enormity of his guilt, and Expect every Instant to undergo the rigorous Tortures which his Crime richly merits; to serve as an Example to deter others.

This I had from a stranger who will conduct those (I send) to the place where this miscreant (or <u>Abyram</u>) is hid. My dear brother this Illus^s chapter is fully convinced of your Zeal, and much disposed to confer higher degrees on you - Now offers an opportunity of your being the first to revenge the craft by bringing this criminal to condign punishment, if pohsible adequate to the Enormity of his crime. -

Do you find yourself disposed to vindicate the Royal Art, and sacrifice this Traitor in Honor of Masonry? answer me? The cand^{us} answers as he thinks proper. then the M^t S: continues:

I must previously inform you, that this man perhaps is one of your friends; nay, he may be one of your most intimate ones. But in such case as this is, Every sentiment must give way to that of revenge, which with you is to stifle every other consideration - Be ahsured that no bad consequences will attend you perpetrating the revenge - besides this is the only opportunity that offers of making us sensible of your Zeal, by which you will be admitted into this degree. Determine immediatly.

A. I am determined.

Then the Mt Sov^n says: Suffer yourself to be conducted and follow the stranger to the place where the criminal is. He is then blindfolded and conducted to the cave, seated on the stone opposite the sleeping murderer - the preparing Brother tells: Be not afraid, I must leave you a while, on which another brother near the cave shakes a parcel of chains and groans as under afflictions and dread of punishment. The preparing brother then places the cand^{es} left hand on the Table, and his head leaning on it, his right hand on his Thigh, and then says: My dear brother I must leave you here alone, but you must promise me on the word of a man, that you will remain in this posture I now leave you in, however alarmed you may be, by any noise you shall hear, attend to what I say, for if you neglect, it may cost you your life. What do you say?

The cand^{us}. ans^{rs}. that he will.

1st Then my brother, as soon as you hear any body knock as a mason, take the Bandage from your Eyes, and closely Examin every object that surrounds you.

2dly When you hear a 2^d knocking in a Masonic manner, drink of the cup near your left hand. But at the 3^d knocking which you shall hear, you shall Exactly follow, what shall be perscribed to you by a voice which will direct you - tho' I leave you alone, believe me that the Eyes of the whole chapter are on you, where fore I beg that you will not fail punctually to comply with these Instructions - fare well, I must leave you.

Then the Terrible Brother leaves him and shuts the door of the cave briskly, and waits for a minute or 2, to his own reflections - he then knocks the first 3, on w^h. the cand^{us} takes the Bandage off, then he knocks the second 3, on which he drinks out of the cup, and on the last 3 knocks a voice is heard which says: Take that poniard and strike the villain first on the head, and then in the heart, cut off his head, take that in your left hand and the poniard in your right and follow me, who brings him thus arrayed to the door of the chapter, on w^h. the door is open'd a little by a brother who asks, who's there? The reply is that Brother <u>Joabert</u> is there, who has discovered where the Traitor <u>Akyrop</u>, or <u>Abyram</u>, had lain concealed, and that he had revenged the death of our Resp^{ble} M^r. H. A. and comes to lay the villains head at king Solomons feet, on which the door is immedially open'd, and the cand^{us} thus arrayed hurry's hastily to the Throne, at the same time striking the head with the poniard, crying out Revenge.

The king looking at him with the greatest Rage & indignation says: <u>"O wretch! what have you done? My orders to you were, that the Traitor should be brought to me, not that you should put him to death. Your disobedience of my orders, shall cost you your life - Stolkin put him to death."</u> on which all the bretheren put one knee to the ground and earnestly entreat the Most Sov^n to pardon him, alledging in his behalf, that it was an Excehs of Zeal and love for the memory of our resp^{ble} Master H. A. that had Certainly prompted him to disobey his orders. Whilst the bretheren interceed for <u>Joabert</u>, Brother <u>Stolkin</u> the Insp^r lays hold of the head, and ready with his drawn Sabre in the other hand to execute his Sovereigns orders; who at length yields to the entreaties of the bretheren and pardons him in Consideration of his Zeal.

Then the Most Sov^n orders him to draw near and contract his ob^{ns} when the Head and poniard are taken from him.

"I A. B. do solemnly promise in the presence of the great Architect of the universe and of the Resp^ble bretheren here present, and who compose this Illus^s. Chapter of elected masters, never to reveal the Secrets of this degree, with which I have been or shall be made acquainted to any person whatsoever, but to a brother known to be of this degree, and in this I bind myself by all my former ob^ns -

"I likewise promise to revenge masonry in general, and in particular the most horrid murder that ever was committed.

"I also promise to protect and support the order and my bretheren, with all my might Credit and power; and also the gr^d Council of princes of Jerusalem etc etc. and if I fail in any part of this my present ob^ns & Engagement, I submit to perish by the same vindictive wapon, which shall now be given me as an honorable mark of this order, and as a reward of my Zeal, fervor and constancy - so God guide my Steps. Amen, Amen, Amen."

After this ob^n the Mt Sov^n raises the cand^us, and gives him the S. T. & Word, and invests him with the apron and Ribbon of the order, then kihses him four times on each cheek, and one on the forehead, and lastly delivers him the Jewel of the order, being the vindictive poniard or Wapon, to make use of when he is ordered to do so.

Sign   The 1st is made, by pretending to strike with the poniard the forehead of a brother (to whom you are going to give the Sign) to which he answers, by Instantly clapping his hand to his forehead and looking at it, to see if bloody.

Sign   the 2^d is made, by pretending to strike your poniard into a broth^rs Heart, pronouncing the word <u>Necum</u>, to which the other answ^rs by clapping his hand on his heart, and saying <u>Nikah</u>.

Token   the Token is given thus: you take the thumb of an other brothers right hand, in the bottom of your hand, and clinch all y^e. fingers of both hands, put up your thumb, which signifies the 9 Elected 8 close together, and 1 by itself. -

gr^d.w^d   The grand word of the m^r. Elected is, <u>Bagulkal</u>, which signifies chief of the Tabernacle, or faithful guardians friends and favorites - this is the sacred word -

After this the cand^us is ordered to sit down with the bretheren, and in the same posture, when the Most Sovereign addrehses him in the following manner.

The Historical discourse by the Most Sovereign

Thrice Resp^ble Brother·Elect, the unanimity and Earnestnehs with which this respectable ahsembly requested your pardon, disposed our heart to grant it, Especially as your crime was owing to an overzeal. In this you have Initiated <u>Joabert</u> - king Solomons favorite, as I am going to inform you.

You without doubt recollect the melancholy catastrophe of our Resp^ble M^r. H. A. whose death is the constant object of our grief and Tears; and in this we take Example from the wisest of kings, (whom I at present represent,) who bemoaned y^e. Imparable Lohs he sustained by his death, - you well know, that Solomon on hearing that he was mihsing, immediately put a stop to the buildings, and swore that no person should be paid his wages, until this great man was found dead or alive. - You will also recollect, that bretheren went in search of him, and that <u>Stolkin</u> at length found him ahsanitrated, and burried under a sprig of accahsia - <u>Stolkin's</u> good luck on the melancholly occasion endeared him to the king, and procured him the most intimate confidence. Nor was <u>Solomon</u> contented with having the Funeral obsequious of that great man Celebrated with as much splendor and magnificence as pohsible; but was also determined to take public satisfaction of the perpetrators of that horrid crime, and sacrifice them to the manes of his Deceased friend.

He Ihsued out a proclamation, promihsing a Considerable to any person, who should detect where the villain or villains lay concealed, who committed this horrid murder; declaring at the same time, that he even would forgive the ahsahsin himself, provided he would appear in his presence, and acknowledge his guilt but must give up his accomplices, so as to bring them to condign punishment, and thus Expatiate the greatest of crimes.

This proclamation was out for a considerable time without his receiving any Intelligence concerning the matter. When one day, when <u>Solomon</u> was sitting in his Hall giving audience to more than 90 masters or other officers of the order, <u>Zerbal</u> the captain of the guards, came in and informed him, that a strange person desired admittance to the king in private, as he had a matter of the utmost consequence and importance to communicate to him - the bretheren were alarmed at the readinehs with which the king consented to this private audience, for fear of any danger to his sacred person; but said audience proved but short, and the kings speedy return removed their fears. - He informed them that this unknown person was acquainted with the retreat of a murderer of H: abif, and had offered to conduct hither such people as would chuse to accompany him to inform themselves to the truth of which he ahserted. the bretheren all to one man stood up, and offered their service on the occasion, the king was highly pleased at their zeal, but declared that among such a number of virtuous bretheren casting of lots, must determine who should have the Honor of being employed on this important matter, to bring him this odious victim, which he intended wreak his vengeance on. The names of all the Intendants of the buildings who were present were put into a box, and he declared, that those 9 whose names should be first drawn from the box, should be the bretheren appointed to follow the unknown man, and bring the Traitor alive in order to make him an Example to the latest posterity. The lots were drawn, and Joy gladden'd the faces of those whose names came out. They received Instructions from the king to follow the unknown man, who wou'd conduct them to the cave, which was the Traitors usual residence since his crime - they obeyd the orders and departed, but one of the 9 namely <u>Joabert</u> (whom you this day represent) annimated with uncommon ardor, and thinking his breth[n] walked too slowly, got a head of them, and was the first that came to the cave or ahsahsins asylum, which was situated near the seaside, not far from <u>Joppa</u>, near which was a Bush that seemed to burn, and a star which had conducted them, seem'd to stand fixed over the cave. <u>Joabert</u> inflamd with rage, enters it, and by the help of a lamp, which hung in the cave, sees the villain asleep, laying on his back, & a dagger or poniard at his feet, which he seizes, and strikes him with all his might first on his head, and next in his heart; on which the villain sprung up with fury, but immediatly dropt down dead at his feet, pronouncing only the word <u>Necum</u>. - <u>Joabert</u> cut off his head, & then quenched his thirst at the spring in the cave, and then was joyned by his bretheren whom he Just was going to meet - They seeing the head of the Traitor cut off, represented to <u>Joabert</u> that he had committed a fault by his over zeal, and that thus putting an end to the villains Life, he has rescued him from the Tortures which Solomon had prepared for him. They ahsured him the king would not pahs unnoticed this his disobedience of orders, and would Certainly punish him for it, but however that they would interceed with Solomon to procure his pardon - then they quenched also their thirst - Joabert took, and all walked back to Jerusalem When they arrived Solomon on seeing them, was going to give orders for the intended Tortures, when he espied Abyram's head in Joaberts hand, at the sight of which he could not restrain his wrath, therefore ordered Stolkin to put Joabert to death, which he would have executed, if all the bretheren had not thrown themselves on their knees and begged him off. Just as the bretheren of this Illus^s chapter have done for you my dear brother.

You see, what a deal of useful instructions may be drawn from the Circumstances attending this History. vizt -

1st By the death w^h the Traitor suffered, you see that crimes never go unpunished, sooner or later they meet with their deserts.

2dly you may learn from the danger which the Impetuous Joabert was in, how unsafe it is to exceed your orders, and that it becomes a necehsary duty literally to comply with the orders of your superiors.

3dly by the pardon procured for this zealous brother, you may also learn, how easily the heart of a good king is Influenced to be merciful; you also see, how useful it is to have friends who Intest themselves warmly for us on Critical occasions

My dear Brother we will put an End to this Discourse by applauding your reception by 8 & 1, and then be attentive to the Lecture or Instructions of this noble degree. Then they applaud 8 & 1.

Lecture or Instructions

Q. Brother Stolkin, are you a Master Elected?

A. The ballot has alone determined the matter, and I have been acquainted with the cave.

Q. What have you seen in the cave?

A. a Light, a poniard and a fountain, with the Traitor Ahyrop or

Q. of what use were these things to you?

A. The light, to dispel the darkneſs of the place, the dagger to revenge the death of our Resp^ble Mr H. A. & the spring to quench my thirst.

Q. where were you made a Mr Elect?

A. In the Hall of audience in Solomon's Palace.

Q. How many Intent^s of the buildings, were made at that time?

A. Nine, of which I was one.

Q. From what order, and number of people, where these 9 chosen?

A. From upwards of 90, mostly intendants of the buildings & some masters.

Q. What motive prompted you to become a Mr Elect?

A. The desire of revenging the death of H. A. by destroying his murderer.

Q. Where did you find the aſsaſsin?

A. In the bottom of a cave, Cituated at the foot of a burning bush, not far from the sea, near Joppa.

Q. Who shew'd you the way there?

A. An unknown person.

Q. What roads did you paſs through?

A. Through dark, and almost inacceſsible roads.

Q. What did you do, when you came to the cave?

A. I laid hold of the dagger which I found there, and with it struck the villain so violintly on the head, and then in his heart that he expired immediatly.

Q. did he say any thing before he died?

A. He only said one word.

Q. What was that?

A. give me the first letter of the 1st Syllable, and I will give you the 1st letter of the 2^d Syllable.

A. C.

Q. What do these 2 letters N. & C. mean?

A. <u>Necum</u>, or <u>Nikah</u> which signifies Revenge.

Q. How was your Election consumated?

A. By revenge, disobedience, clemency, and 8 & 1.

Q. Explain this?

A. By revenge, I distroyed the Traitor, by disobedience I Exceeded the orders given me by the king - by clemency, as through the Intercehsion of my bretheren I obtained the kings Pardon and lastly by 8 & 1, as we were only 9 chosen for the businehs.

Q. What did you do, after having killed the Traitor?

A. I cut off his head, and quenched my thirst at the spring and being fatigued, laid myself down to sleep, until my 8 Bretheren entered the cave, crying out revenge.

Q. How did Solomon behave and receive you, when you presented him the Traitors head?

A. With Indignation, as he had proposed to himself much gratification in puneshing that villain, and even doomed me to death, but on account of my zeal forgave me.

Q. What did the dark room represent, into which you were conducted before your reception?

A. It is the representation of the cave, where the Traitor was found by me.

Q. How came you there to be left blindfolded?

A. To call to my mind the Traitors sleep, and how often we may think ourselves secure after committing a crime, when we are in most danger.

Q. How do the Elected walk?

A. Darknehs obliged them to put their hands before their Eyes & heads to prevent being hurt, or knocking themselves against any thing, and as the roads were bad an uneven, they were obliged often to crohs their legs. and it is for this reason, when sitting in y^e. chapter they have their legs acrohs one another.

Q. What does the dog represent, that you see on the road near ye Cave?

A. The unknown person, or the good citizen, who conducted us Elected.

Q. What does the naked bloody arm, with a poniard mean?

A. That revenge ever attends guilt.

Q. What does the black ribbon, with the poniard to it, means?

A. The grief still subsisting, For H. abif, though one of his murderers was punished; and as it was done by Masons, and some as yet unpunished.

Q. What Emblems do you use, to Exprehs the number of 9 Elect?

A. 1st by the 9 red roses, at the bottom of the order or black ribbon
2dly By the 9 lights in the chapter.
3dly By 9 strokes of the Scepter and mallet.
4thly By the 9 kihses, 4 on each cheeck, and one the forehead, these are the emblems of the 9 Elected, and the red is the Emblem of the precious blood that was spilled in the Temple, & ordered to remain, till revenge was fully completed.

Q. How do wear that large black Ribbon?

A. From the left shoulder to the right hip, with the poniard hanging to it at the bottom, being the order and Jewel of the degree of Elected of 9. -

Q. of what colour is your apron?

A. a white skin lined and bordered with black, spotted with red and on the flap wh is turned down, must be painted a naked bloody arm, holding a bloody dagger, and as if said arm came out of the clouds

Q. with what is the chapter of the Elected hung?

A. with red and white, and mixed with flames, white flames on the red, and red flames on the white. the one Indicates the blood that was spilled, and the white the ardor and purity of the Elected.

Q. Why have you no more then one warden?

A. Because the chapter were always held in Solomons Palace, where was no body permitted but his favorite, who was privy to what pahsed.

Q. What more is to be done now?

A. Nothing, as every thing is atchieved & H. A. revenged.

Q. Give me the pahsword?

A. Necum, or Revenge.

Q. what is the great word?

A. <u>Bagulkal</u>, a word w^h signifies faithful guardian, or chief of the Tabernacle, friend and chosen favorite.

Q. Is there no other pahsword?

A. Yes, there are 2 more. by which we know one another, vizt <u>Joabert</u> & <u>Stolkin</u>.

Q. at what time did the Elected set out on their yourney to the cave?

A. Just at Dusk.

Q. when did they return?

A. at day break.

Q. How old are you?

A. 8 & 1, Perfect.

End of the Lecture.

To close the chapter.

The Illus^s Sovereign, makes the Sign by putting his hand on his forehead. and says: my bretheren, Let us renew our Ob^ns

All the bretheren make the Sign with the poniards together, first, as striking at the head, and then at the heart. then the Most Sovereign strikes 8 & 1, which is repeated by Brother <u>Stolkin</u>, and then by all the bretheren with their hands and then the chapter is closed -

End of the 9th Degree.

10th Degree
called
Illustrious Elected of 15

This chapter must be all in black, spread with red and white Tears. In the East a Skeleton representing <u>Jubulum Akyrop</u>, by some called <u>Abyram</u> by others Hoben; In the West a Skeleton representing <u>Jubella Guibs</u> and in the South a 3^d Skeleton representing <u>Jubello Gravelot</u>, of the two last the flies have sucked their blood. each of these skeletons are armed with that Tool, with which they perpetrated the horrid murder.

(To open) The Most Illus^s Master strikes 5, when 5 candles are lighted at his left side. Then the Insp^r or Senr Warden strikes 5, on which 5 more candles are lighted and placed before him. Then the T:P: says:

Q. Brother Insp^r what's the clock?

A. Most Illus^s M^r it is 5.

Then the Most Illus^s says: if it is 5 my dear bretheren it is time to begin the work. Give notice that the chapter of Masters Elected of 15 is open. The Insp^r repeats the same, and the chapter is open.

Form of a Reception

There can be no more then 15 Masters Elected in a chapter when a reception — If more then 15 the eldest remain of that number in the Lodge or chapter, and the others withdraw till the reception is over. The Junr. warden conducts the cand^{us} from the antichamber to the door of the chapter, and knocks 5. on w^h the Insp^r orders a brother to go and see, whose there? he opens the door a little, and asks, who's there? the Junr Warden on the outside answers, a Brother Elect of 9, who wants to know the 2 other Ruffians of our Resp^{ble} Mr H. A. and to arrive to the degree of Illus^s M^r of 15.

Then the door is shut, and reports the same to the Inspector, who acquaints the chair of it; when the Thr: Ill^s orders the cand^{us} to be Introduced, on which he enters and makes 15 Steps in a Triangular manner and advances to the altar, holding a head in each hand, all the bretheren stand with their daggers ready to strike, then drop their poniards enterlace their hands with the backpart of the hands to the forehead, and beg pardon for the cand^{us}. The Ill^s T: P: says: how is this? they answer, he is not blameable. then the T: Ill^s replies, if he is not guilty why do you ask pardon for him? The Insp^r then answ^{rs} 'T is a grace we ask for him to be admitted in the degree of illus Mr Elected of 15. the T: P: asks, is he qualified? when all the bretheren answer, he is.

T: P: - If so, tell him to kneel - then the Thr: Ill^s says to him - the Ill^s masters Elect here present, beg me to admit you to the degree of gr^d Mr Elect in order that you should become equal with them - do you feel yourself able to keep the secrets of this degree, and will you take a solemn obligation - he answers yes. then the wardens take the heads from him, and putting his hand on the Bible he takes the follow^g

Obligation

"I A B. do promise and swear on the Holy Bible never to reveal where I have Received this degree, nor never tell who ahsisted at my reception - and further promise never to receive a person in this degree without a full power from my superiors, nor to ahsist at any reception unlehs in a regular chapter of this degree, to keep exactly in my heart all the secrets that shall be revealed to me - and in failure of this my Ob^{ns}, I consent to have my body open'd perpendicular and to be exposed for 8 hours in the open air, the venomous flies may glutt on my Entrails, my head to be cut off, and put on the highest pinacle of the world - and I will always be ready to Inflict the same punishment on those, who shall disclose this degree and break their obligation - So may God maintain me, Amen."

After this Ob^n the cand^{us} rises, and the T: P: gives him the Sign, Token & word - NB: there are 2 Signs.

1st Sign is, you take the poniard and touch your chin with your hand as if you would open your own Belly, on which the other answers

2^d Sign, by the Enter'd app^{ces} Sign, but the fingers clinched.

The Token is - you put your fist against each others body, the thumb upwards as if you would cut each others belly open.

the pahsword is: <u>Eleham</u>.

the words are: one says <u>Zerbal</u>, and the other ans^{rs} <u>Benaya</u>.

History of this degree.

My dear Brother, you have learnt in the degree of Elected of 9 which you have past, that Jubulum Akyrop, one of the Ruffians was killed in the cave. that Skeleton in the East was him, you see him armed with a setting mawl, with that Tool he knock'd H.A. down, whose head Solomon had embalmed in order to keep, to be Exposed until the other 2 were found out.

Six months after Akyrop was killed, Bengabee one of Solomons intendants made enquiry in the country of Gath or Cheth, tributary to Solomon, when he learnt that Jubella Guibs and Jubello Gravelot the 2 other ahsahsins of H. A. had retired there thinking themselves in safety -

Solomon having learnt this wrote immediately to king Moacha of Gath, desiring him to deliver these 2 villains to the people he shoud send, in order to receive at Jerusalem the punishment due to their crimes.

In consequence of w^h. Solomon elected 15 of the most worthy bretheren and zealous masters, in which number were included the 9, that went to the cave of Akyrop.

They began their march on the 15th of the month, w^h. answers to the month June, and arrived the 20th of the same month in the country of Gath, and delivered Solomons Letter to king Moacha, who trembled at the news, and ordered immediately a strict search to be made for the 2 Ruffians, and if found to be delivered to the Israelites, and that he should be happy in having his country cleared of such monsters.

For 5 days there was a strict search made, when Zerbal & Elehad, were the first that discover'd them in a quarry of Bendaca, where they chain'd them together, and loaded them with Irons, on which was engraved the crimes they had been guilty of; to have their approaching fate before their Eys.

They arrived at Jerusalem on the 15th of the following month, when conducted to Solomon, who having charged them with the most striking reproaches of their black Crimes, order'd them to be put in the Tower of Achizar, till the day that they were to be Executed by the most Excrutiating torments and death proportionable if pohsible to their crimes - When on one morning at ten of the clock they were tied to 2 stakes by the neck, middle and feet, their arms behind them, when the

Executioner open'd them from the breast to the os Pubis and acrohs and were left in this condition for Eight hours, in which time y^e. flies and other Insects sucked their blood - their groans and complaints were so lamentable, that it even moved the Executioner, who cut off their heads, and their bodies were thrown over the walls of Jerusalem to serve as food for the crows and wild beasts of the Forrest. Now listen to our -

Lecture

Q. Are you a gr^d M^r. Elected?

A. My zeal and my work has procured me this degree.

Q. Where have you been Received?

A. By Solomon himself, in his audience chamber.

Q. When did he receive you, and on what occasion?

A. When he sent me with my companions, to find the 2 other Ruffians.

Q. Was you enquiring after them yourself?

A. Yes, Most Ill^s Sov^n, and if I had not been named by Solomon, I should at my own Expences have gone, to shew my zeal in revenging the death of H. A -

Q. You felt a great Joy, when you saw the villains Executed?

A. The 3 heads I wear on my order is a proof of it.

Q. What signifie these 3 heads.

A. They are the 3 heads of the ahsahsins of H. A.

Q. What you mean by 3 heads, and Just now you told me, you went in search two villains?

A. Because of the villains, had already suffered, before the other two were taken.

Q. What was the names of the 2 you brought to Jerusalem?

A. One was called <u>Jubella Guibs</u>, and the other <u>Jubello Gravelot</u>.

Q. How were they discoverd?

A. By the Deligence of Bengabee, Solomon's Intendant in the country of Gath.

Q. What method did Solomon take to take them?

A. He wrote a letter to <u>Moacha</u> king of <u>Gath</u>, desiring him to make a strict enquiry for then.

Q. Who carried and deliverd Solomon's letter to Moacha?

A. <u>Zerbal</u>, king Solomon's Captain of the guard.

Q. Did king <u>Moacha</u> hesitate to grant Solomon's request?

A. No, on the contrary, he gave us guides and a guard.

Q. Where were they found?

A. In a quarry, called Bendaca's quarry.

Q. Who was this Bendaca?

A. one of Solomon's Intendants, who had married on of his daughters.

Q. How came the 2 Ruffians discovered?

A. By means of a shepherd, who shew'd us their retreat.

Q. Who perceived them first?

A. <u>Zerbal</u> and <u>Elehad</u>, after a search of 5 days.

Q. How were their chains made?

A. In form of a Rule and square, on which was engraved the crimes they had committed, to have their approaching death before their Eyes.

Q. What day did you return with them to Jerusalem?

A. The 15th of the month, which ans^{rs} to our month July.

Q. How long was you upon that voyage.

A. A month Exactly.

Q. How many masters were Elected by Solomon, to go on this Expedition?

A. 15 in all, of which I was one.

Q. Was there no body else with you?

A. Yes, king Solomon sent troops to Excort us.

Q. What did you do with the Ruffians, after your arrival at Jerusalem.

A. We carried them directly in the presence of Solomon.

Q. What orders did Solomon give about them?

A. After he had reproached them bitterly for the enormity of their

Crimes, he ordered <u>Achizar</u>, gr^d M^r of his household, to confine them in the Tower that bore his name, and that they should be Executed the next day at 10, o'clock.

Q. With what kind of death were they punished?

A. They were tied naked by the neck and heels to two posts, their Bellies cut open from the breast to their privies, and acrohs.

Q. Did they continue any time in that Condidtion?

A. They were thus exposed for Eight hours in the hott sun, that the venemous flies and Insects should suck their blood, which them suffer even more than death itself; they made such lamentations, & cries that they even moved the Executioner.

Q. What did he do to them afterwards?

A. The Executioner moved by their Cries, cut off their heads, and flung their bodies over the walls of Jerusalem, for food of ravens & wild beasts.

Q. What did they do with their heads?

A. They were fixed on poles by order of Solomon, and exposed to public view, with that of Akyrop, in order to give an Exemple as well to the people as to the workmen of the Temple.

Q. What was the name of the first villain?

A. According to the 9 Elect, they called him <u>Abyram</u>, but that word is only an Emblem, as it signifies either villain or ahsahsin, but his right name is <u>Jubulum Akyrop</u>, and was the eldest of the 3 brothers.

Q. On which gates, where these heads Exposed?

A. On the South, East and West gate, that of Akyrop on the East gate, that of <u>Jubello Gravelot</u> on the West gate, and that of <u>Jubella Guibs</u> on the South gate.

Q. For what reason were these heads Exposed on these gates of Jerusalem?

A. Because they had each of them used their violence on H. A. at these gates of the Temple, for when <u>Jubella Guibs</u>, had struck him at the South gate.with a 24 Inch gauge, Jubello <u>Gravelot</u>, struck him with a square at the West gate and <u>Jubulum Akyrop</u> gave him the finishing blow with a setting mawl at the east gate, w^h. kill'd our Resp^{ble} M^r. H. abif.

Q. What is the Pahsword of the gr^d. M^r. Elected?

A. <u>Zerbal</u> & <u>Benaya</u>.

Q. What is the pahs?

A. <u>Eleham</u>.

Q. Which are the Signs?

A. Here they are, you comprehend me. (he gives the Signs)

Q. Which are the Tokens?

A. here they are. - ans^r. me.

Q. What's the clock?

A. Six in the Evening.

Q. Why 6 in the evening?

A. Because it was that hour when the 2 last ahsahsins Expired, by which the death of H. A. was Revenged.   End of Lecture

To close the chapter.

The Thr: Illus^s Sov^n then says: My bretheren since the death of our most dear & resp^{ble} Master Hiram abif is revenged by the Cruel death of his murderers, we ought to be satisfied and rest ourselves.

He then knocks 5, the Insp^r. 5, the Junr. warden 5, & then all the bretheren 5, and the chapter is closed.

End of the 10th Degree

11th Degree - A chapter
called
Sublime Knights Elected

The degree of Sublime Elected, is looked upon as the superior and the chief of the preceeding degrees, and a recompence to those Elected who are the most Instructed and deserving by their Zeal fervor & constancy.

Solomon presides and is stiled Thr: puihsant - In the room of wardens, there is an Insp^r and M^r of Ceremonies.

To open the chapter.

Q. Kn^t Insp^r, what is your duty in this chapter?

A. To see that we are secure.

Q. Are you a Kn^t Sublime Elected?

A. T. P. my name will convince you.

Q. What is your name?

A. <u>Emerk</u>.

Q. What do you mean by that name?

A. A true man on all occasions.

Q. at what time is the chapter of Sub: Elect^d: Kn^{ts} open?

A. Full 12 of the clock at Midnight.

Then the T: P: strikes 7, and says, Kn^{ts} Senr & Junr Warden since the chapter of Kn^{ts}. Sub^{me} is open at Midnight, and it is now full 12 o' clock, give notice to the Sub^{me} Knights, that the grand chapter is open - which is repeated by the Insp^r and the chapter is open.

Form of a Reception

The chapter is open, the T: P: says: Illus^s Wardens have you any thing to propose in this chapter?

A. Ill^s Thr: puihs^t, my brother the M^r of Ceremonies, comes to inform us, that there is in the antichamber a M^r El^t of 15, who has past through all the preceeding degrees, and beseeches you to confer on him the Degree of Sublime Elected.

Q. Has his conduct been without reproach, and are the Illustrious Kn^ts satisfied with it?

A. Most Ill^s Thr: Puihs^t The M^r. of Ceremonies says, that all the bretheren Illus^s Kn^ts here present, are satisfied with his conduct.

Q. Then let him be Introduced in a proper manner - on which the M^r. of Ceremonies goes out to the cand^us who is alone in the Chamber of reflection, and conducts him to the chapter; puts him into a chair between the 2 Wardens, puts his naked sword acrohs his body and gives him a compahs in his left hand, the points to his heart. Then the T: P: asks him the following questions?

Q. Brother what do you want?

A. I beseech, the Most Ill^s Sub^me Kn^ts to confer this Sublime on me.

Then the Thr. Puihs^t says: Ill^s brothers wardens, make this brother approach -

Then the Insp^r. makes the cand^us deliver the sword and compahs to the Junr. Warden, then crohses his 2 hands on his breast, makes him kneel 4 times, first at the west door, and says <u>civy</u>, then the T: P: says <u>Ky</u>, he then kneels a 2^d time at the south, the 3^d time at the north, and the 4th time as the East, where he contracts the following

Obligation

"I A, B, promise and swear, on the same obligations I have already taken and contracted, to keep secret the degree of Sub^me Elected Kn^ts, with which I am going to be intrusted as well in regard to masons under this degree, as to the profane.

"I further promise, to adore God, to be faithful to my king, to be charitable to my neighbours and brothers, submitting myself in case of any infraction of this my obligation, to have my body severed in two, my memory lost, and looked upon as infamous and forsworn - So God and his Holy Evangelist be my help - Amen, amen, amen, amen."

After this the Thr: puihs^t gives him the foll^g S. T. & W^d -

The Sign is: you crohs both your hands on your breast, clinch y^r.

fingers and put up your thumbs.

The Token is: you take the right hand of a brother, and give 3 knocks with your thumb on the middle finger.

The pahsword is: <u>Stolkin</u>, - (the running of water.)

The great word is: <u>Adonai</u>.

Then the Thr: puihs^t. puts his sword 3 times on the cand^{tes} head, and decorates him with the order of this degree, which is a broad black ribbon from the left shoulder to the right hip, with a sword of Justice instead of a poniard to it, and on said Ribbon painted or embroidered 3 Inflamed harts, opposite the breast.

A white apron lined with black, with a small pocket in it, and on the middle of the pocket, a little red crohs.

Then the orator gives the following

History

My dear Brother let your heart intirely be devoted to Enjoy, the Extasy of Innocent Joy, which springs of full satisfaction to feel all the motions that it will inspire you with Blehs Thousand times this happy day, which will open to you the perfection you desire, in short, congratulate yourself with having reached the degree of Sub^{me} Kn^{ts} Elected, which we Just have given you

Do not think, that it is one of the Imaginable & proud Titles which have neither origin or ground for it.

Open the sacred books, search in the Holy histories, and you will find the Epocha of your state, there you will see the Excellency and priviledge of it. - I, should without doubt, pahs the limits of an ordinary discourse, if I was to take upon me, to let you know the whole Extent of it.

I will leave the natural Curiosity, to those who ought to be willing to know perfectly the state which they have embraced, with care, to make the necehsary Enquiry for the knowledge to ought to pohsehs. -

The promise you have made Just now, and contracted in the quality of Sub^{me} Elected Kn^t. is the greatest and the most solemn of them all. - I will not speak to you, of the prudence, with which you have already so often laid the law of to yourself, you know that virtue too well with the practice of it. It must be so familiar to you that it would be needlehs to you to Exhort it, and for that reason we fear no violation from your side. I shall only renew to you the Importance of the promihses, you Just now have made, and which are the chief matters, of your obligation.

There is nobody in this degree who has not submitted like you and in short, if all men have Indispensably fulfilled those duties you Just now have imposed on yourself, with what zeal, what eagernehs and what ardor should not a Sub^{me} Elected Knight acquit himself.

We have first promihsed to love and adore God; this is the Natural law, which is engraved in us. — I say more, which came with us in the world; and who is he that could transgrehs this duty? and not render the Lawful tribute to him, which is owing from us the vile creatures that he has formed? Sustaining us only by the means of his power, which he may distroy & annihilate without being able to accuse him of rigor or Injustice —

This is my Ill^s Knight, the first of your duty, and I say it is the most Ehsential and the most Indispensable duty that reason teaches, truth shews and Justice establishes to us.

You have also promihsed to be faithful to your king — is there any among us who do not feel it perfectly, and is not well convinced with the necehsity of this obligation of Loyalty? as we conform ourselves to the custom, which has thus been established for all those who as you attain to a degree as Eminent as this in which you are now cloathed, and to whom is trusted the glory of Justice, w^h you have in your hand.

We now must learn you the names of the letters which were shewn to you when you was Initiated in our sublime degree & mysteries. It is not one of the common names, which has neither sense, Reason nor signification — It is a name, which is as those in use, in the Eastern Nations, shewing the virtue of those they have found worthy of having it. Yours in the quality of Sub^{me} El^d Kn^t is <u>Emerk</u>, a Hebrew word which does signifies, <u>A true man in all things</u>; can there be any better or a more glorious name? and would it not be a terrible shame and disgrace on any of us, which should Expose himself to do any thing and be capable of degenerating from it -

Now let us come to the alligorically explanations of the figures which you see in the draft represented; they will serve you in instructing the sense of science of your state and learn you to unfold by little and little the moral sence they contain, & precepts you ought to follow, and the principles on which you ought to act and the duties you have to fulfil.

The Elected as you know were those Solomon chose to watch the work w^h was done in the Temple, of the death of H. A.

The Temple was at last finished and compleated to its last perfection - God appeared satisfied with this building which was consecrated to him. The cloud that came down on the Ark of Alliance in the Temple, was a mark of Certainty that the Dedication of it was agreeable to him. It is that cloud, in which they have been willing to trace the Image of God in this draft, by the Triangle you see in the cloud.

Therefore it is very easy to make from these two figures a Just and true application.

Our hearts are the living Temples, where are erected Altars, which ought to receive Sacrifices which we make to the Lord. It should always be a Temple worthy of him; we can never know too much how to employ our time for its construction, neither can we apply ourselves too much to carry offerings which may be agreeable to him, to render ourselves worthy of his favors, that we ought to compare to that miraculous Cloud which spread itself over the ark, by which God shewed the favorable alliance he had made with his people, which is the chief object of the draft now before you. -

In that box which hangs at the Top of the draft, were deposited the hearts of the victims that were offered to the Lord, and which were accepted sacrifices - If the gift you make of your heart, is pure it will become a true figure of it, and he will not regret the offering of it, if all what lays in it is worthy to be offered him.

You see an Urn, it is that in which Solomon deposited the precious heart of H. A. that authentic mark of esteem & tendernehs he had for him is without doubt a very urgent lehson, w^h. invites us to re=inflame our endeavours in conducting our actions of life that we may be able to leave behind, a memory worthy to be consecrated with respect, esteem and veneration.

The pair of scales you perceive to be an attribute of Justice, is here exposed to your sight, to make you remember, that it is with that you ought to weigh your proceedings and projects if you are inclinable to deserve the glorious name of Emerk.

The sword with which you are actually armed with, given you Just now, by the T: P. has been remitted you lehs for a mark of Honor & distinction, then to be employed to serve and be used in order to fulfill the solemn obligation you have contracted.

The Key, which you also see in the draft, is a Symbol to learn you to keep religiously in your heart, the secrets with which you are intrusted; as it is a sacred trust that these Illus^s bretheren have reposed to you.

The zealous charity you ought to have for your bretheren, is figured to you by the emblem of an Inflamed heart, a true symbol of it.

As it is the principal object and the most indispensable duty of a mason to devote himself to practice virtue, what care ought not an Elected Kn^t Sub^{me} to have, never to go from this principle - He, who is in the superior degrees ought always to act effectually to render himself worthy of that distinction - charity is of all virtues the principal one, w^h satisfies humanity the most -

Instead of an Inflamed heart which at the time of the written law was a distinctive Mark of the Sub^{me} Elected. but at this day, we wear a crohs, the form of w^h is here traced to you, - It is the happy Epocha of the law of grace we live in, since upon a crohs was spilled ye precious blood of the sovereign redeemer, to whom we are all indebted. We are all obliged to wear it, not as a mark which may please our vanity or our affection, but as one of the attributes of our condition, and a striking object capable continually to recal us. - That divine author of nature, that sovereign master of our days, has been willing to render himself the victim for ye Iniquities of our fathers, and with drawn them from the Everlasting tormints they had but too much deserved -

You see also two palm trees very high and lofty, which seems to spread their branches over the Tomb of H. a. - as Solomon made place in the Temple for a monument, which was Erected for that great man, in memory of his knowledge and virtue, a man whose conduct had been without reproach & of an upright reputation, who by his deserving actions had required the price, which had been put on them. - They are also the Emblem of the everlasting palm, at which we all aim, and which we shall enjoy, if we never scatter ourselves from the views which are traced for us, to be deserving of it.

These are my Illus^s. brother the chief objects of our draft to which you ought to keep up and study the same, and be always and ever the subject of your reflection.

We flatter ourselves (having so fine a road before you) that you will follow it: and never enter any other dangerous path to scatter you from the many great duties you are to fulfill; you will find the Execution so much the more Easy for it. In short, keeping firm to your obligations, and faithful in your promihses, we shall find in you a brother ardently zealous and officiously charitable, worthy to have the respectable name of a Sublime Elected Knight, which you have now received.

End of the Discourse.

Lecture

Q. Are you an Elected Sublime Knight?

A. T: Ill^s puihs^t., my name will inform you.

Q. What is your name?

A. <u>Emerk.</u>

Q. What means that name?

A. A true man in all things.

Q. How was you arrayed when Introduced in the chapt^r of Sub^{me} Kn^{ts} Elected?

A. I had a sword in my right hand acrohs my body and a compahs in the left, the points of which rested on my breast.

Q. Why the sword acrohs your body?

A. To remind me, that my body should be severed in two, if I was vile Enough, to reveal the mysteries of masonry, and this degree.

Q. And why the compahses points to your breast?

A. To shew that my actions were compahsed, as I was found worthy to receive the degree of Sub^{me} Elected Knight.

Q. How was you reported, in that chapter?

A. By 7 knocks.

Q. What signifie these 7 knocks?

A. The seven years that were employed in the construction of the Temple and its ornaments.

Q. What is your sacred word in quality of Sub^{me} Kn^{t} Elt^{d}?

A. <u>Adonai</u>, which is God.

Q. And the pahsword?

A. <u>Stolkin</u>, the name of him, that found the body of H. A. -

Q. What is the Sign, of the Sub^{me} Kn^{ts} Elected?

A. To crohs both your hands on your breast, fingers clinched and thumbs up. -

Q. What signifies this Sign?

A. The promise I made, to wear always the crohs in remembrance of my faults, since they are defaced thereby.

Q. What is the Token of acknowledgement?

A. To take the right hand of a brother, and strike 3 times with the thumb on the middle finger of the brother.

Q. What signifies this Token?

A. Love to God, Fidelity to my king, and charity towards my bretheren and neighbours.

Q. What did you see on entering the chapter?

A. Twenty four lights.

Q. What do they signifie?

A. The 12 Masters elect, and the 12 Tribes of Israel.

Q. What are the names of the 12 Masters Elect?

A. Joabert, Stolkin, Tercy, Morphy, Alquebert, Dorson, Kerem, Berthemer & Tito, These were the 9 Elected, who went with the Stranger in search of Akyrop to the cave; Zerbal, Banachad and Tabor, are the 3 others to make the number of 12 Masters Elect.

Q. What employ did Solomon give them?

A. To superintend all the Masters, and therefore named them Inspect^{rs} that they might be able to give him an account, of what was dayly done, in the construction of the Temple.

Q. In what manner were these 12 Inspectors employed to survey the conduct of so many workmen?

A. 1st Joabert had the Inspection of or over the Tribe of Judah
    2^{d} Stolkin — — — — — — — — — — of do. Benjamin
    3^{d} Tercy — — — — — — — — — — — do. Simeon
    4th Morphy — — — — — — — — — — do. Ephraim
    5th Alquebert — — — — — — — — — do. Manahsah
    6th Dorson — — — — — — — — — — do. Zebulon
    7th Kerem — — — — — — — — — — — do. Dan
    8th Berthemer — — — — — — — — — do. Asher
    9th Tito — — — — — — — — — — — do. Naphtali
    10th Zerbal — — — — — — — — — — do. Ruben
    11th Benachad — — — — — — — — — do. Ihsachar
    12th Tabor — — — — — — — — — — do. Gad

These 12 Masters rendered daily an account as Insp^{rs} to Solomon, of the work done by all the respective tribes, and they received the amount of the pays to be distributed to all the workmen of every Tribe.

Q. What signifies the Tomb at the west door of the Temple?

A. It is the Tomb where the body of H: abif our dear deceased M^{r} is deposited — Solomon had it placed at the Entrance of the Temple, to shew the Israelites, how much he was affected at the lohs of that great man, and did it in honor to him whom he regarded and esteem'd as himself.

Q. What signifies the I H S, which you see in the draft?

A. The I, is the Initial of <u>Jeva</u>, the first pronunciation of the antient Masters word - the H that of <u>Hiram</u>, our Resp^{ble} M^r and S means Stolkin, who discovered the Body of H. a.

Q. give me a discription of the urn, which is on the Top?

A. In that urn, is the heart of our Dear Mr H. a. Embalmed.

Q. What means the 2 Letter X & C on said urn?

A. <u>Xinchut</u>, a Hebrew word, signifying the seat of the soul.

Q. And what means the Key?

A. The Symbol that we only have the secret & dipositary of the masons secret, and ought to rule our conduct so, to shew by Examples that we are worthy of the Trust and charge reposed in us.

Q. And the Ballance?

A. Calls to our remembrance of the obligations laid on us, to be Just to our brothers & neighbours, since we are those whom king Solomon has put all his confidence, by giving us the power of Exercizing Justice, and terminate disputes which might arize, among masons from the apprentice to the degree of Sub^{me} Kn^{ts} El^d w^h is above them all.

Q. And the sword?

A. To make use of it as we ought to those who do not walk in the path of virtue, and are so vile, as to reveal the secrets they are entrusted with.

Q. How long did it take to compleat that Temple?

A. 7 years in the whole to compleat it, and 1 for the ornaments of it, and its Dedication.

Q. How long was that building?

A. 60 cubits.

Q. What hight?

A. 120 cubits.

Q. How wide?

A. 20 cubits.

Q. How many precious things have you in the chapt^r. of Sub^{me}. Kn^{ts} Elected?

A. 5.

Q. What do call them?

A. The ark of alliance, the golden box, the 2 palmtrees, the candlestick with 7 branches, and the veil which is drawn up.

Q. What signifies the ark of alliance?

A. It was the figure of Solomons Temple consecrated to God & contained the 2 Tables of the Law, w^h. God gave to Moses on the Holy mountain, when he contracted an alliance with the people of Israel.

Q. The candle Stick with 7 branches?

A. Represents the 7 planets, and the 7 gifts of the Holy Spirit.

Q. And the veil of the Temple?

A. The figure of the Babylonian Tapistry, which Solomon placed in the Temple, to separate the Holy places, from the most Holy and sacred place.

Q. And what the golden box?

A. In that golden box were deposited the hearts of those victims whose sacrifices had been agreeable to God - We also ought to deposite our hearts, if our actions are as agreeable to him.

Q. And the palmtrees?

A. they represent the cherubims, w^h. did cover the Holy ark with their wings, as also the Joy Solomon felt, to see a superb monument Raised to the glory of the Lord.

Q. and what signifies the Triangle with the A D ?

A. The cloud that spread over the ark when Solomon Consecrated the Temple, to shew to Solomon 't was agreeable to the Lord. and the letters signifie <u>Adonai</u> - God.

Q. What reward did Solomon bestow on the 12 M^{rs} after the consecration of the Temple?

A. He stiled them his beloved. Instituted them Sub^{me} Kn^{ts}. Elected decorated them with a broad Ribbon, with 3 enflamed hearts on it and a sword of Justice to it. Saying to them: you have been the conductors of the works of the Temple, which I have consecrated to the Lord - Be now the supporters of it against the Infidels.

Q. What denotes the 3 Inflamed hearts?

A. That our hearts ought to be charitable to our brothers & neighbours.

Q. Explain me the 5 letters, you have on yours crohs ?

A. The C, is the Initial of <u>Civi</u>, (to kneel) K, that of <u>Ky</u> (to rise) E, that of <u>Emerk</u>, S that of <u>Solomon</u>, and A in the Centre <u>Adonai</u>.

Q. What signifies the 4 genuflections you made before you came to the foot of the Throne?

A. The 4 gates of the Temple, and the respect we should have to Enter a place consecrated to God.

Q. What signifies the word <u>civi</u>, that the S: E^d utter when the T:P: goes to the Throne?

A. Kneeling before the great arch^t of the universe.

Q. And the word <u>Ky</u>?

A. Rise, and receive the reward that your Zeal and Labor has deserved.

Q. What denotes the 3 knocks given with the sword on the cand^{tus} Head before it is delivered to him?

A. <u>Strength</u>, <u>charity</u> and brotherly love, we ought to have for our brother.

Q. Why have the Sub^{me} Kn^{ts}. Elect^d naked swords in their hands, in this chapter?

A. To be always ready to run to the ahsistance of our bretheren, in their defence, and that of religion against Infidels.

Q. Why is not your chapter opened till midnight?

A. Because some of the Sub^{me}. Kn^{ts}. Elected employed the day by fighting the Infidels, and the others in deeds of charity and hospitality, & at Midnight they met, to account of what they had done.

Q. Why is the chapter closed at break of day?

A. To Execute during the day, what is ordered by the chapter to be done.

End of the Lecture.

To close the Chapter.

Q. Are you a Sub^{me} El^{d} Knight?

A. My Name will inform you.

Q. What is your name?

A. Emerk.

Q. What signifies that word?

A. A true man on all occasions.

Q. What time do you close the chapter?

A. At dawn of day.

Q. What's the clock?

A. The day appears.

T:P: says: as the day appears, give notice, the chapter of Sublime Elected Knights is closed — This is repeated by the Inspect^{r} and close —.

End of the 11 Degree.

12th Degree
of
Grand Master Architect

This lodge must be decorated with white, spread with flames - The M^r is stiled grand M^r arch^t, decorated in white & priest robes, with a large blue ribbon from the right shoulder to the left hip, at the bottom of which hangs a perfect square in form of a medal; on one side is engraved 4 half Circles facing 7 Stars, and in the Center a Triangle with CA there in. On the other side of said medal or Jewel must be the 5 orders of architecture, a Level at Top, and below a square and compahs acrohs, and in the middle of the compahs and square the Letters RM, the first and last letter of the word Rabucim.

The gr^d M^r presiding must at least have the attributes of perfection about him. He sits with his hatt on, his apron white Lined with blue, and a black pocket in it to carry the drawings.

A Case with mathematical Instruments on a table before him.

The warden are decorated as the gr^d M^r arch^t with the level and perpendicular, the same aprons, and on their black pockets in white, they wear besides the attributes of their higher degrees.

The rest of the bretheren wear only a small blue ribbon, with the Jewel to it round their necks, & every one must have a Case Instrum^{ts}

In the North of the lodge must be an Illuminating Star, w^h gives light to the Lodge, and under it a Table with a case with mathematical Instruments.

The grand master arch^t In the East will open the Lodge in the following manner vizt.

To open the Lodge.

Q. Brothers wardens, do your duty?

A. Gr^d Mr Arch^t the lodge is well Tiled, and the prohane cannot penetrate our mysteries.

Q. Are you an architect?

A. I know perfectly well, all what is Inclosed in a perf^t mathematical Case.

Q. What is inclosed in it?

A. a square, a simple compahs, a compahs with 4 points, a rule, a drawingline, a Compahs of proportion, a scale, a folding rule, a drawing pin and a Semicircle.

Q. Where was you received a M^r architect?

A. In a white place, figured with flames.

Q. What signifies the white with the flames?

A. The white signifies the purity of the heart, and flames the Zeal that all the Masters arch^{ts} ought to be pohsehsed of.

Q. What represents the Star in the north?

A. The virtue that should guide all good masons, as the north Star guides the mariners in their navigations.

Q. What's the clock?

A. Lucifer - Morning Star.

G: Mr A. Since it is so my dear bretheren let us work. He Strikes 1 & 2, the Two Wardens do the same - then the gr^d. Mr Arch^t says: This lodge is open.

Form of a Reception

The cand^{us} must be decorated with the ornaments of Sub^{me} Elected Kn^{ts}, they tell him to knock . & .. on the door, on which he enters immedially, and goes from the west to the south where he admires the north Star for a little while, then returns to the west again, where he is interrogated in his former degrees, then he is ordered to walk by 3 square steps - first one by itself and then 2 quick, which brings him to the altar, where he kneels, and the following

obligation

"I A. B. Sub^{me} Elec^d Kn^t of the 12 Tribes of Israel do promise to God and this Royal Lodge of gr^d. Mr Arch^t. never to reveal the secrets of this degree which I am to receive, but to a true grand M^r arch^t, if I him to be one - and I never will suffer or give my consent to admit of any cand^{us} to these mysteries, but comformable to the Laws Statutes and the Secret constitutions of the order.

I further do promise a submihsion to all the regulations which may be given or sent me from the Sovereign princes of the of the order, and an obedience at all times upon the notices Received from the grand council - and if I fail in these my present Engagements, I consent to suffer all the penalties I have imposed on myself in all my former obligations. My name to be wrote in Red letters, in order that posterity may remember me as an Infamous & perfidious man - O God grant that may keep myself in righteousnehs and Equity Amen. Amen amen."

After this obl^n the gr^d M^r architect gives the following

Discourse.

My dear brother, Solomon being willing to form a school of architecture for the Instruction of those who conducted the works of the Temple (and to encourage and improve the true masons in the Royal Art, in order to promote from that school those, whose zeal and discretion had made them deserving the highest perfection) created this degree under the Title of gr^d M^r architect.

This wise king always full of Justice and foreseeing the events was willing to recompence the zeal, knowledge and virtue of the Sub^{me} Kn^{ts} of Emerk, in order to make them approach more and more to the Celestial throne of the great arch^t of the universe - by his divine foresight made him cast his Eyes on those last made Illus^s Kn^{ts} and brothers, in order to effect the promise God had made to Enoch, Noah, Moses & David, that if even through ardor they penetrated the Bowels of the Earth it would not satisfie unlehs the divine providence did permit it.

The attachment that you will make to appear in the study of Geometry (to which you will now be intirely consecrated) will procure you the means of unfolding the most sublime knowledge.

Then the cand^{us} is ordered to walk to the Senr Warden with 3 Steps in the same manner as before, to learn the S. T. & W^d - after he makes the first Step, he stops to admire the Star, and retreats 3, Steps backwards, as being surprized by its splendor. then he makes 2 other Steps, which brings him to the warden.

Sign — The Sign is: you strike or slide your right hand over the inside of your left hand, then stop a little, then slide twice more quickly the fingers close, the thumb extended; after this you do, as if you draw a plan with the right hand in the left, looking often at the gr^d M^r architect for a subject to draw by. —

Token — The Token is: you enterlace the fingers of your right hand with the left of a brother, putting at the same time your left hand on your hip forming a square the thumb before the hip, and so reciprocally —

P. W. the pahsword is, <u>Rabucim</u>, which is, I am an architect.

S^d. W^d. the sacred word is: <u>Adonai</u> (id est) the first name of God.

Then the Senr. Warden decorates him with the blue ribbon and Jewel, which he wears as a collar, cloaths him with the apron, embraces him and wishes him Joy upon his new acquisition — Then tells him to go to the grand M^r arch^t and give him the S. T. & W^d. and from thence to all the bretheren, after which he is seated, and listens to the Doctrine of this degree in manner of a —

Lecture.

Q. Which is the 1st of all the Arts?

A. Architecture where of Geometry is the Key, as well as of all Science.

Q. How many Sorts of architecture are there?

A. Three, civil, Naval & Military. Civil architecture is the art of Building, Houhes, Palaces, Temples, Altars, Steeples, Triumphant arches etc in order to decorate & beautify Cities.

Naval architecture, is the art of building ships of war, and all other sorts of vehsells for navigation, Traffic etc.

And Military architecture is the art of Fortifying cities, Towns etc to sustain the attack of greater numbers with lehs, and to dispose the work in such a manner, that they can not be easily cut through, to strengthen them with Trenches Ditches etc In short to render ons selfs master of the best prepared and easyest to be defended fortifications whatsoever.

In the art of Civil Masonry, the Masters are only to be Masters of Civil architecture - The 2 others serve only as attributes to Masons, but if pohsehsed of them it shews their great Zeal and virtue.

Q. Which are the sciences that a perf^t M^r arch^t ought to pohsehs?

A. There are several which have a connection one with the other. And you cannot dispence with any one alone to Exercize architecture in all its parts - The foll^g a gr^d M^r architect ought to pohsehs the knowledge of. vizt

1st	Arithmetic	11th	Hydraulics
2^d	Geometry	12th	Geography
3^d	Trigonomitry	13th	Cronology
4th	The optics	14th	cutting of stone
5th	The catoptrical	15th	Cutting of wood
6th	The Dioptric	16th	Measure
7th	Designing	17th	Physics
8th	Perspective	18th	Music &
9th	Mechanics	19th	Architecture
10th	Statics		

Q. What is arithmetic, and of what use to Masons?

A. As it is the art of Calculating, and is called <u>arabe</u>, because the characters we make use of, are come to us from the <u>arabians</u> - and that what they call <u>algebra</u>, is also an arithmetic, but a great deal more abridged, and not much liked by those who begin to learn it; but those that are masters of it, know the delight & usefulnehs of it. - as thereby it is easy to find the incomprehensible quantities, unknown proportions and their Roots; In short resolve by little work all the problems of geometry. The algebra Characters are $+ = \sqrt{\ }\wedge$, more, lehs, equal greater, smaller etc. one may make use of the first letters of the alphabet for the known quantities and the last for the unknown, and for the nomenator Characters you may use the arabian Cyphers.

Arithmetic is the attribute of a good mason, because he ought to multiply his Benevolence and knowledge to all his Bretheren, and to look on the recompence as a Cypher of the arithmetic, because he has satisfied himself the first, in doing a good action. -

Q. What is <u>Geometry</u>, and why that science an attribute to masons?

A. <u>Geometry</u>, is the 1st of the Sciences, founded on that of the preceeding one - It came from the Egyptians to us; who being in danger of being drowned by the yearly overflowings of the Nile, did find themselves every time confused in the bounds of their lands by every Innundations of that River, for which reason they invented measure and Limits, whereby they could know their respective bounds, after an overflowing of that great River - This art was called by the greeks <u>Geometras</u>, or measure for land, so that Geometry is the art of measuring land on the surface or Superfices, but no solids. and from this is derived the Science of measuring Solids, having several Superfices, vizt hight and depth.

Geometry is an attribute of a good mason, as he ought continually to measure his proceedings, which should have no other end, But the glory of the great architect of the universe and to edifie and keep his brother.

Q. Is Trigonomitry also necehsary to a mason, and as how an attribute to him?

A. Yes, grd Mr Archt, That Science is indispensable from the preceeding - By that they measure <u>angles</u>, <u>Tangents</u> & <u>Secans</u> lines. 'T is by this knowledge of Triangles that they find infallible measures of the unknown sides, the arithmetic and ye algebra. The discovery of this art we owe to <u>Pethagoras</u> -

The Most Ehsential explication of all the Trygonometry's problems are cited in the first proposition of <u>Euclid</u> - This learned Philosopher did sacrifice one hundred oxen to the Gods in acknowledgement of that discovery - He would have deserv'd a place among the Masons, if he had not been an Idolator.

Trigonometry is rather an attribute belonging to the great archt of the universe than a mason, and will make him tremble, when he thinks that the great archt of the universe will Judge him by the same problem of <u>Pythagoras</u> -

All our actions put in Signs will form a Triangle of which 2 Sides only will present themselves to our Consience, viz: the Good and Evil. But the great arch: of the universe will alone find the Top by opening the angles of our hearts which is only known to him.

Q. of what use does <u>optic</u>, <u>catoptric</u>, and <u>dioptric</u> treats, and how can these Sciences be any attributes to masons?

A. They treat of Sights, and reasons of direct lights. it is by these Sciences that we Judge <u>well</u> of things, not because they appear so at a distance, or by the reflections of glahses and looking glahses, from us, but because they are commonly so.

They are attributes to masons, as every Mason ought to look at his own faults, even with glahses that enlarge the subject; and not to see the faults of his brother, but with glahses that diminishes the object and remove it. - He ought continually to study his thoughts and discourses as in a looking glahs of prudence; to use himself never to do any thing which may displease or be a prejudice to any of his Bretheren.

Q. We know what drawing or designing is, but how comes that likewise an attribute to masonry?

A. As drawing is done by a pencil, and the most perfect design has been begun by a sketch, so should masons if they find any good qualities in a brother, acknowledge him as a sketch, after which they should copy in following as much as pohsible his Example, by which they may come to perfection; Provided the great architect grants him that power and favor. -

Q. What is the perspective, and why an attribute to masons?

A. Perspective, is the art to render the object in an accurate proportion from which may appear in their distances or approach as much of their Diminutions as their colours. - a well understood perspective will make the beauty of a picture, which flatters the first sight in giving the true point in view. Thus should masons have for an only point in view, a true one, in the whole course of his Life the pleasant prospect of a future life and of an Everlasting happinehs.

Q. Let us go to the mechanic's.

A. Michanics, is the art of machinery, by which they can raise and put in the most Elevated places the most heavy burthens, with little seeming strength and view people; as with <u>Levers</u>, vices, <u>dommcerachts,</u> Rollers, Cranes etc. By this art, Mills are constructed, as also clocks, Jacks and thousands of other machines are composed, who move by springs and weights.

Thus the great Spring of a Mason ought to be in his heart, and if he does not take Care to wind it up, raise and set it agoing continually to practice virtue, he cannot be considered but as a vicious machine of which the main spring is broke, which Cannot be rectified but by the gift and favor of him, who never refuses to those that ask for it.

Q. Of what use, is Static's to masons?

A. The <u>Static</u> has a connection with the mechanic Science, as it is the knowledge of weights and moving Forces - The art of steelyards Ballances & Equilibriums - Thus the Judgement of a Mason should always be weighed by Equilibrium, and no Consideration whatever of Interested reason, of any part or party work, can make them Deviate from equity, Truth and sound reason.

Q. What is the Hydraulic, and of what necehsity to a mason?

A. It is the art of conducting, governing, draining and discharging of water, necehsary for health and Life, as well as benefits of manufatures and commerce, as also to the delights of palaces, gardens aqueducts, Fountains etc. which an architect conducts by his art, through canals, causeways etc. and gather them in ponds Cisterns and reservoirs, and from thence conduct them again into gardens, Fountains, and also for the use of citizens.

An architect, knows how to drain by canals, the fields and meadows of water for agriculture, and by making of canals through mountains he brings remote seas together for the Benefit of commerce and Navigation. - In short by the knowledge of Hydraulics, one can form a place of the greatest delight, which formerly was a mud pool, or depart.

The mind of a mason shoul be as a brilliant open canals, as the surest way to Join oneanother with sweetnehs, not as open Seas

Separated by the highest mountains, but like two brothers who are often disunited by a false mistaken Interest to Sacrifice, expecting and aspiring each of them to give away to the other, till a mediator who penetrates with a masonic wit, and give away to one of them, by which he renews among them a friendship which was nearly at an end, and w^h without that reconciliation, would perhaps have been totally extinguished, and very likely (and what was mostely to be feared) turned into hatred and mortal Enmity. For the same reason an hydraulic architect, should never let any water be standing to putrifie itself and become his poison, of sweet and wholesome as it was before - Thus a Mason should never let his friendship be a sleep among his Bretheren, but in the contrary animate them every where by the canal of his wit which may furnish him by those means of society, with Humanity, Reciprocal Services, and obliging discourses, advices and Instructions.

Q. What is geography, and of what use to masons?

A. Geography is the knowledge of all places by land, and even by Sea, Inhabited or uninhabited places, the capital & inferior Cities in every Kingdom; of Rivers and great Rivers w^h waters them, and the mountains that Separates them. In short all what may be Interesting to it, and of which one may discourse by maps, and Terrestral Globe.

Though there is but masonry on earth, there are different Temples and divers places where the good masons ahsemble to work at their mysteries, and under the same Statutes sing the praise of the great architect of the universe and the sweetnehs of their Innocent pleasures -

Those Temples, are called lodges by us; and a good mason ought to pohsehs the masonical geography to know all the regular Lodges and their numbers, and have as much as pohsible the most Intimate Correspondence with them; in order for him to know ye true masons, their qualities, virtues, distinctions, Talents, in masonical works - In fine, to render them the respect due to their merits.

Q. Do you place chronology, in the number of Indispensible Sciences of an architect mason?

A. Yes. For as chronology is the Science and knowledge of past times, a mason should be pohsehsed of it, for the following reasons: to be ready to name those masons who have distinguished themselves from ye very Creation of the world; of Kings, Princes, Pontifs, and all those in power who have supported masonry - The various events and revolutions of Masonry, which should model us in Patience, constancy and resolution.

Q. What do you mean by cutting in Stone?

A. I mean by that the most Ehsential Science to an architect, which is the art of discribing by means of the Square all the stones, which are to compose an Edifice, even weighing it, not to revise it again, that there is no lohs upon the whole, and that is sound on its natural lay, as it has been drawn from the quarry - No man in any academy of the world can attain the quality of an architect of any qualification and condition whatsoever without he has himself Cut drehsed and even fixed his stones.

Thus in the Royal art of masonry, no brother can attain to the Eminent degree of a grand M^r. arch^t. Exept he has disposed his heart (which used rather to be carried by weaknehs to evil than to virtue) prepared and cut in the manner of the stone, to become himself one of the materials to the Edification of the Temple which is Dedicated to the Lord. - 'T is also in the Royal art of masonry why no brother, is he a king or prince can attain to the degree of gr^d. M^r arch^t unlehs he has begun with the degree of an Ent^d appr^{tice}, and so on tnrough the other Degrees gradually preceeding this -.

Q. And the cutting in wood?

A. I will tell you as much of this as cutting of stone. The only difference I shall make between them is the stuff itself. The Timbers ought to be cut ready to be fixed on and in the Edifice without being in need to revize it for the proportion of Joyning them, as the first cutting ought to be exact - So a mason ought to have used his will exactly to that of his brother, which forms the exact Joyning of masons, the exactnehs and unanimity of their deliberations, the brightnehs of their works, and the sweetnehs of their Innocent pleasures, should always Joyn.

Q. What is Measure?

A. As an architect is always to Judge of Masons, he ought to know by measuring of their work, what pay is due to them. He is also to measure the materials, to pay the providor according to the quantity - and no Intendant of the building can pay any money, but by orders of the gr^d M^r architect.

For that reason, a mason who knows the measure in hand, should look at it, as the centre of Justice, the use of which he must render an account of to the great arch^t of the universe, who will Judge him accordingly.

Q. How can physic be of any use to a gr^d architect?

A. Not to build or lay a foundation for any building, before he has considered the Situation of the ground and the air. To avoid mashy and muddy places. and not to build near any copper mines, Standing waters or Stinking pools; to place and dispose the windows in such a manner that the building may receive the most wholesome winds and purest air. In short he should know how to remedy against all matters that might hurt the constitution - and if any pools or Standing waters, to drain them.

A Mason also should physically vanquish, the difficulties that a disordinate Stomach opposes to his health, which might hurt his constitution; or if he should be of a weak body and habit, by prudence deprive himself of some of the pleasures which might be prejudicial to him, tho' not to others. This conduct has more virtue in itself then all the physic. -

Q. of what use can music be to an architect?

A. The knowledge of music, was very necehsary to an architect in the time of the antient Romans, in constructing of Saloon, Rotunda's and other places to perform vocal and Instrumental music, as they used by art to place columns, vaults, Cielings alcoved, and even used to place Brahs vehsells in those cielings, to get an Echo to encrease ye sound of concord and Harmony - Some artificial sounds were also put on the cornishes, which also embellished those saloons etc. But as in our present days music is come to more perfection, the Rooms for it made lehs, which occasions the harmony to be kept more agreeable and nearer to the Ear, for which reasons the Ceilings are proportioned to the Extent of those rooms, by which the vibration is kept at the required distance.

Thus music is certainly an attribute to masons, comparative, for as music by the concordance of the different sounds inspire the soul, and charms the sentiments by its various turns of Discord and Concord - so likewise should alone reign among bretheren, to charm one another, and their friends also, to make them Enjoy some unexprehsible pleasures, and at the same time make the profane in wishing, because they cannot partake of it.

Q. Are these all the sciences as mason ought to be pohsehsed of?

A. Mathematic!s is a general term, by which one may comprehend a great many other sciences, besides those I have already given a full account of - This term alone makes a compenduous attribute to a mason - for when he says that he is master of the Mathematics, it signifies he has a heart Zealous for mas^s & masonry.

Q. How many orders of architecture have you?

A. There are 5, vizt. The Tuscan, Doric, Ionic, corinthian & coposite.

Q. What difference is there, in these orders?

A. The Tuscan and the Doric are the most revealed and lehs adorned, the corinthian and composite, are the finest and most adorned - and the Ionic, is more adorned then the two first, but lehs then the 2 last. -

Q. Are there any other sorts of architecture?

A. An Infinite number of which I will mention some vizt the Prostite, the Lamphiprostite, the Perintere, the predoptitere the Deptere, & Longotere, - besides these there are the Iostile the perstile, and the De-estill and a great many more.

Q. on which depends the stile of building?

A. on the proportions of the columns, their distance to their magnitude, the ornaments of Niches, pannells etc. in short the Standing rule of true architecture must be adhered to, in compiling an Edifice to be well finished.

Q. Is this Certain rule of building necehsary to a mason?

A. Yes, gr^d M^r arch^t. It Signifies masonically that we must not mind the country, the quality or the degrees that a broth^r pohsehses, who is in want of ahsistance.

Q. You have told me before my brother that Naval & Melitary architecture are necehsary attributes to a mason, how can that be?

A. They are both attributes, because masons should work as well at sea as on land, for the propagation of the Royal Craft, and the relieve of his brothers - and in the Military, he should serve as a rampard for masons, who are attacked.

Q. Did Solomon Pohsehs all these Mathematical Sciences?

A. Without doubt. Since the great architect of the universe by a Liberal gift gave him that wisdom, for which he was called the wisest of kings - and as God had fixed on him to build a Temple according to the proportion that God had given him.

Q. what is the great attribute of a gr^d arch^t ?

A. 'T is a case with mathematical Instruments, in a small compahs, which contains all the Instruments for the various designs that an arch^t may invent, at the opening of w^h is presented to your view a very Sensible draft, and an Energy of all the Virtues of which a mason ought to be pohsehsed.

Q. Explain these Instruments and their use to me?

A. First there is one, that shews at once the 3 symbolic Jewels of an Ent^d appr^{tice} and Fel: Craft, after having been used to open a right angle - he may also see a level and perpendicular, beside a square level and plumb, all precious Jewels to the masons, which presents continually to their mind the mildnehs they should act with, their conduct on the square of Justice on an unchangeable level of equality among all unanimity of sentiments of mind; and upon the perpendicular of charity, to shew his benevolence directly and without examining such a mason, who is in want.

The simple compas, serves to take dimensions, dividing lines in equal parts, denote paralells, to make sections of Triangles, equiangular and Lateral - In short it may be used in an Infinite number of mathematical proportions too long to enumerate, but its use is well known; by the mathematicians, and being the principal

Instrument in the mathematics, and is therefore the Jewel wore by a master of a symbolic Lodge of masters. - with what satisfaction must not a mason look on this Jewel, when he remembers how close it was to his heart, when by his obligation he was preparing to see the light, and the use he has since made and found of that Instrument. Therefore a good mason should fix his points of the compahs in his proceedings, always accordingly to the Law of the great architect of the universe and the Statutes of the Royal order -

There is another compahs with 4 points, of which one is Inmoveable, and may be altered as necehsity requires - This compahs Serves to draw circles or parts of Circles; the inmoveable point being always the fixt or centre. On the different occasions of drawing you may use a pencil, a pen or a roller on the moveable point - This compahs by drawing some circles tells you that the whole Earth or world is the masons; and by the 3 moveable points is represented the 3 Divine virtues, by which a good mason will be acknowledged by all the Bretheren over the 2 Hemispheres.

Then you come to the compahs of proportion, which is a folded rule; this Instrument is almost an universal one, as you find all operations there; which saves you a good deal of calculation, being most a general Table in which you find the equal parts, the plans, the Poligones the cords of solids the weights of Metals, as also of Bullets with their sides and magnitude - The line of equal parts serves to divide a Line pursuant to a line given - the Line of Planes to diminish or encrease to his mind - The Poligone line is to discribe a Circle, a poligone of such numbers or planes of angles - The solid lines to encrease or diminish a solid according to a reason given - The line for metals to know the difference and proportion between the Six metals - This Instrument is the finest attribute to a mason, especially for one who has attained to the degree of gr^d. arch^t., as it is incumbent on him to have his heart engraved with all the Divine, Moral, Heroic & natural virtues, and that he has proved himself solid and firm.

The Rule and drawing pen, are 2 Instruments which must be used together to draw a straight Line, w^h is also an attribute of Masons; as a mason's behaviour should be always fair and straight, in the Benevolence of his Heart, that his inclination's should coincide with his Duty, and be connected together as these 2 Instruments.

The quadrate is commonly made of Copper & Horn, and is used in opening of angles, to take their Hight and to divide the roses of the simple compahs - which is the Jewel of a perfect Master, and makes him to wear it remember, never to make use of it on any occasion exept he has a point of perfection in view -

End of the Lecture.

To close the Lodge

Q. Give me the Sign of a gr^d M^r architect?

A. He gives it (drawing a plan in his left hand).

Then the gr^d M^r arch^t opens his case of Instruments and says: Let us work - He then ranges the Instruments on the Little Table, and puts his left hand on the compahs of proportion, and leaning on his right hand and says:

Q. do you only know this work?

A. I comprehend an other.

Q. give me the Token?

A. He goes to the gr^d Mr Arch^t and gives it.

Q. give me the word?

A. Ra-

Q. go on?

A. Bu-

Q. make an End?

A. cim.- Then the gr^d M^r makes a Triangle with the compahs and says: My bretheren we finish - on which all the bretheren put their Instruments in their respective cases, and say: we finish.

Q. what's the clock?

A. The beginning of night.

Then the gr:^d M:^r arch^t knocks . & .., and says give Notice, this Lodge is closed - The wardens and all the bretheren knock each . & .., and the lodge is closed. -

                    End of the 12th Degree

===

13th Degree
called
Royal Arch.

The place where this Royal Lodge or colledge is held, ought to be in a very secret place, and should be under ground vaulted, without either door or window, with a small trap door at Top, big enough to let a brother through.

In the centre of the vault must be a Triangular pedestal made hollow inside, on the Top and all 3 sides of which must be cut through the great name of God יהוה , that when a light is placed in the said pedestal, that said name appears on all sides and on the Top. - This vault should be painted white.

There must be 2 officers who are principals, and three Inferior, to fill the necehsary functions when a reception, and to give the instructions vizt.

1st The Thrice puihs^t who represents <u>Solomon</u>, crown'd under a rich canopy in a chair of State, a scepter in his hand, drehsed in Royal Robes of yellow, and a vestment reaching to the elbow ermined of blue Sattin, with a grand purple ribbon from his right shoulder to his left hip, a golden Triangle thereto. In the East -

2dly At Solomons left hand, also in the east, is <u>Hiram</u>, king of Tyre drehsed as a Traveller, his Hatt on, with the same ribbon & Jewel, his naked sword in his hand - NB. these 2 gr^d. officers should at least be princes of Jerusalem -

There must be 3 other officers, to form the number of 5 to hold a lodge of this degree as:

3dly The gr^d. Treasurer representing <u>Guibelum</u>, who was the first depositer of the precious Treasure of Masons, decorated with a small key to a narrow white ribbon, to wear to the 5th Button hole of his Jacket, with these letters I. V. I. L. which are the Initials of <u>Inveni verbum in ore Lionis</u>. In the North.

4^{thly} The gr^d. Secretary representing <u>Joabert</u>, In the South, who perform'd this function, when the 2 kings renewed their alliance, as has been mentioned before, in the degree of Intimate Secretary. He sits with his hatt on.

5thly The grand Insp^r representing <u>Stolkin</u>, In the West, these three last officers wear their Jewels in form of a collar, their arms to be naked. and if any more brothers then the above mentioned 5, they must sit at the lower end of the lodge, as the number of 5 are only to be at a reception.

When a reception you must always make the Ceremonies at the opening of a lodge - and Brother Stolkin the gr^d warden and Insp^r in the West, answers all the questions that the Thr: P^t. Mast^r shall ask -

To open this lodge, by Way of a Lecture.

Q. Broth^r Insp^r, what place are we in?

A. T. P. we are in the centre of the most sacred place in the Earth.

Q. How came you in this sacred place?

A. By an effect of Providence.

Q. Explain this to me?

A. I dug in the antient Ruins of <u>Enoch</u>, I penetrated through 9 Arches under ground, and in the End found the Delta △ w^h God had promihsed to the Holy Patriarchs should be found in fulnehs of time.

Q. What is the Delta?

A. A gold Triangle, replenished with a great light, on w^h. was engraved By <u>Enoch</u>, the great & mysterious name of the great architect of the universe.

Q. who are you?

A. I am, what I am, my name is Guibelum.

Q. Do you know the true Pronunciation of that great name?

A. It is a sacred name, only known by the gr^d. El^t Sub^m. & Perfect Masons.

Q. What is your quality?

A. Knight of the Royal arch.

Q. How was you Received in that quality?

A. Solomon, in company with the king of Tyre, to recompence my Zeal, & constancy, created me in this degree with <u>Joabert</u> and <u>Stolkin</u> my companions.

Q. what are your Signs Token and word?

Sign.   A. The 1st Sign is that of admiration, Extending your arms with open hands, your head leaning on your left shoulder, on one knee; the answer to this or 2^d

Sign   2^d Sign is, to Fall on both your knees.

Token   The Token is mutual, to help & raise each other by the hands & Elbows.

word - The word is, <u>Hamal aheck Guibelum.</u>

Q. what signifies that word?

A. It signifies, Guibelum is a good mason, we must help & recompence him.

Q. Have you any thing else to desire?

A. Yes, the Sub^{me} Masonry, known by the name of Perfection.

Q. God will permit perhaps one day, that your wishes may be accomplished and recompence you, according to your deserts.

A. Amen, amen, amen! The T: P: then says: Let us Pray.

Prayer.

Great Architect of the universe, Adorable God in all, be so kind and exalt our desires in this moment, when we beg thy Divine goodnehs. - In thy self is the true wisdom, to which we aspire; and by the Strength of thy favor we may hope for. Thy wisdom shall make the Beauty of the Temple, that we dare to consecrate to thee, that is to say itself may purifie our hearts, in which we desire continually that you may reside. Amen, Amen, Amen.

After this Prayer, the T: P: strikes first 2, and then 3 more with his hand, w^h are repeated by king Hiram of Tyre and then by each of the 3 officers - Then the 2 kings kneel down at the Divine delta, with the Sign of admiration - after a little while they help each other and Rise. Then all the bretheren shall do the same, and then by a knock the T: P: shall give, they all shall help and raise one another. when they are all risen, the T: P^t shall say: Brother Insp^r. give notice, The Royal Lodge is open, which is repeated by the Inspector.

Form of a Reception

NB: Three brothers may be received at a time.

The cand^{us} or cand^{tes} must be in the antichamber, above and near the trap door; and having knock'd as a gr^d M^r. Arch^t & is asked by some of the guards at the trap door, what he wants? when he or they answer, to be received kn^{es} of the Royal arch; which being reported through a Hole, the guard is answered, "it is not pohsible yet" but that they must petition God to permit it - a 2^d Petition is made, and the same ans^r given; but the 3^d time their request is granted. when the brother conductor takes the cand^{us} and leads him to the Trap door, and then asks him or they if willing to descend into the Bowels of the earth to seek for Treasure? if he consents a rope is put or fixt round his body, and when the trap door is lifted up and all the lights below darken'd, when he is let down twice and hawled up again, and when he is let down the 3^d time, they throw down some stones and mortar, when all the lights below are shewn by 5 times 5 round the Delta. - then the grand warden makes him kneel by the Delta in admiration, the trap being shut. and the 2^d and 3^d cand^{us} are singly let down in the same manner as the 1st, and when all 3 are below on their knees, the Thr: Puihs^t speaks to them thus:

The great arch^t of the universe, hath done you the greatest of favors; it is him that hath chosen you to discover the most precious Treasure of Masons; and you are his Elected; I give you Joy of it; come to me and contract the most solemn obligation, and I will reward you, for your hard Labor. they then kneel, and take the following obligation

Obligation.

I A. B. do promise before the great arch^t of the universe and this puihsant Royal ahsembly, never to reveal the secrets, which are going to be trusted to me, especially what is to be revealed to me of the sacred mystery - I do promise to renew my zeal for masonry and my friendship for my bretheren and never to separate myself from this Royal Lodge, but by leave from the most powerful gr^d M^r. and of his gr^d officers.

I promise never to receive, nor consent that ever a mason be received to this Eminent degree, but according to our Laws.

I further promise to observe at all times the Statutes and regulations which shall be perscribed to me by this Royal lodge, and acknowledge at all times the council of princes of Jerusalem and of the Royal Secret, for the Sovereign chiefs of the Royal art If furnished with authentic Titles; and submit myself to their decrees, to Sign my Submihsion to the most authentic act of it -

And if I fail in these my present engagements, I consent to suffer all the pains and penalties, of all my preceeding obligations - my Body to be exposed as food to the ferosity of the wild beasts - So God keep me in Righteousnehs & Equity Amen, Amen, Amen -

Historical Discourse of the Royal arch

My dear Bretheren to continue the History of masonry which you now have received the Elements of, it will be necehsary to acquaint you, with things that have past many ages ago.

<u>Enoch</u>, the son of <u>Jaretn</u>, was the sixth generation of <u>Adam</u>. He lived in the fear of God - God appear'd to him in a dream, spoke to him by Inspiration and communicated to him as follows:

"As thou art desirous of knowing my name, follow me and I will acquaint and Teacheth thee". after this, a mountain seemed to rise to the Heavens, and <u>Enoch</u> was carried there, when God shewed him a golden Triangular plate, Enlighten'd brilliantly with these הוה characters, his ever blehsed name, and gave him strict orders, never to pronounce it - after that <u>Enoch</u> seemed to be carried under ground perpendicularly through 9 Arches, and in the 9th or deepest, he saw the same brilliant golden plate, with the same characters, and flaming light round it, which he had seen before -

<u>Noach</u>, being full of the Spirit of the most puihsant God - built a Temple on the Spot, under ground, dedicated to God, accompanied with 9 arches, one above the other; in the same manner as what he had seen in his dream or Reverie.

Methusalem, his Eldest son was the architect of that construction, not knowing at the same time, the reason why it was built.

This Edifice was Erected in the land of <u>Canaan</u>, which was since the land of promise, and afterwards Jerusalem the Holy land.

<u>Enoch</u>, made a gold plate of a Triangular form, a Cubit long on each side, enriched with the most precious stones - he incrusted this plate on a stone of <u>Agate</u>, of the same form, and transported it afterwards, in the 9th arch, and Engraved thereon the same characters God had shewn him; and put the whole on a pedestal of white marble of the same figure.

After <u>Enoch</u> had finished this Temple under ground, God appeared to him again, and said: make a trap door of stone, on the first arch, which must be laid down with an Iron ring thereon, to lift the same occasionally, because he was under the necehsity, to Exterminate every living thing on Earth.

The 9 arches thus finished and exactly closed up, no person could penetrate or enter into them, only <u>Enoch</u> alone knew the precious Treasure those arches contained, and only himself knew the true pronunciation of the great name of God. -

The wickednehs of mankind encreased every day, and God threathened the world with universal distruction.

<u>Enoch</u>, foreseeing, that the knowledge of the arts would be lost, by the universal distruction that was then to happen, and being desirous of preserving the principles of the Sciences to the latest posterity, of those whom God should be pleased to save. He therefore built two great columns (on the highest mountain near him) one of brahs to resist the water, and the other of Brick to resist the fire. He engraved on the brick column Certain hyrogliphics intimating, that near it was a precious Treasure under ground, which he had Dedicated to God; and he Engraved on the Brahs column, the principles of the Liberal arts, and particularly that of masonry -

Methusalah, was the Father of Lameth, and Lameth the father of Noah, who was pious, in always loving God. His virtues gained him the love of God, who thus spoke to him: "I will punish all mankind, in general with a deluge, and order thee, to construct an ark, to contain, thyself and family, with apartments for a pair of every other living creature, for those, and only those I will save from the punishment, I am now about to Inflict" and then gave him the plan by which the ark was constructed.

Noah was 100 years in constructing the ark, he was 600 years of age, and his son Seth 99. It was but a little while before his father Lameth and, aged 777 years.

There was not one of the antient Patriarchs alive since Adam, Exept Methusalem the grand father of Noah who was then about 969, who died a few years before ye flood, and Lameth 5 years before it -

God directed Noah with his family and a pair of every kind of Terrestial animals to retire into the ark he had built.

The deluge happen'd in the year 1656, and every thing on the Earth perished by the Deluge which ensued - The most superb monuments were distroyed, with the brick column, which Enoch had raised, by by the Divine will and permehsion of God, the Brahs column resisted the force of the waters, by which all the liberal arts have been communicated to us, and masonry takes from thence its antient state -

The History of the Bible teacheth us the succehsion of the times, and the doctrine of the Holy men Instructs us, that the people of Jerusalem were slaves to the Egyptians, and were redeemed by Moses their leader, to go and take pohsehsion of the promihs'd Land.

We also learn from the annals deposited in the archieves of Scotland (and only to be revived by us) That in a Certain Battle, the ark of alliance was lost in a Forrest, and the same was found again by the Roaring of a Lion, who Ceased to roar and couched on the approach of the Israelites - which Lion before by Instinct had Devoured a great many numbers of the Egyptians who attempted to carry away the same, he keeping secure in his mouth the Key of the ark, and on the approach of the High Priest, he dropt the same and retired to a distance

Couching and Tame, without offering the least violence to the chosen people.

The History of the Bible also Instructs us, that Moses was well loved and cherished by God, That he spoke to him on Mount Sinai in a burning bush, communicating to him, his Divine laws, and many promihsed, Renewing an alliance with him, and, then gave him the True pronunciation of his Holy name, by which he would be always invoked - and it was at this time, that Moses replied: Who art thou? God said: is my true name, by which he would be always invoked, which is,: I am a Strong & Jealous God, most Mighty Puihsant.

The pronunciation was Corrupted in after ... the different Traditions because as God had directed Moses and his descendants never to pronounce it. but had promihsed that in fulnehs of time some of his posterity should find it engraved on a golden plate.

The same History Informs us of the different movements of the Israelites, to the time of their having pohsehsion of the land of Promise - and in the beginning of the city of Jerusalem, we observe, that David never could begin the Temple of God, which Honor was reserved for his son Solomon the wisest of all kings on the Earth -

Solomon remembring the promise that God had made to Moses, of finding his Holy name in fulnehs of time; his wisdom inspired him, that the same could not be found, until he should consecrate a Temple to the Infinite God, In which he could deposit the precious Treasures already set aside for his worship - He followed the plan that David his father had communicated to him; on the Model of the ark of alliance, and begun the building of the Temple in the 4th year of his Reign, and laid the foundation on the most healthy and beautiful plain in all Jerusalem -

They found in digging the foundation an antient Ruin, of a very large Edifice, and a quantity of Riches, such as vases, gold and silver urns, marble, porphery, Jaspers and agate Columns, with a number of precious stones, which were all Carried to Solomon.

This virtues king, presuming that on that spot before the Deluge, perhaps a Temple had been erected, and fearing to the service of some false god; and least the true Diety might be profaned in that place, he would not build there; therefore went and made choice in the plain of Arunia. And on abandoning this place, they did not find any more precious things.

The Temple of Solomon was built as we are Instructed by Masonry, and as we know by the melancholly Event & death of H. A -

Solomon having given directions to build a Cavern under ground like a Cave, he gave it the name of the secret vault In the centre of which was erected a pillar of white marble, w^h supported the Sanct^m Sancto^{um} of the Temple, and called it by Inspiration the Pillar of Beauty, for reason of the beautiful ark, which it was bound to support, and the sacred Treasure that providence had design'd to be encrusted thereon.

To arrive in this secret vault, you was obliged to pahs through a long narrow close entry of 9 arches following one another by a communication under ground from y^e. Palace of Solomon. And to this place Solomon used to go in company with Hiram king of Tyre, and H. A. privately to Enter secretly on Holy matters.

The lohs of H. A. deprived the 2 kings of this satisfaction as the number of 2 was Insufficient to enter in there, 3 absolutely necehsary - and they were at a lohs who they should chuse to compleat this number.

Some Masters Intendants, Sublime Elected, and gr^d mast^{rs} architects, were informed that the king of Tyre was at Jerusalem; and they were not ignorant, that when H. A. was alive, that Solomon had a particular place under ground which was called the secret vault, only known to the 2 kings and the Deceased. They went to the 2 kings and Entreated that some of them might be Introduced in to that secret place, when these 2 kings were renewing their alliance.

Solomon answered them with arms extended and head reclining: You cannot expect it; God will permit one day, that you will come to the knowledge, of what you now desire.

Some days afterwards Solomon sent for the 3 Masters Joabert, Stolkin & Guibelum, and gave them orders to search once more in the antient Ruins, where they had already found many Treasures, in hopes of finding more. - They departed in order to fulfil the kings orders. One of the 3 namely Guibelum, in working with a pickax met with a large Iron ring; which he remarked to his bretheren, and companions; they presumed there must be something Extraordinary deposited in that place, They therefore worked all of them with much ardor and zeal, with shovel and crow to clear the Earth that covered the ring, when they found that it was fixed to a perfect square stone, which with great labor and pains they lifted, and then found that it covered a most ....

Guibelum proposed to them that he would descend, & for that end fixed a rope round his body to let him down, and when he should shake the rope, they shou'd raise him - His 2 companions strictly observed his directions - and after Guibelum descended, he found himself in an arch'd vault, on the pavement of which he found another opening; he descended into that, and then found also a 3^d opening, through which he went which brought him in the 3^d vault, and made the like observation of a 4th opening but was afraid to pursue his search, therefore shoock the Rope and was hawled up by his 2 companions.

He acquainted them with the observations he had made, and proposed, that they should descend by turns, to make further observations, but they refused, and therefore he again undertook the task on the following conditions: That through every arch he should descend, he would slightly shake the rope, and when he would be hawled up, he would shake the rope greatly.

He then was let down again, and paht 3 other arches, and when in the 6th, he shoock the rope and was hawled up again.

He acquainted his 2 companions, that he had been in 6 arches, and that he still had observed an opening to descend further and now proposed for one of them to descend, as he had worked hard and was afraid to venture further or deeper.

This frightened and Terrified both Joabert & Stolkin so much, that they absolutely refused to go down, which raised the Zeal of Guibelum, and again with courage took a lighted flambeau and descended on the former conditions.

When he was entering the 9th arch, a parcel of stones and mortar fell suddenly down from the Top, and his flambeau went out, when he perceived the rays of the sun to penetrate lively, briskly and directly on a gold plate of a Triangular form adorned richly round with precious stones –

The brightnehs thereof so affected Guibelum, that it almost deprived him of his sight, on which he made the sign of admiration, which was the same as Solomon & Hiram of Tyre made to him and his 2 companions, when they went and desired to be admitted into the secret vault, and Subl^{me} Degree –

Guibelum fell prostrate on his knees, his right hand before his Eyes, his left hand behind his back, shaking the rope three times – on which Joabert and Stolkin drew him up, and he recounted to them all the amazing things he had seen in ye 9th arch.

By this account they proposed to descend together by a rope ladder made for that purpose, – after they arrived in the 9th arch, they did the same as Guibelum had done, and being amazed at the brightnehs thereof, they also fell prostrate there at, and after having got the better of their surprize, they went and raised Guibelum (who still continued prostrate) and both said Hamalahech Laheck Guibelum, which signifies Guibelum is a good mason, we must help and recompence him. They then examin'd the golden plate, on which they perceived some characters, which they did not understand. –

Said Triangular golden plate was encrusted on the Top of an agate stone of the same form; they admired the plate with respect, and conceived that the Characters did mean, the sacred name of God, which name was only known to Solomon, Hiram of Tyre, and H. A., and it seemed to them, that after the death of Hiram abif, the 2 kings not being a sufficient number, could never bestow this degree, on those who aspired thereto; which now they hoped to receive by the Circumstances of their finding this precious Treasure –

They determined among themselves, to raise the cubic stone, on which this golden plate was fixed, and carry it to Solomon. It was at break of day when they arrived; the king of Tyre being with Solomon in his apartment. The 2 kings on seeing this precious Treasure, were struck with such admiration, that they both naturally made the Sign of admiration to the 3 masters, (as what they had made in the 9th arch) and fell down on their knees – Solomon got up first from his surprize, and seeing king Hiram still on his knees not come to himself as in

Extasy, raised him and said <u>Hamalaheck Guibelum</u>. Then examin'd the characters on the gold plate, he found it to be   , but would not explain any part thereof to the 3 elected.

Solomon told them that the great architect of the universe had bestowed on them the most singular favor - He has chosen you to discover the most precious and rare Treasure of Masons; you are his Elected, and I wish you Joy - and in recompence for their Zeal fervor and constancy Created them knights of the Royal arch, as they were the only that discover'd the same, and by which discovery that arch was Called the Royal arch; promihsing them to give an Interpretation of the sacred and mysterious characters which they saw on the golden plate, after they in company had fixed it in the place destined for it, and thereby would discover to them the most high and sublime degree in Masonry.

The 3 Elected observed to Solomon, that the first word that he and the king of Tyre spoke to them, was the same they had naturally pronounced in the 9th arch on seeing the Treasure, and then recounted Every thing they had done and seen; by which they precizely found the Sign token and word of this degree, since by the Title of kn^{ts} of the Royal arch.

Solomon then explained to them, that the promise of God was accomplished, that he had promihsed to <u>Noah</u>, <u>Moses</u> and <u>David</u> that one day the true name of him, by which he was to be Invoked by - should be discover'd on a gold plate; and that they should defend to write it, and only to have the liberty to letter it for their consolation but never to pronounce or speak it, and in the lettering of it, they must do it with great Circumspection.

<u>Solomon, said, you know the masters word was lost on the construction of the Temple, by the Tragic Scene of H. A. our great M^r architect, and this word never came to us but by Tradition (till now) and that corrupted succehsively, but never the True one.</u> Now we are so very happy my dear bretheren to have at this present moment the True characters, which we very soon will give you the Interpretation of as well as the pronunciation. -

We have now nothing to do, but to recompence you with Justice to the merits due to your works - you are now stamped by the Divine hand and Certainly doth merit this signal favor -

The 2 kings and the 3 kn^{es} took the precious Treasure and went to the secret vault, by the private way through 9 arches of which no body had any knowledge but themselves, they arrived at the pillar of Beauty, and thereat worked together, to encrust ye golden plate on the pedestal; and the 2 kings seemed gloriously rejoiced to work with the Trowel (having their arms bare) on that thing, which God had only destined to be done by their hands -

After they had done or finished the work, they all 5 prostrated themselves to adore the great arch^t of the universe, giving him Homage, thanks and praises for his favorable decree in their favor.

The Brilliancy of the plate, the splendour of the Ruby's and Diamonds, placed one on another, was sufficient light for this place for there was no other artificial light.

'T was in the moment after the work was done, that the 2 kings changed the name from secret to sacred vault, known only by the gr^d El^t perf^t and sublime Masons. -

But mark the different ages of Masonry, which was 3, 5, 7, & 9, which when multiplied by the calculation we know, makes 81, which will be fully Explained to you in the general Instructions of our doctrine.

It was now time to recompence the virtue of the 3 Masters and kn^{es} of the Royal arch, Guibelum, Joabert & Stolkin, therefore the 2 kings gave them the degree of gr^d El^t Perf^t Mast^{rs} & Sub^{ms}, Explaining the sacred word engraved on the Triangular golden plate, which was the True name of the most sacred omnipotence; and told them that was the name by which he would be Invoked - a pronunciation which had suffered much, and hath greatly corrupted.

Here follows the method of pronouncing it before, and remark always the number of letters, or characters, which compose those words. in which degree they are broke - some mysterious numbers in Masonry of which you have only the True pronunciation when you arrive to the Intire degree of perfection.

The Names and words which compose the mysterious name are

	Letters	
Jub	3	All Puihsant.
Jeo	3	Divine light.
Ina	3	Striking light.
Hayah	5	It is, what it will be.
Gotha	5	God himself alone
Jeeva	5	God Eternal.
Adonaii	7	oh. you that is Eternal.
Jackinai	7	Sustain us oh God! by your great force, that we always may ahsist each other.
Jehovah	7	Brilliant God.
Heleneham	9	Mercy of God.
Ichabulum	9	In God is my faith
	9	The Lord almighty. I am that I am.

The last is the appellation among us, w^h you will know when you are Initiated in the Sub^{me} degree of Perfection.

It is very Certain that from the diffirent varieties of this word the Moors have taken their Juba, and the Latins their Jupiter as the true pronunciation was not a little lost of the greatest of Names. Moses having been Taught by the great architect himself relative to Efficacy of this great name, and he thereby provided in Egypt against draught, hunger and Sicknehs.

They could see this sacred name in the Temple in the time of St Jerom; It was wrote in the antient Samaritan characters unknown to strangers, which was the reason that the word could never come truly to them; neither could it serve them in their Necromances or Magic Experiments - as they would have been well pleased to have employed it, as the Roman pagans had already done; being well perswaded of the great power thereof - Thus you see the true pronunciation only vested in the hearts of the Sub^{me} Mast^r. Masons.

This mysterious word is covered by 3 pahswords, and by 3 touches preceeding the figurative Signs to the Incidents before you arrive to the true one. -

The new Elected Bretheren, Guibelum, Joabert and Stolkin, Took their

Obl^s before God and the 2 kings, never to pronounce that word fully, and never to admit any mason to this Sublime Degree, before he he had given long proofs of his Zeal and attachment for the craft, and to use the same Ceremony to commemorate this mysterious History of the Divine Delta, near the B. B. where God made the antient Father promis the same. –

The number of the grand Elected begun by 3, afterwards there were 5 from what had happen'd, & they remain'd a long time at that number, namely: Solomon, Hiram of Tyre, Guibelum, Joabert & Stolkin. –

When the Temple was finished, and Solomon had Dedicated it, He recompenced, with the degree of Perfection the 12 Masters that had commanded the 12 Tribes, since the death of H. abif. – 9 other antient masters elected who were Distinguished by their virtue, they were chosen and formed the Sublime Lodge to be admitted to the degree of the Royal arch and in a short time to the degree of perfection.

The 9 kn^{ts} to be admitted to the secret vault, were oblig'd to Tyle the doors of the 9 arches, which lead from Solomons Palace to said vault – the most antient was placed at the door nearest the sacred vault, and the others by degrees to the 9th door near Solomon's Palace or apartment, never permitting an entrance to any but the gr^d El^t perf^t & sub^{me} M^s giving the Sign Token & word of each arch. From this reason the knights take their quality, because from the sacred vault to have an entrance in the Royal Palace. – Here you have the pahsword for each arch:

1st	Jub	4th	Hayah	7th	Jackinai
2^d	Jeo	5th	Gotha	8th	Heleneham
3^d	Ina	6th	Adonai	9th	Johabulum

The Brother that gives on the inside the sacred word, was oblig'd to give another pahsword besides, which is, Sciboleth 3 times with an aspiration.

At this time the number of antient's M^r. Masons were 27, being the number of 3 times 9, vizt

```
    Two kings, Solomon and Hiram of Tyre . . . . . . . .  2
    Three kn$^{ts}$ of the Royal arch . . . . . . . . . . .  3
    Twelve antient M$^{rs}$ Command$^{rs}$ of the 12 Tribes . . . 12
```

    Nine Elected antient masters 9
    one Antient gr^d M^r architect 1
                                       makes in all 27. –

There were besides the above 3568 masters who had served in the construction of the Temple, who became Jealous, on seeing a preference given to the above 25 bretheren, as they saw them often in the Kings apartment, which was shut to them, and which chagreen'd them much – Therefore sent Deputies with their complaints to Solomon, why those 25 masters should have such preference given, above them.

Solomon heard them with Patience, and replied with much sweetnehs: "Those 25 masters deserved this preferment by their Zeal in working the most hard, and having shewn invulnerable constancy therein; that therefore he loved and cherished them; but that their time was not yet come" go (said he) God will permit that ye shall be one day recompenced, as ye deserve" One of ye Deputies being transported with pahsion (not being contented with the soft and sweet reply of Solomon) said, Have we any businehs for a higher Degree? We know how the word has been changed, we can travel as masters and receive pay as such. – Solomon was struck with this reply and being always full of wisdom and goodnehs would not rebuke him but by Inspiration spoke to him thus: "The antient masters deserved this degree of perfection, as they have been in the antient Ruins and penetrated into the Bowels of the Earth which frightened them, and from thence took an Emence Treasure to Embellish and Decorate Gods Temple. Go, in peace, and do as they have done! Work, to adorn the Temple of the mighty God, he will recompence you, as you deserve."

Those masters being proud and vain, made a report of their Ambahsy, and not having received a reprimand, ambition being mixed with Jealousy, they agreed to go all together to ye antient Ruins to search under ground, and departed for that purpose ye next morning at break of day, and as soon as they arrived at the antient Ruins, they discovered the Ring to lift the Trap, and with a ladder of ropes entered the arches with lighted flambeaus.

God having a design, to recompence those masters for their ambition, and to give a clear proof of his Justice and providence pronouncd their Doom for their Insolence, in so much that when the last of them had entered, the arches fell in upon them succehsively one after the other, with all its apurtenances, so that they were heard of no more, by which the antient word that had been Corrupted was intirely lost with them, and no person since knew it in any wise, being only known and kept by those masters of which you have heard this history. -

It was not long before Solomon heard what had happened therefore sent the 3 brothers Guibelum, Joabert and Stolkin to Enquire, and inform him what had happened. -

They departed at break of day, and when they came to the place, where this disaster had happen'd; they found such strange things, that they knew not what to make of it, and were at a lohs to find the prestine state of the arches, neither could they perceive any remains of the presumptious masters, who had gone in search of the Treasure - they imagined that they were all Eveloped in the Ruins, which they saw were fallen in.

They Examined the place with attention, & consulted what could be the meaning, that they were mihsing, not finding any thing but a few pieces of marble, on which were some characters in Hieroglyphic's, which they took and Carried to Solomon, and reported every thing they had seen. -

Solomon placed the pieces of marble together, and sent for some brothers who could decipher those Hieroglyphic's, by which they learn'd that the ruins they had seen, and which had distroyd the presumptious masters, was the Temple Enoch had built and consecrated to the true God, which had been built before and distroyd in the Deluge, which had swept away every thing, but the 9 arches under ground, were was deposited the Delta or Treasure so often spoke of to Moses and David by God, with the Brazen Pillar, from which history of the antient masters is taken this true and Interesting history, of which the Bible speaks so little and we can not Illustrate at large upon.

Solomon caused all the pieces of marble to be put together, and order'd them to be kept in the sacred vault. the brother who explained the Hieroglyphic's was Abdamon.

I Exhort you my dear Bretheren to meditate on the grandeur of our mysteries, - you are not come to get the ultimate of knowledge of that you want to be acquainted with, but you must expect it by your zeal fervor and constancy.

End of this 13th Degrees History.

Then the Thr: Puihst says: By virtue of the power which has been transmitted to me, I decorate you with the Jewel of the order of this degree. It represents the Delta found by your antient Brothers; you'll carry it suspended round your neck to hang on your breast by a purple Ribbon, which colour exprehses the Love & Friendship that you ought ever to have for the order, and your bretheren in general -

Go to the grand Inspr, and he will Instruct you with all that is necehsary for you to know. he goes, when he is shewn the Sign of admiration, The Token, to raise one another, and given the word <u>Hamalaheck Guibelum</u>. -

To close this Royal lodge

Q. What remains for you to desire of me, Respble brother Inspector?

A. Perfection, and Eternal happinehs.

Q. God will permit one day, that your wishes may be accomplished?

A. Amen, Amen, Amen.

Q. What's the clock?

A. 'T is Evening.

Q. acquaint the Respble Bretheren, I am going to close this Royal Lodge, by the most perfect and mysterious numbers.

A. Respble bretheren the Most Puihsant is going to close this Royal Lodge by the most perfect and mysterious numbers.

Then Solomon knocks 3, times 3, the king of Tyre the same. The grd Inspr. the same, the grd Treasurer the same, and the grand Secretary the same. after wh the grd Inspr. says to order, bretheren

Then the 2 kings and all the bretheren fall on their knees and make the Sign of admiration. before they get up they make the Sign with their right hands on their back, after which they help each other to rise; the kings first, and then the other bretheren who after this make all an obedience to the kings - then Solomon says: this Royal Lodge is closed with all its Honors -

NB: There is a Jewel wore in this degree of a round form like a medal to a purple Ribbon to hand on the breast, on one side of which must be a square hole, and the Trap with an Iron ring on it, Two people standing over the Hole with their heads together letting Guibelum down the Trap with a Rope round his body; -

on the reverse of said medal or Jewel must be in the Centre the Delta and the following Initials round near the Edge of it, of these words Regnante Sapientehsims Solomon, Guibelum, Joabert & Stolkin, Invenerunt Pretiosihsimum Thesaurum artificium Subter Ruines Enoch A° 2995. -

End of the 13th Degree.

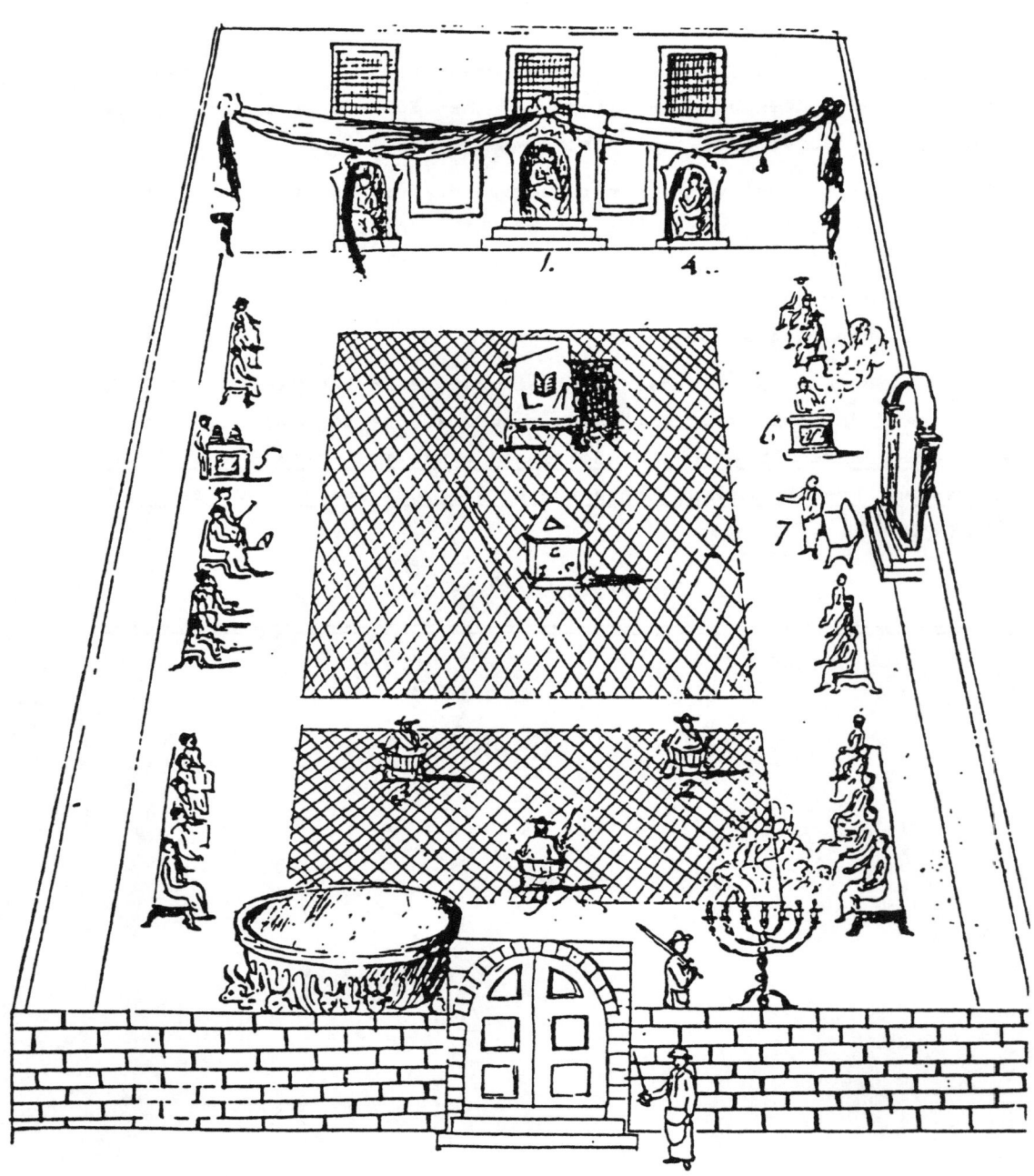

14th Degree
called Perfection
The Ultimate of Symbolic Masonry

The lodge of gr^d El^t perf^t and Sub^{me} Masters, represent a Subteraneous vault, of a red Colour, with many columns of a firy colour.

Behind the M^r, who represents Solomon and is Stiled Thrice Puihsant must be a transparent light, which Illuminates the whole lodge and shines through a Delta or △ of the B. B. with the hebrew characters הוה therein.

There must be besides the following lights, to shew the different degrees of Masonry vizt. at the Head of the Vener^{ble} Junr warden 3, at the head of the Ven^{ble} Senr warden 5, in the South 7, and behind the T: P: 9 -

The T: P: is placed in the east under a Delta, below which must be painted some Ruins, and before him a pedestal as if broke.

All lodges of gr^d El^t Perf^t & Sub^{me} ought to be composed of 9 grand officers, and a number of bretheren not exceeding 27 in all vizt

1st The Thr: Puihs^t in the east under a canopy, on his right hand a Brother representing Hiram king of Tyre, in the absence of the grand Insp^r or his deputy - - - - - - - - N. 1.

2dly on the left of the T: P: is the gr^d Keeper of the Seals represent^g <u>Galaad</u> the son of <u>Sophonia</u>, chief of the Levites - " 4.

3dly In the North before a Table of Shew bread, is the gr^d. Treasurer Representing <u>Guibelum</u>, Solomons confidant - - " 5.

4^{thly} In the South near the Table of perfumes is the gr^d orator representing <u>Abdemon</u>, who was the brother that Explained the several Enigmas w^h Solomon proposed to him, as also in the fullest manner the Hieroglyphic's on the pieces of marble that were found in the antient Ruins of <u>Enoch</u> on mount <u>Ancheldama</u> after the distruction of the 3568 presumptive masters - - - - - - - - - - - - - - - - - " 7.

5thly In the South before the Table of perfumes is the gr.d Secretary <u>Joabert</u>, a favorite of the 2 kings, and Intimate Secretary to their new alliance - - - - - - - - - - -   N. 6.

6thly In the North the gr.d mast.r of Ceremonies representing <u>Stolkin</u> also a favorite of Solomon - - - - - - - - - - -   " 8.

7thly In the West the Sen.r Warden Adoniram, the son of <u>Abda</u>, Prince Harodim of Libanus.- before the death of H. A. he had the Inspection of all the workmen at Libanon; and was the 1st of the seven Secret Masters - - - - - - - -   " 2.

8thly on the left hand of the Sen.r Warden is the Jun.r Warden <u>Mohabon</u>, the most zealous master of his time, and a great friend of H. A. - - - - - - - - - - - - - - - - - -   " 3.

9thly Behind the 2 Wardens, in the centre of the west is the captain of the guards, who represents <u>Banaja</u>, or <u>Zerbal</u>, - 'T was him, who acted in that post, when the alliance was formed by the 2 kings to which <u>Joabert</u> was Intimate Secretary -   " 9.

Each grand officer in dignity ought to be decorated besides the Jewel of perfection, with a Jewel of dignity in office.

The must be 2 Tilers, one without, and one within doors, to prevent the gr.d Wardens the necehsity of quitting their Seats -

All the Bretheren must be decorated with the Jewel of perfection. - the aprons lined and bordered with silk of a firy red colour, a double narrow blue ribbon round the edge of the apron - The flap down, on which must be painted or embroidered in gold, the Jewel of the order, and on the area or middle of the apron must be painted a square stone with a ring on the middle of it.

When there is a Reception, there must be on the Table with the perfumes, a small silver Hod and a gold Trowel, with oil to annoint, and on the Table of shew bread must be 7 loaves, a cup with Tint or red wine for libation. a gold ring for every cand.te with this discription on it. <u>Virtue unites, what death cannot Separate</u>; besides all the Jewels necehsary for the candidates.

The lodge being thus well prepared and Tiled, the Thr. P.t gr.d M.r shall make the foll^g questions, to prepare the bretheren to open the lodge of Perfection:

Q. Most resp^{ble} Brother Senr gr^d Warden, are we Tiled in this sacred vault?

A. Most Ill^s & most Puihs^t we are here well Tiled, and in Security.

Q. Since we are well Tiled and in Security from cowans, my most dear bretheren, let us pray the great architect of the universe that he may Enlighten and Inspire - Let us pray. They all put one knee on the ground -

Prayer.

"Sovereign architect of this vast universe, who by the great Divinity doth penetrate in the most secret thoughts of mortals, purifie our hearts by the sacred fire of thy love - guide and direct us in the in the path od virtue - cast from thine adorable sanctuary all impiety and preversnehs - we pray thee intirely to occupy us in the great work of our perfection, which will be a sufficient price of our Travel.and that peace & charity may closely link us in the band of union; and that this lodge may be a faint resemblance of the happinehs w^h the Elected will enjoy, in thy Heavenly kingdom - give us a Spirit of Holy discernment, to distinguish the good and refuse the Evil; and that we may not be deceived by those, who are to be mark'd with the Formidable Zeal of Perfection - and finally we might have no other design, but Thy Glory and our advancement of good works, in the reign of True masonry. Amen, Amen, Amen! God Blehs the King and our works"-

After this prayer there is a Silence for a couple minutes, and then the T: P: asks the foll^g questions:

Q. Ven^{ble} Br^r Senr Warden, who conducted you hither?

A. Thr. Resp^{ble} & Puihs^t it is the love of masonry, my obl^s and a desire to the perfection of Masonry.

Q. What have you brought here?

A. A Heart zealous for friendship, and love of virtue.

Q. What are the proper qualities, for you acquiring this?

A. The 2 first conduct us imediatly to the thir, and when these are properly attained, they lead us to happinehs and perfection.

Q. What is the disposition of a true elected perfect mason?

A. To divest his heart intirely of Iniquity, Vindictivenehs and Jealousy to be always ready to do good, and never to employ his Tongue to calumniate, detract against his Brother.

Q. How are you to behave in this place?

A. with a profound respect.

Q. How comes it, that Rich, poor, prince and subject are here always friends and brothers?

A. Because there is something in that Delta (pointing to it) repeated on the pedestal and firmament, that's greater than you.

Q. why is the Delta the subject of our respect?

A. It contains the sacred name of the Divinity, known revered & Exalted in Heaven & Earth, by the name of the great architect of the universe.

Q. What age are you?

A. Three times 3, the perfect number 81, when properly repeated by our mystirious calculation.

Q. How so my brother, can you demonstrate this?

A. I am a perfect sublime mason, my Trials are finished and 't is now time to reap the fruits of my labor.

Q. What did you contract, when you was made a gr[d] El[t] perf: & Sub[me] mason?

A. I contracted an alliance, with virtue and the virtuous.

Q. What mark have you to shew this?

A. This golden ring, a Symbol of purity.

Q. What's the clock?

A. High 12.

Q. What do you understand by High Twelve?

A. Because the sun darts its rays perpendicular into this lodge for us to work efficaciously the end of our perfection, which is the time to profit of it, by its generosity.

Q. Where will you find materials?

A. In the Treasury of virtue of perfect Masons, in regular composing my actions in my heart by the square and the compahs of the Divine wisdom.

Q. Where will you find divine wisdom?

A. In the heart of every brother which composes this Resp^{ble} Lodge of which you are the supporter.

Then the Thr: Puihs^t says: It is on you my most Resp^{ble} bretheren that I am going to enforce your disign; to this effect, my Venerable Brother Senr. Warden, announce that I am going to open the Lodge of gr^d. El^t perf^t and Sub^{me} by the mysterious numbers of 3, 5, 7, & 9.

This being announced by the Senr. grand Warden, the Junr. gr^d Warden Strikes 3. Then the Senr. gr^d. Warden 5, and then the Thr: puihs^t 7. after which a profound Silence is kept for a minute, - then the Thr: puihs^t says: to order my bretheren. Then he strikes 3, on which all the bretheren make the Sign by hawling the right hand from the left side of the Belly to the right side. Then the T. P. Strikes 3 more, on which they all make the Sign which is, to bring the back part of your right hand opposite your left cheeck, sup the elbow with the left hand, this represents the imprehsion the B. B. had on Moses on Mount Sinai to shelter his Eyes from the brilliancy there of, as that light was too great for his eyes to bear.

Then the Thr: puihs^t strikes 3 more, which makes 9, on which all the Bretheren make the -

3^d Sign, which is that of admiration, by Extending your arms, the head reclined, and then put 3 fingers of your right hand on your lips. Then He says: This lodge is open. He then salutes the lodge, which they all return, and the lodge is open. - Then they all cover their heads & take their places - when the minutes of the last lodge are read by ye Secretary.

Form of a Reception

The cand^{us} must be in a chamber near the narrow pahsage, with all the decorations of his former degrees upon him; the gr^d M^r of Ceremonies gives the cand^{us} the 1st pahs, w^h he gives to the brother that guards the door, and repeats 3 times <u>Schibboleth</u> with an asperation, on which that broth^r says pahs.- In the middle he meets another brother, who asks a 2^d pahs, when gives <u>Mohaben</u>, that brother says also, pahs, which brings him to the door of the sacred vault, where he gives <u>Heleneham</u> to ye brother that guards that door - Then the M^r of Ceremonies tells him to knock 3, 5, 7, & 9 on the door, which numbers are alternately repeated by the Junr Warden, Senr Warden & T: P. who then says, broth^r Junr gr^d Warden See who knocks at the door in the manner of a gr^d El^t perf^t & Sub^{me} mason? The Junr Warden goes and opens the door a little, and demands, who's there? The M^r of Ceremonies answers a Sub^{me} Kn^t of the Royal arch desires perfection, in being introduced into the Sacred vault. - The Junr gr^d Warden then shuts the door, and carries the report to the Senr Warden, and he to the T: P. who gives orders to let him be Introduced in a proper order.

When he Enters a brother on the Inside as well as a Master of Ceremony's put their swords to his breast and so lead him between the 2 gr^d Wardens; when they whisper him to make the Sign of admiration to the T: P: on which a Silence for a minute is observed, when the Thr. puihs^t addrehses him thus:

Q. What do you want here my brother?

A. T: Resp^{ble} & puihs^t gr^d Master, I ask the perfection of Masonry.

Q. Do you consent my bretheren, that this our brother a Kn^t of the R. arch should be pahsed to the degree of perfection?

A. All the Bretheren give their consent, by lifting up their right hands.

Q. Before I Initiate you my dear brother in the sacred mysteries of our perfection you must ans^r ye questions, I shall propose other wise you must be sent back

1st are you a mason, brother?

A. T: P: my bretheren know me to be such.

Q. give the S, T: & word to the Junr. grand Warden

A. He gives them.

2^d
Fell'
Cr^t
Are you a fellow Craft?

A. Yes, I have seen the letter G, and know the pahs.

Q. Give the Sign T. & w^d to the Senr gr^d Warden?

A. He gives it.

Q. Are you a master mason?

3^d.
A. I know the Sprig of accahsia, and everything it consumates.

Q. give the pahs, S. T: & W^d to the Junr gr^d Warden.

A. Tubalcain. M: B: N

M^r
(as soon as he gives the word, every brother is presenting his sword to him, and the T: P: says to him)

What have you done: you afright us my brother on speaking this word so high; we are always ready to punish the Indiscretion of the person, who pronounces this word so high and aloud, for fear that some of the profane or cowans might hear you; but as you did not do it with a bad intention, and mean'd no harm, we forgive you

---

Q. Are you a Secret Master?

4th
S. M^r
A. I have past from the square to the compahs. I have seen the Tomb of the Resp^ble H. A. and have shed my tears there at.

Q. give the S. T. & W^d to the Senr gr^d Warden?

A. He gives it.

Q. are you a perfect master?

5th
A. I have seen the 3 circles and the 3 Squares, put on the 2 columns acrohs.

Q. give the Sign Token & W^d to the Junr gr^d Warden?

P: Mr A. He gives them. and as soon as he pronounces the word <u>Jeva</u>, the T: P: and all the bretheren cry: What do you say? We are always afrighted, when we hear this word given, and ready to put a man to death who dares to pronounce the least syllable of the sacred and mysterious name. let us pahs to the 6th Degree.

6th
I:S:

Q. Are you an Intimate Secretary?

A. My curiosity is satisfied, which had almost cost me my life.

Q. give the S., T., & word to the Sen.r gr.d Warden?

A. He gives it.

7th

Pr.t & Judge

Q. Are you a provost & Judge?

A. I render Justice to all the workmen without destinction.

Q. give the Sign, Token and word to the Jun.r grand Warden?

A. He gives it.

8th

Intend.t of the build.s

Q. Ar you an Infendant of the buildings?

A. I have made the 5 Steps of Exactitude, I have penetrated in to the inmost part of the Temple; I have seen the effect of the great light, in the middle of which I perceived in Hebraic characters ....., which were unknown to me.

Q. give the S: T. & word, to the gr.d Sen.r warden?

A. He gives it.

9th

El.d of 9

Q. Are you an Elected Knight?

A. A cavern received me, a Lamp lighted me and a fountain refreshed me.

Q. give the S. T. & word to the Jun.r gr.d Warden?

A. He gives it.

10th

Q. Are you a grand M.r Elected?

A. My Zeal and labor, has procured me this degree.

Q. Where was you received in this degree?

Eld of 15

A. By Solomon himself in his Study.

Q. When was you received and on what occasion?

A. When he sent me with my companions to search for the two other Ruffians, who distroyed our Dear gr^d M^r. H. A.

Q. How came they discovered?

A. By the Industry of Bengaber, Solomons Intendant in the country of <u>Gath</u>.

Q. give the S: T: & w^d to the Senr gr^d Warden?

A. He gives it.

11th

Q. Are you an Illus^s Subl^{me} Elected Knight?

A. My name will inform you.

Q. What is your name?

A. <u>Emerk</u>, is my true name.

Q. give the S: T: & w^d to the Junr gr^d Warden?

A. He gives it.

12th

Q. Are you a grand M^r architect?

A. I pohsehs all the Sciences of the Mathematic's, I know also all the attributes.

Q. give the S., T., & word to the Senr gr^d Warden?

A. He gives it.

13th

Q. Which is the most Sublime degree, which you have received in Masonry?

A. The 13th, which I have rec^d by an effect of Providence.

Q. Explain this my Brother?

A. I searched in the unknown Ruins, and in the End, found the Divine Delta, which had been promehs'd to the Holy Patriarchs, one day Should be found.

R: A.

Q. What do you understand by this Delta?

A. It is a Triangular plate of gold, filled with Rays, on

which was Engraved by <u>Enoch</u> יהו, the sacred name of the Divinity.

Q. I Suppose you know that mysterious word, my brother?

A. I do not know it as yet, as my time is not expired. — That sacred name is only known by the gr^d. El^t. perf^t & Sub^{me} Masons. All my hopes are in God, and am in hopes I shall have the knowledge of it in fulnehs of time.

Q. What is your quality?

A. Kn^t of the Royal arch.

Q. What is your name?

A. <u>Guibelum</u>.

Q. give the Sign T., & word to the Senr grand Warden?

A. He gives it.

Q. What do you now desire my brother?

A. The Sub^{me} Degree of gr^d El^t Perf^t & Sub^{me} mason.

On which the T: P: makes the Sign of admiration and says: My Brother retire, God will permit you this day to receive what you so much Crave — Then the Senr Warden orders the M^r of Ceremonies, to take him a way till he is wanted.

Then the T: P: says, my bretheren do you consent that this kn^t of the Royal arch shall receive perfection? on which all the bretheren lift up their right hand, as a mark of consent.

The T. P. then says, let us applaud it by 3, 5, 7, and 9, after which the cand^{us} is ordered to return, when the door is opened and he is Introduced by the M^r of Ceremonies between the 2 gr^d Wardens again, when the T. P: Interrogates him, thus.

Q. Do you know in your concience my dear brother of any thing Since you have been made a mason, of any falsity to your broth^r or hurting him in his character or family, your Religion or your king? ans^r me, ans^r me, ans^r me?

A. Never, Never.

Q. you have never communicated or let escape from you, any of our mysteries to cowans. — What would you have done to the ahsahsins of our Resp^ble Master H. A. had you lived in those days, would you have revenged his death, be sincere, and ans^r me?

A. I would have done as <u>Joabert</u> did.

Q. Have you always been truly mind full of your obl^s you have contracted in the presence of the great arch^t of the universe,? ans^r me?

A. I have.

Q. Did you ever find any thing in your obl^s which was contrary to your religion, the State, or yourself, or any other thing that might hurt your delicacy? do, ans^r me.

A. Never.

Then the T: P: continues: Remember my brother, if you approach cool and Indiffirent to our sacred mysteries, you will be the more blameable after receiving this degree of G: E. P. & S. Mason than you could have been heretofore, and will have more to answer, at the great and awful day of Judgement, where the Secrets of all hearts, shall be disclosed.

This Degree my brother, is the <u>End</u> and full measure of Masonry, to which you are now going to be attached, & particularly by some indispensable obligations, which are now unknown to you I therefore hope, you will fix them in your heart when communicated and demonstrated by us, to you. Your goodnehs by a steady pursuit of virtue and close united love for all your bretheren, particular for us, who are your fellows and Superiors. What do you say?

A. I will. —

Q. Do you desire to be contracted by these new Engagements?

A. I do most cordially.

Q. If you do, my brother, go and wash your hands in that Brazen Sea, to prove your Innocence, that you have never violated any of your Engagements; Remember, our forefathers used the same ceremony when they were accused of Crimes; and by that proved themselves Innocent & guiltlehs.

Then the M^r of Ceremonies shews him the brazen Sea, in which he washes his hands, then returns between the Wardens again, and the T: P. proceeds thus:

You are now Introduced my venerable brother in the most sacred place of Masonry - the sacred mysteries which are now to be revealed to you, and the ramparts of this has been properly guarded by the strict Care of the grand Elected, against every vile discoverer, whereas the first 3 degrees has been laid open to the public eyes of the world.

We are now going to confirm you in our grand Secret, as we are Certain of your discretion, and have no doubt among us Concerning you - come then my dear brother and add to our Tranquility, swear Inviolable fidelity to us.

Then the M^r of Ceremonies, makes him take 8 Steps quick and 1 slow, which brings him to the T: puihs^t, with the Sign of an Elected master on him, he falls on his knees and takes the follow^g

Obligation

"I N. N. do swear on the Holy Bible, and in the presence of the great architect of the universe, and in this Respectable lodge of gr^d El^t perf^t and Sub^{me}, to be Eternal faithfull in my Religion -

I promise, never to take arms against my king, nor to Enter directly or Indirectly into any consperacies against him or my country, or to know of any without making it public -

I further promise that I never will reveal to the gr^d architect or knight of the Royal arch, or to any person whatsoever, to whom it doth not belong, the mysteries of this most high degree, or any matter that shall occur in this our lodge; or any of our laws and regulations; under every penalty of ye different obl^s by me heretofore Taken -

I promihs if pohsible, at least once a year, to meet together, and that on St John the Baptist, or St John ye Evangelists day; and meet this lodge as often, as my affairs will permit it.

I promihs an Equal regard, for my bretheren of this Royal Degree, without the distinction of Riches, poverty, Noble or Ignoble; and of making no other distinction, but that of being the greatest in virtue; and will never refuse of acknowledging a brother, who is a good man and Mason, in what ever State or condition he may be. to support him in Indigence, provided he is virtuous, and on making it appear sufficiently.

I promihs to visit my bretheren in sicknehs, and to help and ahsist him, with my council, purse and arm, whether in affliction or pain; and in case of life or death, to give him consolation as much as in my power. -

I never will give my voice for an admittance of a Candidate in these our mysteries, without being scrupelous circumspect and having an exact knowledge of his life & conversation, as near as I can.

I Swear I never will lay with the wife of my brother, nor dishonor his sister, or any of his family known then to be such, and I never will break this my present engagement I am now contracting.

I will never make, nor ahsist in making in my presence, any person to be a gr^d El^t P. & S. M^n who is not, or has been an officer in a regular and Legitimate constituted lodge; and promise never to receive or cause him to be received, but on the following conditions, vizt

1st By the permihsion and unanimous consent of all the G: E: P: & S M^s who compose this Resp^{ble} lodge, and are members there of, or by their permihsion in writing under their hands -

2dly or by Patent and power Invested in me, by the gr^d Inspector or his Deputy; and then at least at the distance of 25 leagues of this or any regular constituted lodge of perfection, that shall be regularly constituted or Established - and in failure of this my oblig^s, I condemn myself, to undergo all the penalties of my former oblig^s - and to have my Belly cut open, my bowels torn from thence, and to be given as food to the vultures - God maintain me in veracity, uprightnehs Justice and Equity. Amen, A, A, A, A.

The cand^{us} remains on his knees, and the gr^d M^r of Ceremonies carries the Hod and Trowel to the Thr:Puihs^t, who annoints the candid^{us} Eyes, lips and heart, and says: by the power committed to me, which I have acquired by my absiduity, Labor, constancy and Integrity, and make sacred your Eyes, lips and heart with the Holy oil that annointed the pious Aaron, The penitent David and the wise Solomon — I now stamp you with the redoubtable Zeal of the great architect of the universe, to the End that you may always live in his adorable presence, and that he may be ever in your mind and heart; and that a fervent Zeal and constancy may always be the rule of your actions.

Then he raises the cand^{us} and presents him the bread and wine in a gold Cup, and says: Eat with me this bread and drink this wine out this Cup with me, to learn to succour each other graciously and mutually — he then Eats and drinks. —

Then the T: P: presents him the ring and says: Receive this ring as a Token of alliance, and that you have made a Contract with virtue and the virtuous — Promise me my dear brother, that this Ring shall never depart from you until death, and you never will give it to any body, but your wife, eldest son, or your nearest friend. —

After this Ceremony all the bretheren eat the bread and drink the wine, and then make a Libation, according to the antient usage, that was practized at the sacrifices — the Libation being finished, the T: P: Decorates the cand^{us} with the ornaments of the order and says: I now salute my dear brother, and give you the Title, of gr^d El^t Perf^t and Sub^{me} Mason, and this with all the pleasure Imaginable that I ornament you — By the Symbol there of receive this ribbon of the order. The Triangular figure represents the Delta, on w^h was engraved by Enoch the Holy name of names, which makes the principal object of our mystery, and which was accomplished by the utmost labor, trouble and danger, without having the knowledge of what it was — the red colour represents 2 things: first the rays that Encompahsed the B. B. when <u>Moses</u> received this sacred name from God on Mount <u>Sinai</u> the first time; and secondly the pre Emince of the gr^d El^d perf^t and sub^{me} over all other bretheren below this degree.

The Juwel which hangs on your breast, give us a great deal of useful Instructions vizt

1st The crown designs the Royal origin of Masonry.

2^d the compahs and circle of 90 degrees represents the operation of the most Important things by w^h the gr^d El^d profit.

3dly The Sun is the design and Superiority of their rank; every one of which is suspended on your breast, to the End that you may continually see the ornaments of your dignity; and that we are never to fail in the duties imposed on us – The Instructions of our history, which we will reveal to you, will accomplish you, in the Study of Masonry.

There are 3 Signs, 3 Tokens, 3 covered words, & 3 pahswords, besides the great word of our order, which I shall give you.

1st Sign: draw your right hand from the left side of your belly to the right Side.

1 Token. Take each others right hand, as the Token in the 6th Degree, & and say. <u>Berith</u>, <u>Neder</u>, <u>Zelemonth</u>.

1 cov^d. W^d – is Guibelum, w^h. signifies a chosen friend, Elect^d. favorite & Zealous brother

1 P: W^d – is 3 times, Schiboleth, with an asperation, and signifies plenty.

===

2^d Sign is, To bring the backpart of your right hand opposite your left cheeck supporting the Elbow with the left hand. This represents the imprehsion, that the B. B. had on Moses, when on Mount <u>Sinai</u>, to shelter his Eyes from the brilliancy there of as that light was too great for his Eyes to bear.

2 Token is: The same as the Masters gripe. Then you ask, can you go further, then slip your hand above the wrist to the middle of the arm below the Elbow, and then to the Elbow, then with your left hand supporting each others right shoulder; pahs it 3 times, as the Secret M^r does 7 times.

2^d cov^d. word is. <u>Mahabin</u>, w^h signifies Silence and respect.

2^d. pahs w^d. is. <u>Helehenam</u>, w^h. signifies mercy of God.

===

3^d. Sign is double. first the sign of admiration, and after that put 3 fingers of your right hand on your lips.

3^d Token is. To seise each others right elbow, and the other hand round the neck, as if you would raise one up.

3d. covd. wd. is. Adonai, which is, O God Eternal.

3 pahs wd. is. Mahacmaharaback, wh. signifies God be praised we have found it.

The grand word is יהוה _____ Never to be pronounced.

Then the draft of the lodge and this degree is laid before him, which he inspects, while he listens to the history of this degree.

Historical Discourse

My dear brother, your good conduct, your Zeal & discretion has determin'd me, to give you in the End the true knowledge of the Perfection - you have now received the name of grd. Elt. perft. & Subme. mason, and we are happy in having great circumspection in giving you this knowledge, without wh. care we should perhaps be liable to the same fatality, of what the 3 first degrees have suffered. -

The application my dear brother, which you have made hath lead you to penetrate the mysteries of each degree which you have pahsed, before you came to this - Therefore we are perswaded & convinced that you pohsehs the Masonic history, even to the miraculous Epocha, when Guibelum, Joabert & Stolkin, by the Divine permihsion did find this Holy Name, engraved on a brilliant golden Delta in the 9th Arch under ground, where Enoch had secretly placed it under the sanctorum of his Temple, under the mountain of Ancheldama in the valley of Tophet, to the south of the valley of Jehosaphat, and mount Sion, called before Christ, the potters land or ground, now called (as said before) Ancheldama, - the bloody field or land.

It would be loosing many precious moments to revert to the circumstances of this history from the beginning - you have penetrated even to that moment when those 3 Zealous brothers (Elected by the providence of God himself to make the discovery of his sacred name) carried it to Solomon, then in his apartment with Hiram king of Tyre, who in recompence for their works, Created them the 3 first knights of the Royal arch; a Title by which the 9th arch is stiled; & promihs'd them to Interpret the sacred name they had adored, as soon as they had fixed it in the sacred place appointed for its reception and then making the Sign of admiration, he said to them God will permit in a short time to recompence all your virtues. and you will be decorated with the sublime degree of gr^d El^t perf^t & sub^{me} Mason.

You know my resp^{ble} brother, that when the Temple of Jerusalem was finished, the masons had achieved great Honor; their society was established into an order; and the delicacy of the bretheren in the choice of proper objects render'd them always respectable - Merit and merits only proved them to be worthy of it; as yours has been my dear brother, which has procured you this advantage.

The G. E. P & S. were not by any Difficulty seduced to determine in favor of Cand^{ees}, but received them at all hazards when they appeared to be worthy -

With these principles numbers of the gr^d El^d masons being able workmen, went from Jerusalem after the dedication of the Temple, and dispersed themselves among ye neighbouring nations, to Instruct them in the truth of the Royal Craft - but with this precaution, of only initiating the males, and those of a free and Eminent degree - notwithstanding this resolution masons of the lower degrees multiplied over the face of the Earth, their numbers encreased beyond measure, by w^h their secrets were disclosed, and their knowledge made common, so that they were held in no esteem - only the gr^d El^d perf^t & sub^{me} masons had so great a Care to conceal the higher mysteries of masonry that they came to a resolution to keep them an Impenetrable secret among themselves, w^h they put in Execution, by not raising any higher then the 3 first degrees -

The generality of those bretheren, made in the 3 first degrees, not being circumspect in their words, actions & lives, was the reason why cowans have frequently obtained their Signs, Tokens & words by their imprudence and Indiscretions - .

These disorders chagreen'd the perfect masons, who luckily were but few in number, which gave them all imaginable trouble, to stop the contagion; but all their endeavours proved quite fruitless; the craft degenerated insensibly, receptions were obtained too easy, the intervals of the degrees were broke into, too hastily, and scarce were they separated by any. - In the end, they were preferred without merit, when they preferring amusements to Instructions, Innovations encreased, and new Doctrines arose, which distroyed the old, to which they ought to have adher'd.

These differences created disputes, quarrels heart burnings and dihsentions, which in the End produced a voluntary discovery of our works, for which we heartily grieve, and by which masonry has lost the 3 first degrees - Happy for us, that we have the consolation of knowing the secrets of the gr^d El^t p. & Sub^{me} masons, of which they are Intirely Ignorant - Let us endeavour to render it impohsible for these other degrees to share the same fate, with the 3 first in Masonry - Let us animate with zeal to obtain that antient perfection - Let us labor, to learn their Science, to Imitate their discretion, and Inherit every part of their noble occupation - The Study and Imitation of the great architect of the universe were always their chief aim -

This grand and sacred word, was the antient masters word - Solomon, chose this word especially and exprehsily, to fill the principal workmen with veneration for him; to whom the Temple was intended to be Dedicated, and also in order to Excite them never to neglect the Execution of their office - So the masters uniformly followed their occupations with this great secret - The Sign, Token and word makes a part of this. -

The sage king knew all the force of this Holy name, he also knew that god had appeared to Moses in the B.B. (near which our lodge is always kept) when he declared to him that this was his name, and he was the only one of the Patriarchs that knew it; and that he would be invoked by no other name in the Temple, which he had ordered to be built in the land of promise, upon the plan and design of the Tabernacle, giving him orders at the same time that the Tables of the Law should be deposited there also -.

This His Holy name having so great a report to the construction of the Temple, made it the masters word.

When Hiram abif, was killed (being convinced of his couragious Discretion, in never disclosing this secret) It was resolved never to entrust a secret of this importance in future to a single person; therefore the Masters Sign, Token & word were changed, as before related, and no one Else but the antient masters knew it, until it was taken by the kn. of the Royal arch from the Delta in the Ruins of Enoch, where was wrote the true name, which makes the principal object of perfection and of Masonry.

Solomon and Hiram king of Tyre being satisfied in having placed in safety this precious deposit of the gr.d El.d p. & Sub.me masons under the Sanct.m Sanct.rum, then named this place the Sacred vault, A denomination truly Just, because there was nothing else on the pedestal but the Divine △ delta, and this column was the 3.d that supported the Temple, of which you never yet knew any thing but vulgarly, and have always been Ignorant of the true situation and the characters upon it, which is that of the great arch.t of the universe; which Pillar is called the beauty of perfection, and which sustains wonderfully the most beautiful place in the universe.

The curious cowans, have never been able to discover the place where this sacred word was deposited, as it was always kept a Secret from all masons, but those of the Royal arch, and of this degree and a very strict guard kept at the door to prevent admittance to any but the gr.d Elected, when they went to contemplate the mysteries of this sacred word, and substituted on in its place. It was impohsible for any greater precaution to be taken by this wise King, to preserve this great word from all other profanation, w.h has always been observed by the gr.d Elected, who have lived after him, and were pohsehs'd of his Zeal; and so has been handed down to each other - Then commenced the union of the bretheren and fraternity, which was sworn to by the gr.d El.d to which this word was a Zeal -

The Temple was finished in the year 3000, being 6 years, 6 months and 10 days from Solomons first laying the first stone, with a pomp and magnificence the most brilliant pohsible. The Temple being finished, Solomon gave audience to all the bretheren for 3 days succehsively.

The first day was for the Elected masters, who were Introduced into the sacred vault, when the kn.ts of the Royal arch took care of the 9 arched vault, or pahsages to guard the Entrance, and at the same time, the gr.d masters arch.ts were in Solomons apartment.

He qualified with the degree of perfection the most virtuous among these 2 orders; and made them promise solemnly to live by themselves in peace, union and concord, to Exercize the works of charity and Benevolence, in Imitation of their Deceased friend & chief, and that like him the Base of their actions, might be that of wisdom Justice and Equity - and to keep a profound silence relative to their mysteries, never revealing it to any one, who did not deserve this signal favor, by their Zeal, fervor and constancy; to ahsist mutually each others want - To punish severely Treason, perfidy & Injustice - on which he gave them his blehsing, and discovered to them the ark of alliance open'd, from which the Eternal arch^t of the universe used to deliver his Oracles. - He then ordered many sacrifices and admitted them to a Holy Libation - He embraced them, and gave each a golden ring as a Token of alliance, that they had contracted with virtue and the virtuous - He gave them many presents, with permihsion to stay in his Dominions, or go else where, as they chose. -

The 2^d Day, he gave admittance, to the masters and kn^{ts} Elected, In the heart of the Temple, and made them promihs, as the others had done, that they never would depart from the principles of virtue, of which their antient master was the model, - He bestowed on them the Degree of gr^d M^r arch^t, and decorated them with all the Honors relative thereto - He made them promihs to be faithfull guardians of their mysteries, never to communicate them to any who did not merit them. He bestowed many favors on them, and permitted them likewise to stay or travel, to their own Decision. -

The 3^d day, Solomon gave audience to the fell^w Crafts and Ent^d apprentices, - He Introduced the F. Cr^{ts} in the Eastern part of the Temple before the Tomb of H. A. at which time the Ent^d appr^{es} guarded the outside of the Temple - He gave those F. Cr^{ts} he thought the most worthy the degree of M^r and the Ent^d appr^{es} that of crafts, and Introduced them into the Porch - He made them promise, never to separate from the principles of virtue, of which their antient was their model, to be always united, ahsisting each other mutually, and keeping secret among them, their Signs, Tokens & words; never to communicate them to others, but those that had received them with goodnehs, and were known to be virtuous - He loaded them with presents and permitted them to stay, or go where they pleased; having given orders to his Intendants, to defray their Expences, till they should arrive in their own country -

Solomon, so wise, so virtuous, this king whom God had chosen after his own heart, became Deaf to the voice of God. Proud of knowing himself the greatest king on Earth, and of having built a Temple, the structure so large, the magnificence of which, was the admiration of the universe, soon forgot the goodnehs of God, and gave himself up to all licentiousnehs - His shameful compliance for a Sex so dangerous amiable, in distroying the Piety of his Father, and profaning by offering the Incence to the Idol Moloch which should have been burnt in the Sanct^m Sanctorum. -

These crimes penetrated the hearts of the good masons, yet they Instructed their children in the path of virtue that they had first received, by the Holy and respectable union that subsisted among them. They endeavoured by their council and good Example to deter their fellow citizens from Impiety and sacriledge, but dispaired of being able to succeed.

They remember'd in the bitternehs of their hearts ye vengeance that God had taken on their forefathers, by the Deluge, they Imagined that Thunder would fall on their heads and that the superb Temple would be laid low - Jerusalem would be distroyed, and that their children would suffer for these Iniquities by a dreadful slavery; which determined the greatest part of the good masons to Banish themselves voluntarly, that they might not be spectators of thic Horror, when ever it should happen. -

The crimes of these people people being accomplished God put it in the heart of Nebucadnezar king of Babylon to lay siege to Jerusalem, which he took, and mastered all Judea, under the command of Nabuzaradan his general, who raised the walls, and even distroyed the foundation of the Temple, where the Living God dwelt. He took the Inhabitants with their king Jehorakim, Captives to Babylon, Exporting with them all the riches of the Temple. This Event happen'd 470 years, 6 months and 10 days after its Dedication -

The gr^d El^t perf^t masons were then at Jerusalem did defend it with Intrepidity, but could not resist the force & vivacity of the conquerors. They were under no concern about the riches of the place, nor had they any Inquietude about the Treasures thereof, only least the sacred vault should be ransacked - these lively apprehensions remain'd in the bitternehs of their hearts to see the Temple ruined and distroyed.

They Intrepidilly exposed themselves to the fury of the soldiers who guarded the door, till they penetrated through the Ruins in the sacred vault, and searched with great ardor, till they found the golden plate on the cubic Triangular stone of agate - They found also there the Body of Galaad, the son of Sophorie (a considerable man among the Perfect masons, and) chief of the levites.

This Galaad, was the guard of the sacred vault, to take Care of the burning lamps, and to adore and contemplate the Ineffable word. He was a man equal to H. A. who 400 years before had lost his Life rather then disclose the secret of the Master - This Galaad preferred being burried in the Ruins of the Temple rather than discover (by his going away) the Treasure to be defiled by the hands of the Barbarians. They all cried Mahacmaharaback, God be blest, we have found it, and this is the 3^d pahsword and the most necehsary to be known by the faithful guardians of the sacred Treasure.

It is difficult to Exprehs the other demonstrations of Joy, with which they were filled at this time - They immediatly set to work to efface this sacred name, that it should no more be legible, to run any risk of it being discovered by the Impious - They put said golden plate in the ark, w^h contained the Tables of the Law and other precious Treasures, broke down the cubic agate stone, (as they found it impohsible to Carry it off) oversetting the column or pedestal, on w^h the sacred name had been deposited; they digged 27 feet deep and there did sink the ark with its covering and contents. - Then took from Galaad the Robes of chief of the Levites, consisting of a Tiara and vestment of fine linnen, and covered him with the marble tables which were deposited in the sacred vault, and found also by Guibelum, Joabert and Stolkin in the Ruins of the Holy Patriarch Enoch, and the retired satisfied, resolving never to trust in the future to any thing, but their memory of Carrying down to posterity by Tradition that Ineffable name; from which comes the custom of spelling letter by letter the most Holy name of names, without ever Joyning a syllable - an usage afterwards observed when the Temple was rebuilt under Cirus, and has been particularly observed among us. The grand Priest in the middle of a small number of perf^t Bretheren who formed a circle like a chain, used to spell it once a year in the Temple, giving orders to the people to make a great noise, lehs they should be heard ba them.

By their having so great a Circumspection, they lost the method of writing & pronouncing this great name. They were uncertain of the number of letters which composed this word, as the true pronunciation was only vested in the gr.^d El^d & perf.^t Masons. For God had ordered that the antient masters who knew this word, but were not Elected before the death of H. A. (who had treated Solomon so Ill), and had formed a blameable project) were distroyed in the 9 arches of Enoch, as before related.

Those gr.^d El^d masons who had penetrated in the Ruins of the Temple of Jerusalem at the time of its distruction for this Inestimable Treasure etc, left Jerusalem & Judea, and went into strange lands and other countries - Some went into Egypt, others in Syria, and Scythia, even some went to the desarts of Thebias - others past the sea, and took shelter in the southern climes, principally in England Scotland and Ireland, who have continued faithful in virtue, ahsisting each other, knowing no superiority among them but virtue; and became the admiration of the people among whom they had taken refuge, practizing particularly their virtues. The Envy of profiting by their good Example; determined many to enter in the society of these good masons, beseeching these bretheren to admit them to be Initiated into their mysteries - .

Some of the few, who preserved themselves from the general corruption, having with regret seen some of their bretheren depart from the road of virtue, took a resolution of keeping and preserving their secrets, and remembring Certain Signs, which the madnehs of their bretheren had made them forget, they separated themselves from them as if they were not even their country men.

The Time arrived when the christian princes were combined together to conquer the Holy land, and to deliver Jerusalem from the hands of the barbarians, who had it in pohsehsion.

The good and virtuous masons worthy the Heritage of those who had built the Temple; voluntary contributed to the Execution of so Holy an Enterprize, offered their service to the confederate Princes, on this condition, that they should have no other chief, but one of their own chusing - The princes accepted their offer; They hoisted their own standard and Departed.

In the Tumult and disorder of the war they retained the principles of virtue, of which their Fathers had given them the model; they lived perfectly united, lodging together in the same Tents, without any distinction of rank; they never knew any general but in the time of battle, retiring on an equality, and giving mutual absistance to each other, and extending their charity, even to the Enemies - .

In all their actions the sustained and gave proofs of their great valor, and frequently resisted the whole force of the Enemies troops. The confederates could not withstand the violent Impetuosity of the Turks, but the bretheren re Established the combat and gained the victory; a memorable Example of their courage and virtue. On signal given, they all attacked, open'd, closed, Rallied and fell on the Enemy with such an Impetuosity and Torrent, that nothing could resist the bretheren. Those prodigies of valor succeeded alternatly - The South wind doth not distroy so fast, as the rapidity of the masons, did on many occasions.

This ardor and Intrepidity in the greatest dangers, Joyned to the wisdom of the bretheren, their union, Charity and disinterestnehs in refusing to partake of the spoils of the field, awaked the attention of the confederates and principally the kn[ts] of Jerusalem, who, when they came to have a knowledge of these Heroes and saw them, intreated their alliance. -

What a moving spectacle was it, to see these Illustrious knights, such worthy deffenders of Religion, throwing themselves in the arms of these masonic Heroes, calling them their fathers, & offering them the Tribute of a greatful acknowledgement - These generous masons replied. "<u>That Tribute</u> was only due to the great architect of the universe. - That they only had taken arms to deffend the common cause - That <u>Judea</u> was their antient country, and that their fathers had been oblig'd to abandon it for many years, the particular Circumstances of which, when they thought thereon brought Tears from their Eyes" -

The princes were surprized at meeting with so great virtue among the bretheren, and desired to be admitted into their society, and to be particularly Initiated into their mysteries. The masons replied, that wisdom Justice probity, peace and good manners, friendship equality and union were their principal Laws; which charmed the knights, and their Zeal and fervor, were recompenced by partaking of the mysteries of which they were worthy by their constancy - .

The kn^{ts} of St John of Jerusalem readily ahsisted to what the masons had laid down to them; and were Initiated into their mysteries, Instructed into their History, and learnt by them that a new light had appeared on Earth, and the age of the great mystery accomplished, as the promise made to Abraham, and his posterity was now fulfilled.

By these new proselites and the Inheritance of the antient masons, Masonry is gloriously perpetuated in all Europe, and part of America, without any revolution, which so frequently changes the form of Empire; but has never affected our glorious profehsions; and is now handed down my dear brother in all its purity.

Let us render our prayer at the footstool of the Eternal architect of the universe, that we may never be devided, Amen, Amen, Amen -

End of the Discours

General Lecture of the Perfection

Q. Who are you?

A. I am what I am, and more; I am a gr^d El^t perf^t and Sub^{me} Mason nothing is unknown to me, my name is Guibelum, a zealous friend and favorite.

Q. Where was you received a gr^d El^t P: & S. mason?

A. In a place, where the Rays of the Sun, nor light of the moon were wanted.

Q. Where is this miraculous place Situated?

A. under the S^m Sanct^m of the great arch^t of the universe.

Q. Who Introduced you in this sacred place?

A. The most wise and Puihsant king, in company with his ally.

Q. which way did you Enter to arrive in this sacred place?

A. In going from one chamber of the kings Palace, I pahsed through a long narrow pahsage composed 9 arches, w^h brought me to the Holy place

Q. How was you Introduced in this subteraneous vault?

A. By 3 knoks.

Q. What signifies these 3 knocks?

A. The age of an Ent^d appr^{tice}, and also the number of the 3 Zealous masons, who have penetrated into the bowels of the Earth and found the precious Treasure of the antient masters.

Q. How do you call the place, where this precious Treasure was found?

A. The Mountain of Tophet or the potters land, it was called thus because it belongeth to some potmakers of arunea, as the Earth that was drawn from thence, was fit to make potts and urns, and said field also served a long time for a burrying place of the antient masons, who died at Jerusalem. - This same field was afterwards called acheldama that is to say the bloody field, because it was bought for 30 pieces, w^h Judas return'd after he had betrayed Jesus Christ.

Cardinal Devitry says, that the Hospitalers of St John of Jerusalem did there burry the poor Pilgrims which died in their hospital -

The Armenians now pohsehs a part of the same of which they have made a burrying ground, where they expose their dead bodies on the surface of the ground only with their scapulary on them, where they dry in a short time without any putrifaction nor Exhale the least offensive -

Some say that land must have been of great Extent, since it was appointed to be a burrying ground, to so great a number of strangers, who died at Jerusalem. They add, that it was near Jerusalem, others say that it did not contain one square of land, though sufficient for a burrying place, because the corps dried so soon there, and besides being unfruitfull, the proxemity of Jerusalem Could not render it more dear, then what the potters perhaps drew from it, thus every one did sell and raise the value of these pieces or deniers.

According to the most probable opinion of Denis the carthesian friar, who says, that the Deniers were pieces of silver which were worth 25 pence of our English money, so that the 30 Deniers for which Christ was betrayed, did make the sum of £ 3.2.6 Sterl^g - Estius believes that each <u>Denier</u> was worth was worth a golden crown - <u>Lucas</u> was of opinion that each <u>Denier</u> was worth as much as an attic mine of silver, which was in use at that time, that is to say 20 S & 10 p^s Sterl^g, so that the 30 made the sum of £ 30.5. Sterl^g

Q. Pray what did these 3 knocks procure you?

A. 5 other knocks, w^h distinguishes the age of the fell^w Cr^t, as also the number of the 5 bretheren, who were compleat, when <u>Guibelum</u> <u>Joabert</u> & <u>Stolkin</u>, arrived with the precious Treasure to the 2 kings who then Joyned themselves with them to deposit it in the place that was destin'd for it.

Q. What answ^r was made to these 5 knocks?

A. 7 other knocks, signifying 3 things 1st the age of the master, 2dly that there were 7 Experiencd bretheren chosen, to replace one, and 3dly that Solomon, Employd 7 years in the construction of the Temple.

Q. what answer was made to these 7 knocks?

A. 9 great knocks, which signifies the age of the perf^t masons, which when often repeated make the number 81, a number, revered by the gr^d El^d p: & Sub^{me} masons.

Q. What derived from thence?

A. It open'd to me a pahsage of the 9 arches, which I pahsed, after having first pronounced 3 times the pahsword <u>Schiboleth</u>, & brought me in the most holy and sacred place in the earth.

Q. what signifies this word?

A. Abundance.

Q. What did you perceive on Entering this Holy place?

A. The most brilliant of all lights, which dazzled my Eyes and struck me with admiration.

Q. What is the brilliant Delta?

A. It is the golden Triangular plate, w^h was deposited sacred by the antient Patriarch <u>Enoch</u> and found in the 9th arch by the 3 zealous bretheren, on w^h was engraved the Holy name of Names, and was placed on a pedestal, in the sacred vault.

Q. What do you call this pedestal?

A. It is called the pillar of beauty.

Q. give me that word?

A. I cannot.

Q. How will you make me sensible that you do know it?

A. Mahabin, was instituted in its place, and the gr^d pahs is Mahacmaharaback, or 3 times 5.

Q. To whom did God first communicate that word?

A. To Enoch before the flood, and by the Care of that Holy Patriarch it is come to us. — afterwards when God appeared to Moses in the B. B. on Mount Sinai, he told him, that it was his true name.

Q. What became of this word afterwards?

A. It was intirely effaced, and the golden plate being put in ye ark and burried 27 feet deep by the Pious Masons, during the destruction of the Temple by Nebucadnezar; as they were afraid that if the sacred name was to fall in the hands of the Impious, that Holy name would be profaned.

Q. What have you perceived, in the Degree of the Sublime Illustrious Knights?

A. 12 great lights.

Q. What do they signifie?

A. The 12 Masters, that were Elected by Solomon, to carry on the work of the Temple, after the death of H. A., and who commanded the 12 Tribes.

Q. What were the names of these 12 masters?

A. Joabert, Stolkin, Tercy, Morphy, Dorson, Kirem, Berthemer Tito & Alquebert. these were the 9 that went in search of the Traitor Jubulum (or hoben) akyrop, one of H. abif's ahsahsins. and Zerbal, Benachad & Tabor, are the 3 other masters Solomon Elected, to make up 12.

Q. How were these 12 masters Divided in the Temple to have the proper cognisance of the work?

A.
1st Joabert, had the Inspection over the Tribe of Juda
2d Stolkin — — — — — — — — — — — — Benjamin
3d Tercy — — — — — — — — — — — — — Simeon
4th Morphy — — — — — — — — — — — — Ephraim
5th Alquebert — — — — — — — — — — — Manahsah
6th Dorson — — — — — — — — — — — — Zebulon
7th Kerem — — — — — — — — — — — — Dan
8th Berthemer — — — — — — — — — — — Ahsur
9th Tito — — — — — — — — — — — — — Naphtali
10th Zerbal — — — — — — — — — — — — Ruben
11th Benachad — — — — — — — — — — — Ihsachar &
12th Tabor — — — — — — — — — — — — Gad

These 12 masters rendered dayly an account of what work was done by their respective Tribes in the Temple, and received the wages due their different workmen.

Q. What signifies the Ivory key of the Secret Master?

A. It serves us, to remember that the gr^d Elected, were the only depositers of antient masonry, which is to be lock'd up in their hearts and are always to rule their actions, and conduct in such a manner, as never to render themselves unworthy of that great trust.

Q. what signifies the Tomb, placed by the west door?

A. In that is reposed the body of our resp^{ble} Mr H. A. which Solomon caused to be placed as a lasting mark to the bretheren, of the Esteem he had for that great man.

Q. What signifies the Ballance in the degree of provost & Judge?

A. It teacheth us, to be Just and Equitable.

Q. what signifies the sword, carried naked by the M^r of Ceremonies, at your entrance in the lodge?

A. It is to be employd in defence of our gr^d M^r and to distroy those, who shall be so perfidious, as to reveal the secrets committed to them.

Q. What recompence Rec^d these 12 masters from Solomon?

A. He chose them for his favorites, and Instituted them Sub^me kn^ts Elected Decorating them with a broad black order, on w^h was an Inflamed Heart, paited opposite their breasts, and instead of a ponjard, gave them a sword of Justice. He did not permit them to travel without this mark of distinction; and said to them: as you have been the conducters of the Temple, you are to deffend it with this sword against all Enemies, who shall attempt to profane it.

Q. What signifies the flaming heart?

A. The ardent charity, we ought to have for each other.

Q. What is your word in quality of Ill^s Kn^t Elected?

A. Bagulkal, w^h signifies, chief of the Tabernacle, or faithful guardian. There are 3 other pahswords proper to be known. 1st Necum or Nikak (revenge) 2dly Stolkin, the name of him who found the body of H. A. under the sprig of accahsia. and 3dly Joabert, who cut off the head of Jubulum akyrop, and brought it to Solomon in company with his 8 companions. -

Q. What signify the 9 lights, 8 together and 1 separate, in the chapt^r of 9 Elected?

A. The 9 Elected masters Sent in Search of akyrop, in company with the stranger, represented by the Dog in the draft.

Q. What was the name of the unknown person who acquainted Solom^n with the place of retreat of that ahsahsin?

A. His name was Perignan; he was a squarer of stone, in the quarry of Guibelim near Joppa, between the sprig of accahsia and the sea, where the body of H. A. was found, beyond the cavern of the Traitor - This perignan was not enrolled among the workmen of the Temple; but for this piece of Service, Solomon recompenced him by enrolling of him, and changing his name to Guibelim, because he continued to work in that quarry.

Q. who were the 2 other villains?

A. They were brothers to akyrop, of the same father & mother, of the Tribe of Dan, and he was the Eldest - The 2^ds name was Jubello

Q. What became of these 2 youngest brothers?

A. They had fled in the country of cheth or Gath.

Q. How came they discovered in that country?

A. By the ahsiduity of Bengabee, Solomons Intendant of that country, Tributary to Solomon.

Q. What method was taken to apprehend them?

A. He demanded them from Moacha, king of that country to whom he wrote on that subject.

Q. Who was the bearer of that letter to Moacha?

A. Zerbal, one of the captains of Solomons guards.

Q. Did Moacha, start any difficulty, on the demand of Solomon to have a search made, for them in his dominions?

A. To the contrary, he even gave troops to Excort them.

Q. And where, were they found?

A. In a quarry called Bendaca.

Q. Had not Solomon an Intendant of that name?

A. Yes, and he was married to one of Solomons daughters.

Q. How came they to discover these 2 ahsahsins?

A. They learned from a shepherd, the place of their retreat.

Q. Who were the persons that discovered them first?

A. Zerbal and Eleham, after being 5 days in search for them

Q. How many masters, did Solomon send on this Expedition?

A. 15, of which number, I was one.

Q. was there no other persons sent by Solomon?

A. Solomon gave them Troops for an Excort, of w^h Zerbal had the command.

Q. In what manner were they conducted to Jerusalem?

A. In chains, with their wrists behind their backs.

Q. what was the form of the chains?

A. It was in form of a Rule, Square and lever, on w^h was Engraved ye crime they had committed.

Q. On what day, did they arrive at Jerusalem?

A. The 15th day of the month Nisan, which answers to our month July.

Q. what was done with them, after they arrived at Jerusalem?

A. They were presented to Solomon, who after having reproached them order'd them to be Confined in the Tower of achizar, and the next morning at 10 o'clock, to be tied naked to 2 posts, by the neck, waist and heels their arms Extended, and then their bodies cut open perpendicular and crohsways, in which condition they remained for 9 hours, in the hot Sun, the flies and Insects feasting all this time on their blood and Entrails, In order that they might suffer the most Excrutiating torments pohsible. Their Cries were so lamentable, that it drew tears even of the Executioner, who in comiseration of their Torments severed their heads from their bodies, which bodies were thrown over the walls of Jerusalem as food for the verocious birds and beasts — then Solomon gave orders to put the head of akyrop on the East, that of gravelot on the South, and that of guibs on the west pinacles of the city gates, in order to shew an Example of their perfidiousnehs treatment of our Resp^ble Master H. A. to the other bretheren and workmen in general.

Q. At what hour, did these 2 ahsahsins expire?

A. At 6 in the Evening, revenge was accomplished.

Q. what is the word of the Elected of 15?

A. Zerbal & Eleham.

Q. How long was it, before revenge was accomplished?

A. one Intire month.

Q. Have you received any mark of distinction, since you have been a Kn^t Elected?

A. As Solomon was willing to recompence the Elected for their trouble he advenced them to the rank of Illus^s Kn^ts; He Joyned to their chapt^r 3 more Zealous bretheren, that it should consist of 12 members; and then shew'd them all the riches of the Tabernacle.

He gave to each a golden ring, and in order that they should be superior among the rest of the bretheren, he gave them the name of Excellent Emerk, a word, Signifying a True man on all occasions; and then gave them the command of the 12 Tribes. -

Q. Have you penetrated any further?

A. Solomon soon after (being full of Justice) Initiated me in the degree, of gr^d M^r arch^t in recompence for my Zeal fervor, and constancy, and in the End, to lead me to the Celestial Throne.

Q. Pray, what signifies B. N: S, which you have perceived in the Triangle, of the 6th degree of Intimate Secretary?

A. The alliance of Moses & Aaron - the same between Solomon & Hiram of Tyre, and the promise which is made by the gr^d El^t perf^t and Sub^{mes}, with the result which is given to their Enterprizing characters by the words, Alliance, Promise and perfection.

Q. what is the word of a gr^d M^r architect?

A. Rabucim.

Q. what signifies that word?

A. Grand Master architect.

Q. What recompence did Solomon honor you with afterwards?

A. Providence looking favorably on us, by the divine promise made to Noah, Moses & David, my ardor was recompenced by the sovereign creator, conducting my steps in the Bowels of the Earth, and thence I took in the End, the brilliant Delta, charged with the sacred name of the Divinity, which dazzled the Eyes of me and my two companions - In recompence Solomon gave me the degree of the Royal arch, & guardian of the narrow pahsage, which leads to the sacred vault.

Q. How was you received?

A. By Solomon, and Hiram king of Tyre, in recompence of my labor, Created me in this quality, with my 2 companions Joabert and Stolkin.

Q. what was your name then?

A. Guibelum.

Q. what is the Sign of a kn.t of the Royal arch?

A. Admiration, and then kneeling down.

Q. What is the Token, and word?

A. The Token is to take each others Elbow reciprocally; and the word is <u>Hamalaheck</u> <u>Guibelum</u>.

Q. What was the recompence, Solomon Honor'd you with, after having Deposited the precious Treasure of the masons.

A. After I had penetrated into the most sacred place of the Earth, I was decorated with the degree of gr.d El.t perf.t and Sub.me antient Master.

Q. What is the name of the sacred place where you have penetrated, to be admitted to this Eminent degree? -

A. It is now called the <u>sacred vault</u>, since the greatest of Treasures is deposited there; but formerly it was called the secret vault.

Q. Where did the gr.d El.t & perf.t work?

A. under the Holy of Holy's of the Temple of Jerusalem.

Q. What is the work of the gr.d El.t Perf.t & Sublime, now?

A. To keep with respect in their hearts the sacred mysteries of Masonry, to sanctifie those that have been Initiated, to practice the purest of morality, and to ahsist and succour your bretheren.

Q. What is the name of a gr.d El.t perf.t and Sub.me master?

A. <u>Guibelum</u>, which signifies, a friend, Elected favorite & Zealous master.

Q. where does the gr.d Elected Travel?

A. In all the 4 quarters of the world, to spread the mysteries.

Q. How many figurative Signs, have the gr.d El.d and perf.t Masons?

A. There are 9 in all; but 3 are the most necehsary.

Q. Give me the 3 principal ones, with their signification?

A. The 1.st is, cutting your belly acrohs with your right hand.
2.d is, shading your Eyes, from the Burning Bush.
3.d is. of Silence. 3 fingers of your right hand on your lips.

Q. Go on, my brother, and give me other 6.

the 4th is, of admiration, and advancing with the Toes of the right foot lifting Hands and Eyes to heaven.

the 5th is, Enterlacing your fingers of both hands, over your head, the palms of the hands uppermost (this is the Sign to call a brother in Emergency).

6th is, also admiration, on which you answer the brother by looking over each shoulder alternatly.

7th is, clapping your hand on your heart, then raise it to its Extent, then clap it on your right Thigh.

8th is, Put your hand Clinched before your mouth, as if you would pull out your Tonge, then clap it briskly on your heart.

9th is, To raise your hand as if you had a poniard in it, and as if you would strike one on the forehead with it; on wh the brother claps his right hand on his forehead - this Sign shews that revenge is accomplished. -

Q. What are the Tokens, and how many?

A. There are also 3 principal ones, besides 6 others vizt.

1st is The Intimate Secretaries B. N: S, signifying <u>Alliance</u>, <u>Promise & perfection</u>. -

2d is, That of Circumspection, first that of Master, then to the wrist and so on to the Elbow, pronouncing the word <u>Guibulum</u>

3d is, Defiance, resistance and remembrance, and advancing reciprocally the hand as in the fourth degree, draw them to each other 3 times, then put the left hand to his neck, as if to raise him out a precipice.

Q. How many and what pahswords?

A. There are also 3 principal ones, vizt.

1st is, <u>Schibboleth</u>, 3 times with an asperation (abundance).

2d is. <u>Heleneham</u>, which is Mercy of God.

3d is, <u>Mahacmaharaback</u>, wh is God be praised we have found it.

Q. What are the cover'd words?

A. The 1st is <u>Guibulum</u>, wh signifies favorite.

2d is, <u>Mohabin</u>, wh signifies, <u>Tis him, he is in dead Silence</u>, this word was pronounced by <u>Moabo</u>, a particular friend of H. A. and a favorite of Solomon.

3ᵈ is, <u>Adonai</u>, wʰ is, <u>oh Thou alone Eternal.</u>

Q. give me the grand word?

A. Thrice Puihsant, I cannot, I am not able to pronounce it, <u>Mohabin is instituted in its place in favorable times, you know what I mean.</u>

Q. How did you enter in the lodge of perfection?

A. with firmnehs & constancy in my heart, the ordinary characteristic of the virtuous –

Q. why do you always stand in a lodge perfⁿ in a posture of Surprize?

A. Because Moses was oblig'd to stand in the same manner, when he receiv'd the Laws from God – Solomon & Hiram of Tyre were seized with yᵉ same Surprize, when <u>Guibulum</u>, <u>Joabert</u> & <u>Stolkin</u>, brought to them the Divine Delta or golden plate with the Ineffable name engraved on it, which Struck them both with Holy respect. –

Q. what signisfies Cutting your belly?

A. In Remembrance of the wounds of our respᵇˡᵉ Mʳ Hiram Abif; and to subdue our pahsions of Shameful desires. –

Q. What are the tools of the grᵈ Elᵗ perfᵗ & subᵐᵉ masons?

A. Shovel, crow and pickaxe.

Q. what use did they put them to?

A. The pickaxe and shovel served to discover the Iron ring on the square stone or trap, which covered the arches of <u>Enoch</u>, in which was the pricious Treasure of the G: E. p. & S: Mˢ, and the crow served to lift the Trap by the ring; it likewise served afterwards to break the pedestal in the sacred vault, in the time of the Temples distruction by Nebucadnezar, in order that the Impious, should always be Ignorant, that <u>that</u> sacred name had been there deposited.

Q. How did Solomon live after the Dedication of the Temple?

A. This wise king, so virtuous, this king whom God had chosen, became deaf to the voice of God – Proud of knowing himself to be the most puihsant monarch of the Earth, and having Elevated a Temple, the Extent structure and magnificence of which was the admiration of the universe; gave himself up to all sorts of Excehses; he forgot the Benevolence of the Lord; His shameful compliance for a sex equally dangerous as well as amiable, Took him from his duty to God; and even profaned the Holy Temple, in offering to the Idol Moloch, the Incence w^h was laid aside for the use of the Sanct^m Sanct^{rum} - He built upon the 3^d Hill of the mountain of olives towards the south, Altars to the Idols Moloch camas & Astarat, false deities of his ammonites, moabites & sidonian concubines; which occasioned several Israelites to fall into the crime of Idolatry; and was a Terrible Scandal to be seen by the true Israelites. - This mountain was called the mountain of Scandal - some say that the false Temple of Milchem or Moloch, Idols of the ammonites was built there; but the other 2 were built upon the great and smallest mountains of olives vizt. That of Astarot Idol of the of Sidonians, upon the middle Hill, and that of Idol camos of the Moabites, upon that to the North, vulgarly called virigaliloi, - there are yet upon mount scandal some ruins of Molochs Temple to be seen, with some remains of the Palace, where Solomon lodged his concubines in the valley of Tophet, which is at the foot of the hill to the South. - one may see there the well of ye Holy fire, commonly called Nehemiah's well, which is covered with a small building, and is famous on account of the event w^h happened there, when the Israelites under the conduct of Nehemias looking there for the fire, that the priest had hid in it by order of the prophet Jeremiah and finding only water, with which having sprinkled the victims, a fire kindled directly and consumed them. This well is of an equal deepnehs, and abundance of water there - at this Time, the Turks have a small mosque, not far from it.

Q. What happen'd after these horrid crimes of Solomon?

A. These crimes of Solomon pierced the good masons hearts, with the most lively griefs; and the major part of them detirmined to Exile themselves voluntary, not to be spectators of the Horrors they expected would fall on Jerusalem. They abandoned Judea, and went in search of new countries among strangers.

Q. How many years did Solomon Reign?

A. Solomon reign'd 40 years, and died when he was 94. He was burried at Jerusalem - His breaking the Laws of God, was the cause of all his misfortunes that happen'd to Jerusalem, and the Masons.

Q. Who was king of Jerusalem after Solomon?

A. Rehoboam, his son.

Q. what remarkable things happen'd in his Reign.

A. The Division of the kingdom of Juda, which God permitted in order to punish the crimes of Solomon, as God himself had threatend to Solom^n saying: "for as much as this is done of thee, and thou has not kept the covenant, and my statutes, which I have commanded thee, I will surely rent the kingdom from thee and give it to thy servant." (1st Kings chapt^r XI verse 11.)

Q. How came this division to be made?

A. By the Cruelty and imprudence of Rehoboam, which provoked the Israelites so much, that Ten Tribes raised against him, and acknowledged Jeroboam for their king; but the Tribes of Juda and Benjamin, remained alone faithful to their kings, and then their kingdom was divided in two - .

Q. what names did they to these 2 kingdoms?

A. That of Rehoboam was called the kingdom of Judea, and that of Jeroboam the kingdom of Israel or Ephraim.

Q. How did these 2 kings agreed together?

A. Rehoboam, was willing to oppose the Division of the kingdom and for that purpose raised an army of 10000 men to prevent the division, but God ordered a prophet to tell him, to let Jeroboam reign in peace, on which Rehoboam ceased the war - But this peace lasted only 8 years, after w^h these 2 princes were afterwads always at war -

Q. Which were the capital cities of these 2 kingdoms?

A. Jerusalem was the capital of Judea, and Samary that of Israel.

Q. and how did Jeroboam live?

A. A wicked, Impious and ungodly life, and an Idolator, hindering his subjects to go to the Temple of Jerusalem; Persecuting the masons who had constructed it; He ordered some golden calves to be made to be worshipped in order that his subjects should be separated from the rest of the Just as much for Religion as for the denomination - .

Q. How many kings has Judea Had?

A. Twenty vizt

1st Rehoboam.	6th Ochorias	11th Joatam	16th Josias.
2^d Abias.	7th Athalie (a queen)	12th Acham	17th Joach.
3^d Osas.	8th Joas.	13th Ezechias	18th Joachim.
4th Josaphat	9th Amasias	14th Manahses	19th Jecconias
5th Joram	10th Osias.	15th Amnon.	20th Zedekia

Q. And how many kings In Israel?

A. 19 In all vizt

	5th Zimri (an usurper)	10th Icha	15th Selieve
1st Jeroboam	6th Amri -	11th Joachas	16th Manchen
2^d Nadab.	7th Achab. -	12th Joas.	17th Phaece (son of Manchen)
3^d Baza.	8th Ochorias	13th Jeroboam 2^d	18th Phaece (son of Ropenehs)
4th Ela	9th Jorom	14th Zachary	19th Ozie - .

Some of the kings of Judea have lived a Holy life, but all the kings of Israel lived in Impurity.

Q. How did the masons behave during that time?

A. The most of them followed the examples of their kings; but God at all times reserved to himself a small number, of the gr^d El^t perf^t & Sub^{me} in both the kingdoms, which have remained faithful and Inviolable bound in faith -

Q. How long lasted the kingdom of Judea?

A. <u>Saul</u>, <u>David</u> & <u>Solomon</u> reigned succehsfully for 130 years, and the 20 kings 387 years.

Q. How ended the kingdom of <u>Judea</u>?

A. The crimes of the Jews having come to their full hight, <u>God</u> raised <u>Nebucadnezar</u> king of <u>Babylon</u>, according to the prophets prophecy - <u>Nabuzaradan</u> his general made himself master of all <u>Judea</u> after 2 years war. The city of Jerusalem was taken at midnight the 11th year the 1st day & month of the Reign of Zedekiah, and 470 years six months & 10 days after its dedication by <u>Neregelian</u>, <u>Aremant</u>, <u>Emegard</u>, <u>Nabazar</u> and <u>Ercarampzaz</u> generals under Nabuzaradan - Nebucadnezar was then at Reblata. -

They marched streight along to the Temple, king Zedikiah with his family and a few friends whom he loved the most left the city, to hid themselves in some narrow pahsage in the dehsart, the babilonians got Intelligence of his retreat by one of those that had quitted him, they pursued and came up with him at <u>Jericho</u>; they took him, his wife and children and the few that had stayed with him, and Carried them to their king.

Q. How was <u>Zedekiah</u> received by Nebucadnezar?

A. The Babilonian king treated him as a perfidious man, as he had violated the promise he had made him, to preserve Inviolably the kingdom for him, as <u>he</u> had put the crown on his head, reproaching his Ingratitude of having forgot his obligation, as he had preferr'd him to <u>Joachim</u> his own Nephew, to whom the kingdom had belonged, and had even employed against his Benefactor the power that he had given him. And Ended with these words "<u>But the great God to punish you, has delivered you into my hands</u>"

He then ordered all the sons of Zedekiah with his relations and friends to be killed in his presence, then had his Eyes putt out, and sent him in chains to Babylon, where he ended his days in a miserable prison - Thus the prophecy of <u>Jeremiah</u> and <u>Ezekiel</u>, which this unhappy Prince had so much despised, were both accomplished - The prophecy of Jeremiah was: That he should be taken prisoner, that he should be carried before <u>Nebucadnezar</u>, who would upbraid him to his face - and the prophecy of Ezekiel was, that he would be carried to <u>Babylon</u>, but would not be able to see it.

Q. What Example do you Extract from all these things?

A. This Example shews and clearly Evinces the most stupid, what the power of the infinite wisdom of God is, who knows how to proceed by diverse means in due time to fulfil what by his inspiration was foretold by the prophets; and this Example, shews also the Ignorance and Incredulity of men which hinders them to foresee, what ought to happen to them, which make them also fall into misfortunes when they least expect it, and only know them when they happen, which are not in their power to avoid.

Such was the End of the Race of David after 21 kings Descended from him, who have succehsfully swaded the scepter in the kingdom of Juda; and all their reigns including Saul, have lasted 514 years 6 months and 10 days. -

Q. what did Nebucadnezar do, after this victory?

A. He sent Nabuzaradan his chief general to Jerusalem, with orders to burn the Temple, after taking from thence all he should find; as also to reduce to ashes the Royal palace; to raise the city and its walls, and to bring all the Inhabitants slaves to Babylon. - Thus in the 18 year of this princes reign, Jerusalem was laid low - .

This general accordingly, stripped the Temple of all its riches and carried away, all the golden and silver vases, the great vehsell of Brahs called the sea; the 2 columns, the Tables, and golden candlesticks etc, and then burnt the Temple and the Palace of Solomon; and afterwards distroyed and Ruined the city intirely -

This Happened, as said before, 470 years, 6 months & 10 days after its Dedication - 1062 years, 6 months & 10 days, since they came out of Egypt; and 1950 years, 6 months & 10 days after the creation of the world -

The people were carried in captivity to Babylon, by order of Nabuzaradan, and he himself carried to Reblatha (a city in Syria where the king then was) the High Priest Sarsa, with cephon the 2^d priest, besides the 3 principal officers who had the care of the Temple committed to them - the 1st Eunuch and 7 officers who had been the greatest in favor with Zedekiah; his secretary of state besides 60 other people of the first quality; whom he all presented to his prince, with all the Riches of the Temple.

Nebucadnezar, ordered immediatly the head of the Highpriest to be cut off, with some of the most Eminent captives, because they would not confehs, what was become of the ark of alliance; the rest of the slaves with Sasadoc son of Sarca attended his Triumphal Entry in Babylon. -

Q. How did the masons behave, during the Siege of Jerusalem?

A. All the gr^d. El^d. perf^t & Sub^{mes} who were at Jerusalem, deffended it with Intrepidity, and the High Priest (Just mentioned) had the precaution (being in the sacred mysteries) to let the Ark down in the sacred vault, which stood over, and hid the Trap door on the 3 Steps (on which the Holy ark stood) through that Trap, for which he lost his head - .

Galaad being on guard in the sacred vault, for 3 days before the city was Taken,- and as the Israelites could not Resist the Force of the conquerors; the masons did not mind so much to see the riches of the Temple carried away; but their inquietude was in case they should come to the sacred vault, which would thereby be profaned; therefore exposed themselves to the fury of ye soldiers, who kept the Palace; and with great ardor fought till they gained the subteraneous pahsage, and went into the sacred vault, and searched for the pillar of Beauty, and with gladnehs in their hearts, found the sacred Treasure, with the Ark and the Tables of the laws. - They, also found the Body of Galaad, son of Sophorie, a considerable man among the gr^d El^t & perf^t masons, chief of the Levites - this Galaad was on guard in the sacred vault to trim the lamps which burnt in that vault constantly, and to contemplate the Holy and Inominable word - He, like H. A. who had 400 years before preferred to loose his life rather then give up the secret of masonry chose rather to be burried under the ruins of the Temple, then by his going away, to discover this great Treasure to ye Impious.

Q. What did they do, when they came in the sacred vault?

A. Being Seized with Transports of Joy, they exclaimed together ma-hacmahaback - God be praised, we have found it.

Q. What did they do afterwards?

A. The broke the golden plate, and broke down the agate pedestal, and put the golden plate in the ark, dug a Hole 27 feet deep, and sunk the ark, with hieroglyphic's of the most important secrets, which were the pieces of marble found by the 3 Zealous brothers in the antient ruins of Enoch, as mentioned in the 13th degree.

Q. what did the gr^d El^d p & S: do, after they had deposited the Ark its contents, and those pieces of Marble?

A. They would have been pleased, if they could have Erected a monument for Galaad to his memory, as Solomon had done for H. A. but the distrehsed situation they were in, only gave them time to take from him his levite's drehs, or Tiara & linnen gown, which they burnt, and burried his body on the Top of the pieces of Marble, and then filled up the hole, or ditch with Earth and Stone; distroyed the lamps, and withdrew with a promise, never to pronounce, write or engrave this Holy word, but only trust to their memory, and pahs it to their posterity by Tradition. From this is derived, to spell it letter by letter.

Q. What did Solomon leave the gr^d El^d p^r masons, to remember him after the Dedication of the Temple?

A. He gave audience to all the workmen succehsively for 3 days; first to the gr^d El^t p & S which he Introduced into the sacred vault, shewed and made them admire the Holy word, and all other Precious Treasures, Inclosed in this sacred place, permitting them to confer their mysteries to those whom they should know to be virtuous; and that they should be received with urbanity, and repeated to them the Sign of admiration and consternation (w^h serves us to know a gr^d El^t p: & S. m) and made them a present of a golden Ring each, which he himself put on their fingers as a mark of alliance which they had contracted with virtue; loaded them with presents, and permitted them to Stay in his Dominions or depart whenever they pleased.

Q. Why is the Jewel of the gr^d El^d a crown'd compahs Inclosing a Sun, a Triangle and a Circle of 90 Degrees?

A. The Triangle represents the Precious Treasure found by the 3 Zealous brothers, who attained by their fervor and constancy to the Sublime knowledge; The crown is the design that the origin of masonry was Royal, when the 2 kings worked together with <u>Guibulum</u>, <u>Joabert</u> & <u>Stolkin</u>, to encrust the golden plate on the agate cubic Stone - the compahs and circle of 90 Degrees, designs also the most important operation, which attends the gr^d El^d & perf^t, and the Sun, is the superiority of their Rank -

Q. Why is the Jewel suspended to a firy red ribbon Triangular on your breast?

A. Its Triangular figure represents the Delta, on which was engraved by <u>Enoch</u> the Ineffable name, which makes the principal object of our mysteries, and which was found by the goodnehs of Providence, by the 3 Sublime knights of our order, without knowing what it was when found. - and the red colour represents viz!

1st The brightnehs that surrounded the B. B. when Moses received the Holy Name the first time.

2dly The Brilliancy of the Delta when first seen by Guibelum & his 2 compans

3dly The pre-Eminence of the G. E. P & S: over all other symbolic masons?

Q. Where do the G. E: work now a days, as they have no more land?

A. In secret places, to re-Establish the Edifice ruined by the Traitors, under the protection of the Sovereign and Sublime Princes.

Q. How long was the captivity of the Masons after the distruction of the Temple, by Nabuzaradan, Nabucadnezars general?

A. The captivity lasted 70 years, and the 2 years that the war lasted makes it 72 years, as had been prophecy'd, by that great Prophet Jeremiah.

Q. How did the Israelites behave themselves during their Captivity?

A. By the Examples of the good masons that were in captivity with them and who served God faithfully; they followed their Examples the more so, as by the prophecies that God had written to support them in their captivity, they were in hopes that they should be freed in fulnehs of time. -

Q. Who were these Prophets?

A. The most celebrated were Ezekiel, Daniel, Habacuck Zephonia Hagai & Malachi.

Q. what is the reward of your succehs?

A. Virtue, and the common concord of the brothers. -

Q. What reward do you Expect in particular?

A. The Totel distruction of Vice; to gain the love and acknowledgemt of my brothers the True Elected.

Q. what will you find in this sacred place, usurped?

A. Some bones, some blood, and an ardent lamp.

Q. what will you do with this ardent lamp?

A. I will put it out.

Q. You then will be in obscurity and darknehs?

A. No, Thr: Puihsant, instead of the burning lamp, I shall be lighted by the most brilliant <u>Delta</u>, the brightest of all Lights.

  Then say all together, God help our design. A. A. A.

     End of the General Lecture

    To close the Lodge of Perfection.

Q. From whence come you resp^{ble} Brother Sen$^{r.}$ warden?

A. T: P: I come from Judea.

Q. what do you bring us?

A. The precious Treasure of the gr^d El$^{t.}$ p & S: m^s which I come to bring you.

Q. Approach then my dear brother.

At this Instant the gr^d Sen$^{r.}$ warden approaches the T. P: with the Sign of admiration, and delivers in his right Ear, the word letter by letter; and after the T: P: has received it, he says: to order my bretheren, on which they all surround the <u>Delta</u> in the middle of the lodge, and form the chain of union, the hands acrohs above their heads, The T: P: gives the first letter to his right, and so goes round when it comes to the T: P: again, and so 3 times, when he says: My dear bretheren, the word that was lost, is found again, let us keep it in the deepest parts of our hearts; let us enter again in Silence, and let us take care not to defile our hearts with any vice.

    My bretheren, Let us pray.

      Prayer

Direct our Steps o Sovereign author of the universe; let us escape the snares, that our Enimies have laid for us; let the light of thy Divine spirit light us, that we may never fall in darknehs. - Give us means to Exercize our charity, and ahsist the poor with the precious gifts of thy liberal providence - Do not render our labors in vain and unuseful - Blehs and sanctifie us, that we may proceed by thy

Divine spirit, in living only for thy glory in continually practizing the virtues which Masonry teacheth us. Amen, Amen, Amen -

After this prayer, every brother takes his seat, and the T: P: continues the following questions.

Q. Resp^{ble} brother Senr warden, what's the clock?

A. T: P: It is midnight.

Q. Why do you say it is midnight?

A. Because after work, comes rest.

Q. Why do we close our lodge at midnight?

A. Because night serves those that work in Iniquities.

Q. What motive brought you hither

A. The desire of practizing the arts of Justice, virtue and charity.

Q. What do you find to attract you here?

A. That Brilliant Divine Delta.

Q. why is this Divine Delta here so often mentioned.

A. To shew the power of the great architect, of Heaven & Earth.

Q. What do you carry away from hence?

A. A great desire to practice virtue.

Q. What does there remain for a gr^d El^t Perf^t & S: Mason to desire more, having attained to this Subl^{me} degree of antient masonry?

A. Everlasting happinehs, for which he ought to sigh continually, and must <u>that</u> require by his good works.

Then the T. P: says: resp^{ble} brother Senr warden, give notice to the bretheren, that I am going to close the lodge of perfection, by the mysterious numbers of 3, 5, 7, & 9. The Junr warden repeats the same to his side, and the Senr to his, then the Junr Strikes 3, on w^h his lights are put out - Then the Senr warden Strikes 5, and his lights are put out - Then the T:P: Strikes 7, and his 7 lights are put out - then there is a Strict Silence for about a minute, after which he says to order my bretheren Then he Strikes 3, on which the First Sign is made by all the bretheren as Cutting their bellies acrohs the he Strikes 3 more, and all of them make the Sign of Sheltering their eyes from the B. B. - Then he Strikes the 3 last Strokes, on which all the bretheren make the Sign of Silence, by putting the 3 fingers of their Right hands on their lips. -

Then he says: My dear and respectable bretheren I recommend to you to retire in peace, to practice virtue, and to endeavour to live always in the presence of the great Architect of the universe. Amen, Amen, Amen -

God Blehs the king and our work, w^h is applauded by all the bretheren by 3, 5, 7, & 9, and the lodge of perfection is <u>closed</u>.

End of the ultimate of Antient Masonry

Finis Coronat opus

15th Degree

Masonry renewed, or the sword Rectified; in the grand Lodges of Pruhsia & France. The Islands of Hispaniola & Jamaica and in the province of New York. vizt Bordeaux, Marseilles Toulon, Cape Francois cayes de Fonds, Kingston In Jamaica and at Albany in the province of New York - Established by the most Illustrious Brother Stephen Morin Pr^{us} of the R: S: etc etc etc Grand Inspect^r general, and revived By Henry Andrew Francken prince of the R: S: Senior Dep^{ty} grand Inspector general of all Superior Lodges, Chapters etc over the two Hemispheres -

From the Council of Kn^{ts} of the East or Sword.

The hangings of the council should be green or a water colour, in remembrance of those events which happened at the River Euphrates (called Starbuzanai) on the return of the Israelites from their captivity. Where of a particular account shall be given hereafter - the aforesaid hangings ought to be interspersed with red in remembrance of the ahsyrian blood spilt there, which tinged that River -

The lights that illuminate the council should be 72, in allusion to the 72 years Captivity of the Israelites at Babylon. But may be done with 7 large and 2 small ones, the two small lights represents the two last years of Sedecias's Reign; and the time the Siege lasted; and the 70 years, that the captivity lasted, from the time that the Israelites were Carried to Babylon by Nabuzaradan, under the reign of Nebucadnezar by whose order Jerusalem and Gods Temple was distroyed - and secondly, on on account of the 72 letters w^h Composes the words of the order of the Knights of the east, & also those of the gr^d El^d perf^t M^{rs} and Sublime, as may be seen by the following Example. vizt

Words of the Kn^{ts} of the East -   words of the gr^d El^d p: & Subl^{mes}

	Letters		Letters
Yaveron hamaim	13	Berith	7
Rafodom	7. -	Neder	5. -
Juda et Benjamin	14. -	Selemouth	9. -
Gabaon	6. -	Schiboleth	10. -
Liberthas	9. -	Elehenam	8 -
Syrre	5. -	Mahacmaharabac	14. -
Libbanus	8. -	Gabaon	6. -
Jachin	6. -	Mahabim	7. -
Boaz	4. -	Adon	6
	72.		72

All the Knights are decorated with a large broad green watered ribbon from the right shoulder to the left hip - on that part of the ribbon w^h comes on the shoulder must be a bridge, either painted or embroidered, and thereon the Initials Y. H. of a firy colour, w^h word is Yaveron Hamaim, and signifies, Liberty of pahsage for free masons.

Said Broad ribbon must be strewed, with heads, Limbs of Bodies new Slain, broken pieces of Swords, Crowns, Scepters etc and the word Starbuzanai divided by single Letters, in two parts at each side of the bridge on said ribbon

At the bottom of said ribbon must hang a small eastern Sabre in its sheath, to a ribbon of a firy Colour

There must be no dead heads or Skeleton bones in   nor any black such having the appearance of mourning, whereas the Kn^ts of the East never ought to go in mourning for any body; and indeed why should he? on the most happy revolution of the masons, when they Triumphed victorious in a combat, in w^h non of them was Slain, but only the   who endeavoured to oppose their pahsage, contrary to the orders of the greatest King in Persia.

The green water'd colour, is the only proper one for them, as well on acc^t of the victory they obtained, as the color of the water or River on whose banks they Triumphed -

The interspersion of the heads, Limbs etc, on the ribbon is a natural representation of what happen'd on the bank and Bridge of the Euphrates. whose green waters were tinged with the ahsyrian blood, and covered, with their limbs heads & bodies -

This River is called by the Kn^ts of the East Starbuzanai which is the name of the chiefs of the adversaries who attempted to oppose the rebuilding of the Temple, w^h in Hebrew signifies Recover'd art, as we are taught in the Talmuth, a signification which wonderfull well agrees with the profehsion of the Kn^ts of the East; a Name, in short composed of 11 Letters, which being added to the other words of the order, form the mysterious number of 81, as shall be amply explained hereafter. -

The apron must be of a white Skin, lined with red, & border'd with green; the flap down, on w^h must be a bloody head, between two swords in a St Andrews Crohs, painted or embroider'd, and in the area of the apron, must be represented 3 heaps of broken chains -

Explanation of the Draft.

First, at the upper end, you see an Eagle up right on his legs, with his wings extended, his head fiercely erected staring at the sun on his right side, and on his left, you see the moon - by his right foot a Large I, and by his left a Large B and at equal distance on either side of him, the Initials of the Compound word Yaveron Hamaim -

2dly Imediatly under the Eagle is a great oblong Square, representing the new Temple; constructed according to the dimensions given by king Cyrus -

3dly In the East part of this oblong Square is represented the Holy of Holies where the ark of the covenant is deposited, covered by the wings of two cherubims, w^h supports the Delta, on which is the name of the Supreme architect of the universe, never to be pronounced without Terror.

4^thly This Holy of Holies, is to be separated from the rest by a veil or Curtain.

5^thly In this sacred place, is to be an altar of the Sacrifices, on the middle of which is an Enflamed heart, the Letters R. O. Initials of two words, which signifies, True Masters, or True Masons (such as those that devote their hearts to God, and the general good of the order.) these two Letters mean Raf odom. on this altar also are to be the Tools & Instruments of masonry, which were employed in the construction of the Temple.

6^thly At the west door, is to be great Stair Case of 7 Steps -

7^thly Beneath the altar of the Sacrifices is the Square of 9, - which

3 times makes 27, and properly multiplied makes the favorite Number of 81, whereof you have here the first Example, referring the Explanation to another occasion, which we will give more ample here after, in order to shew, why this number of 81 is so peculiarly dear to the perfect masons.

This square of 9, which gives 3 times 27, Explains the Tripple alliance & Ehsence of the Divinity, marked by the Tripple Triangle, whereof, we here give you the figure - its Explanation is 9 virtuous attributes to, the 3 first of the Triangle Composes the number of 81 Letters, viz:-

Boundlehs mercy	Creation	Almighty
Justice -	omniscience	perfection
Immensity	Beauty	Eternity
3 virtues	3 virtues	3 virtues

These virtues being added together makes   9. -
Applied to the Tripple Triangle - - - - 27. -
and in Letters makes - - - - - - - - - - 81. -

The Example.

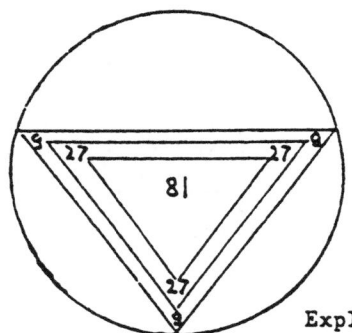

3 words of engagem:t   Explanation of Engagements viz:t
B - - -
N - - -   Here follows the square of the words
S - - -
                                                    1st alliance
  3 pahswords   2d   promise
S - - - 11.   3d   perfection

B	E	T	E	A	R	B	B	I
E	R	S	S	M:	R	A	I	E
R	S	C	H	M	A	L	N	E
I	E	H	E	A	B	O	A	H
T	L	I	L	C	A	N	D	O
H	E	B	E	H	C	M	O	O
N	M	B	H	M	H	A	N	O
E	O	O	E	A	G	H	A	a
D	a	L	N	H	A	A	I	H

E - - - 8   3 pahswords viz:t
M - - - 14.   1st abundance, or run-
                                                         ning of water
  3 current words   2d   Mercy of God.
G - - - 7   3d   God be praised, we
M - - - 7   have found it.
A - - - 6
       ___   3 current words.
        72   1st favorite or Zealous
the gr:d word 9   Elec:d master
       81 Letters   2d   Silence & Respect
                                                    3d   oh, thou Eternal -

8thly without side of the Temple, on a line with the ark, below the Sun stands mount Hebron, known by all masons; represented by the Initial Letter H. - under the moon on the Left side stands Mount Gabaon, exprehsed likewise by its Initial G - on this Mount were the sacrifices made before the construction of the new Temple.

9thly At the south gate is a hand holding a Trowel and 5 Steps opposite this gate is a hod, for the Carrying of Mortar, and under neath the 5 Steps is a heap of Cubic Stones - a little further a heap of Rough Stones, destined to fortifie the building.

10thly At the North gate is a hand with a sword & 3 Steps, under which is a Trophy of arms, for the use of the builders in case of necehsity -

11thly Lower down, are the vases, urns and other adornments of the new Temple, the Molten Sea, and the Table with the bread of proportion, the candlestick with 7 branches; the Altar with perfumes is placed immediatly below the 7 Steps, and Invironed with the Instruments of the sacrifices -

12thly In the Center beneath the 7 Steps, are the Bible Square & compas

13thly Still beneath on another line at the right hand are represented, a shovel, Lever, & Cutting hammer; and in a third line on the same side a Level, perpendicular, Cube Triangle & a quadr. angle so disposed that they may occupy the whole Lodge, from North to South on the same side.

14thly upon another line is placed Triangular wise, the rule, chihsel and Mallet; and on the Center on the void upon the bank of the River the word Judea, or its Initial -

15thly In the North you see a Square Stone with its Ring and the opening wh. said stone Covered, being the representation of Enoch's Temple, with the Nine arches under ground - and in a perspective in ye south you see an Egyptian Pyramid -

16thly The lodge towards the west end is traversed from North to South by the River Euphrates, Called Starbuzanai by the Knts of the East, over which is built a wooden bridge, for the pahsage of freemasons, to get into Judea and on said bridge are seen the two Initials Y. H., signifying free pahsage for Freemasons -

17thly The aforesaid displays, and is full or Strewed, with heads, Limbs Crowns, Swords, Scepters etc -

18thly on the void and west side of the River opposite the bridge, you see the word Syria, and at each extremity (the same side) is represented a collar of chains of Triangular links, and in the middle of these chains the 7fold Candlestick overset -

19thly on the right is a Mount with the Letter T, representing the quarry of Tyre, from whence the stones were drawn for the construction of the Temple - and on the Left a mount with the Letter L, representing Libanus, from which the Timbers were taken for the same purpose. before the letter L is a little oblong Square with a proportionable little Triangle in the Centre, representing the Tomb of Zedekias the last king of the Race of David -

20thly In the Centre, are the 2 Columns of J & B acrohs & broken

21stly Intirely at the bottom of the draft, is represented part of the plan of the City of Babylon, as if in Ruins -

22d underneath the quarry of Tyre is a heap of Triangular chains broken, and paralell with the Tomb of Sedecias - each article of the explanation of this draft includes a mysterious Sence, a part of which shall be explained in the Instructions which will be given you - The rest must remain an Onigma until that moment when Truth shall be wholly unveyled. happy moment, when True masons shall be solely attached to the first principles of masonry, as the only, that can direct every amusement in to a solid and permanent end of Everlasting happinehs; but how small is the number of those who are happy enough to be initiated here in, & Thrice happy those, who Can merit so to be - .

All the Bretheren are Stiled Princes by the Sovereing, and among themselves, they have the Title of Excellency. The candidate represents <u>Zurubbabel</u>

The door of the Council must be guarded by the two youngest knights, arm'd with Pikes; one within, and the other without the door - and all the Kn^{ts} ought to be armed with Javelins, and when the Sovereign Enters, they form and arch therewith, for him to pahs trough

Form of the Council

1st The Soverain who represents <u>Cyrus</u>, Darius, etc places himself in the East under a Canopy, in <u>his</u> Royal Robes -

2dly The grand keeper of the seals, Called <u>Nehemias</u> places himself on the right hand of the Soverain. He never leaves his place, not even when Princes of Jerusalem visit; who take their places at his Right -

3dly The grand General Called <u>Satrabuzanes</u>, takes his stand at the West End of the Council, a little to the right of the Sovereign -

4^{thly} The grand Treasurer Called <u>Metridates's</u> place is likewise in the West on the right hand side of the grand General -

5^{thly} The grand orator, or minister of State, Called Esdras, places himself on the left side of the Sovereign - The other brothers knights place themselves Indifferently on Either Side - NB: if any of the 5 gr^d officers are absent, the Sovereign nominates them out of the bretheren present. There are no wardens in the Council, yet their function is neverthelehs complied with -

To open the Council.

The gr^d gen^l in the west, shall open the Council, by saying Bretheren Knights, The Sovereign ahsembles us, to hold a Council. here he Comes, Let us be attentive, to what he will propose to us - The Sovereign then Enters Suddenly, and pahses through the arch, up to the Throne, and Striking the footstool of the throne with his naked sword, says: princes this Council is open. He salutes the knights by putting his right hand on his heart and bowing a little, having either his Hat or a crown on - all the knights return the salute in the same manner holding their hatts in the left hand, and the points of their Lances to their hearts, making an obedience, and then sit down

Initiation of a Candidate

The candidate stands at the outside of the door, covered with a Large black Crape from his head to his breast, in such manner that the guard within can hear his Sighs, who on hearing him, opens the door a little to see, who it is; and seing a man in mourning shuts the door briskly, and acquaints the gr^d gener^l of the army of it, who rises from his Seat, without uttering a word, he goes to the Candidate and asks him the foll^g questions, (which the Cand^{us} answers being prompted by the guard without)

Q. what do you want here? (pronounced with a firm voice).

A. I beg, if pohsible that you would procure me the Honor of speaking to the King?

Q. who are you?

A. A Jew by nation, a prince by blood, descended from the Race of David, and of the Tribe of Juda.

Q. what is your Name?

A. Zurubbabel.

Q. what is your age?

A. 81 years.

Q. what motives brings you hither?

A. The tears, and distrehses of my bretheren - Then the gr^d gen^l says: wait a while, I will go and interceed with the King for you - Then Striking the bottom of the door with his foot very hard, it is opened by the guard within, who recognizing the general, gives him admittance, who goes to the foot of the Throne, and relates what he has heard; on which the Sovereign, orders Zurubbabel to be ushered in with his veil, on which the gr^d gen^l makes a profound obedience to the King, then goes to Zurubbabel, and says: You have found grace before the greatest king of the Earth, he permits you to appear veiled in his presence - then the gr^d gen^l gives one stroke on the door, w^h is open'd and he Introduces Candide veiled, (being search by the guards that he has no Conceal'd wapons about him by which he might attempt the Life of the King) the gr^d gen^l makes him walk to the foot of the Throne where falls on his knees. NB when the Cand^{us} Enters all the kn^{ts} are Standing with their lances or Swords in their hands, their hatts on - Then the minister of State gr^d orator of the Council advances to him, and asks the following questions? the answers being prompted him -

Q. what brings you hither?

A. I come to implore the bounty and Justice of the King.

Q. on what occasion?

A. To beg grace for my bretheren masons, in Captivity these 72 years.

Q. who are you?

A. Zurubbabel, an Hebrew prince, sprung from the blood of David.

Q. what is the grace you would ask?

A. To Set my bretheren free, to suffer us to return to Judea, and restore the Temple, revive the laws of God of Battles and the ordinances of Moses. - After this the Sovereign makes a signal for Surubbabel to retire, when the gr^d gen^l conducts him to the door, out of w^h he is escorted by the guard, and the door being shut - The Sovereign addrehses himself to the knights in the Following manner. vizt Princes, I have a long time meditated to give the Captive masons their liberty. it troubles me to see them people in chains. Their God, whom they call their mighty God has appear'd to me in a vision, and me thought, this God threatneth me like a raging Lion, ready to fall upon and devour me - I thought I heard two words from his mouth which signifies in our languish: Render my people their Liberty or thou shalt die. From you therefore beloved princes I expect Council what I must do in regard to the people of Zurubbabel? The King having ceased to speak, the whole council observe a profound Silence and in the interim the minister of State gathers the Suffrages of each knight, and reports the same in the Kings right Ear - who then commands the gr^d gen^l to Introduce Zurubbabel, being decorated with a white Robe, girded with a broad green ribbon, and in this State brings him up to the Throne, where he falls on his knees, when the King lays his Sword on his shoulder, and says: "Rise, I grant your request, I consent that Israel may be Set at Liberty, even that they are permitted to return to their own Country, or remain in my dominions, and that you may go and build a Temple to the Almighty God; and that the vases and all other ornaments of the old Temple be all restored you, for the advancement of the New. Further, I appoint you, chief of all the Jewish Nation, & command that they obey you as such; and as an authentic of my good will for you; I shall arm you with a Terrible Sword, to combat against your Enemies, and make you formidable to such of your brothers that might cabal against you - I command my general Satrabuzanes to Instruct you in the art of war".

As soon as the king has armed Zurubbabel with a Sword, he is conducted by the gen^l, who teaches him the method of making himself known; and then asks the following questions - the answers of which are prompted him by Metridates -

Q. where is your Country Situated?

A. Beyond the Euphrates, to the west of Syria, its name is Judea.

Q. what are the names of those, that are Captives there?

A. Israel, divided into Tribes, that of Benjamin & Juda.

After these questions, Satrabuzanes says to him: my dear Brother I Rejoice at the favors you have received from our sovereign, by his bounty you and your nation are become free; he has armed you with a sword to defend you against your Enemies - by the authority he has given me, I will decorate you with this Ribbon, to which you may suspend the sword, and you must wear it from your right shoulder to your left hip - These are the Sign, Token & word, by which you will be known to be a Knight of the East.

1st The Sign is, to Carry your hand from the right shoulder in a Serpenting manner downwards to the Left hip, where the Sabre hangs - which you draw out the scabbard, and raise it, as if you are going to engage an Enemy - the other answers to same -

2^d The Token is, you clinch the fingers of your left hand, with the Brothers left hand, as if you repulse an enemy to obtain a free pahsage - then put the points of the Sabres reciprocally on each others breast. - One says: Juda, the other ans^{rs} Benjamin

P:W^d The pahsword is: Yaveron Hamaim. Liberty of pahsage.

NB: In order to make yourself known in a council, you must give the great word: which is Raf odom, signifying true Master - after this the foll^g Ob^n is tendered the Candidate in the following terms - vizt

I A: B. promise & Engage Solemnly in the presence of the great architect of the universe, and before all the Bretheren Kn^{ts} of the East here present & ahsembled, on the faith of an honest man and free mason, to be faithful in my religion, and Laws of the State as far as in my power; never to reveal the mysteries of the order of Kn^ts of the East; and never receive or Initiate to this Eminent degree any brother mason, but conformable to the antient Statutes and Constitutions of the order. all under the pain of being dishonor'd and Loosing the Title of Freemason, and being deprived of the advantages of this Council. I also promise to recognize in any part of the Earth, the princes of Jerusalem as chiefs of masons and masonry; to render them as such all the Honors & homages due to their dignity, and to do my best to merit and aspire to that most Eminent degree - <u>So God maintain me in uprightnehs and Justice, Amen</u> -

Origin of the Knights of the East

The Kn^ts of the East, draw their origin from the Captivity of <u>Babylon</u>, where the Israelites remain'd 70 years after 2 years Siege -

They had their liberty given by <u>Cyrus</u> King of Persia, by the Solicitations of <u>Zurubbabel</u>, a prince of the Tribe of Juda descended from the Race of <u>David</u>, & <u>Nehemias</u>, a holy man of a distinguishing family. - <u>Cyrus</u> permitted them to return to <u>Jerusalem</u>, to restore the Temple - he caused all the vases, urns and ornaments that had been Carried away at the distruction of <u>Jerusalem</u>, and Solomons Temple, By <u>Nabuzaradan</u>, <u>Nebucadnezars</u> general, being in number 7410, to be restored to them, & entrusted the whole to <u>Zurubbabel</u>, Commanding him, that the new Temple should be 70 Cubits high, and as many broad - He ihsued an Edict, enjoyning all his subjects, to let the Freemasons pahs freely through his Dominions without causing them any molestation under pain of death to such as should infringe his commands.

He ordered <u>Satrabuzanes</u> his general, to teach <u>Zurubbabel</u> the art of war; he armed him knight, and gave him power to confer the same degree, to those of the masons, he shou'd chuse worthy.

on which <u>Zurubbabel</u> ahsembled all the Israelites, the number of whom amounted to 42360 exclusive of Slaves - he made choice of those Freemasons that escaped the fury of the soldiers at ye distruction of the Temple, and choose 7000 whom he armed all knights, put them at the head of the people, to fight such, as would oppose their pahsage on the Road to <u>Judea</u>. The march of the Israelites was prosperous unto the bank of the <u>Euphrates</u> or <u>Starbuzanai</u>, w^h Separates <u>Judea</u> from <u>Syria</u> - The kn^ts masons who arrived there first found troops armed to hinder their pahsage, on account of the Treasure of the Temple, w^h they carried with them - Neither the Remonstrances of the kn^ts nor the Edict of Cyrus was able to restrain their insolence; and they fell on the kn^ts masons, who on their side repulsed them with such ardour, that they were all, to a man, either drowned or Cut into pieces at the pahsage of the Bridge - after this victory, <u>Zurubbabel</u> Caused an altar to be Erected on the field of Battle, on which he offer'd an Holy caust to the God of armies, who had fought for Israel; and they took the word <u>Yaveron Hamaim</u> for a pahsword, as it Signifies Liberty of pahsage.

After this the Israelites pahsed the River and arrived at Jerusalem (after a four months pahsage) on the 22^d of June at 7 of the clock in the morning - and after 7 days rest, the 3 architects with their ahsociates began to lay the foundation and work of the new Temple, they divided the workman into Clahses, each of which had its chief and two ahsistants -. Every degree of each clahs was paid according to their rank in the works, and had each of them their respective words - the word of the first clahs was <u>Judea</u> and were paid at the column, w^h stood at the Entrance of the Temple.

The word of the 2^d clahs was <u>Benjamin</u>, and received their pay, in the <u>Portico</u> -

The 3^d Clahs Received their wages in the middle of the Temple after pronouncing the word <u>Yaveron Hamaim</u> - The same order was observed in the construction of the 2^d Temple, as was practiced at building the first -.

The work was hardly began, when the kn^ts masons, were disturbed by false bretheren from <u>Samaria</u>, who, Jealous of the glory which the two Tribes of Juda & Benjamin were to acquire being now Free, resolved to war against them, in order to defeat their Design of Rebuilding their Temple. <u>Zurubbabel</u> being informed of their intentions, ordered that all the workmen should be armed, with the Trowel in one hand and the sword in the other, that whilst they worked with the one, they might defend themselves with the other, and repulse the Enemy when they should present themselves.

The construction of the new Temple last 46 years, it was begun in the Reign of Cyrus, and was finished in that of Artaxerxes; and was consecrated in the same manner as the first by <u>Solomon</u>. The Decalogue and ordinances of <u>Moses</u> were observed anew, and a chief was appointed to govern the Nation, and whas chosen from the knights masons, Called the knights of the East, Because they were freed, and Created kn^ts by Cyrus King of Persia.

This 2^d Temple having been distroyed by the Romans, the Kn^ts Masons of the present age and descendents of those that constructed it, are oblig'd under the Conduct of a new <u>Zurubbabel</u> to raise a 3^d to the glory of the great architect of the universe.

The Doctrine of the Kn^ts of the East.

Q. are you a kn^t of the East?

A. I have received that Character, my Name, my Robe, my Sword and my firmnes will ahsure you there of.

Q. by what means did you arrive to this high degree?

A. By my Humility, my patience & frequent Solicitations.

Q. To whom did you apply?

A. To a king.

Q. what is your first name?

A. <u>Zurubbabel</u>.

Q. what is your origin?

A. I am an Israelite, of the Tribe of <u>Juda</u>.

Q. what is your profehsion?

A. Masonry.

Q. what building did you Erect?

A. Temples, & Tabernacles.

Q. where did you Construct them, being dispohsehsed of Land?

A. In my heart.

Q. what is the sirname of a Kn^t of the East?

A. That of a most free mason.

Q. why are you a most freemason?

A. Because the masons who wrought in the Temple of Solomon were qualified Such, and of course they and their descendents were declared Exempt from every charge & duty, even of that of going to war; their families being called free by Excellence, but in procehs of time, having been subdued, and only recover'd their right through the bounty og king Cyrus, who conformed it to them - 'T is therefore they are called most free.

Q. why did Cyrus give them their Liberty?

A. Because God had appear'd to him in a dream, and gave him a charge, to set his people Free and at Liberty, that they should rebuild the Temple which had been Demolished.

Q. what are the duties of a Kn^t of the East?

A. To love and adore God, to hold Tradition in Honor, to succour our bretheren in Necehsity to anticipate their wants; to receive with friendship strange brothers, to visit the Sick and Confort them, to aid in burring the dead, to pray for those that are under persecution, Love mankind in general, avoid the vicious, never to frequent places of debauchery nor women of imfamous life. To be religious in adoring your maker and an exact observer of the prince & state; and in fine to follow the precepts of Freemasonry in all its points; and render Justice & Honor to the princes of Jerusalem, and respect them to all superior orders -

To close the Council.

The sovereign says: Princes, the Council is over. he then Strikes the footstool of the Throne 7 times with his sword, on which all the Kn^{ts} say together: Glory be to God, Honor to our sovereign, and prosperity to the Kn^{ts} of the order - the sovereign is the saluted by all the Kn^{ts} as at the opening of the council & close.

Feasts of obligations of the Kn^{ts} of the East

The Thrice Illust^s Knights of the East, shall celebrate the feast of the Re-Edification of the living God the 22^d of march and 23^d September at the Equinoxes, or at the renovation of the short & long days, in commemoration of the Temple being built twice by the masons -.

NB: The Kn^{ts} of the East, when they visit a lodge of perfection or Royal arch, are always received with Honor of the <u>arch</u>; and if the master of said Lodge is not a Kn^t of the East, he offers the <u>Hiram</u> and Seal to the Knight, who may accept or refuse it - if he accepts it, he only seats himself in the Seat for a little while, and then returns it again, and then seats himself at the right hand of the Thrice puihsant, who offers him the inspection of the minutes & transactions of said Lodge

If more visitors then one, they take their Rank to the right and left seats of the Thr^{ce} puihs^t - and he that has the Superiority in the degrees, has only the honor of being offered the <u>Hiram</u> & seat -

16th Degree.
Draught of a grand Council of the Illustrious & most valiant Princes of Jerusalem

Form of a grand Council, when a reception

1st This council must be divided in two parts, with an arch in the middle the first part in the west must be decorated with red, representing Babylon, where the most Illustrious & most valorous Sits under a red Canopy, with a small square Table before him; on the top of which, is a naked sword, a Ballance and a hand of Justice with a Roll of paper; he being crown'd with a Scepter in his hand.

2d The part in the East, must be yellow, and represents Jerusalem. The Sovereign of Sovereigns placed under a yellow Canopy; before him a Triangular Table, on wh. must be also a naked sword, a Ballance & Shield, a Scepter & a candlestick with 5 branches - he has a large broad water'd yellow ribbon, suspended from his Left shoulder to his right hip, and a Jewel of the order suspended there to; which is an equal Ballance with 5 stars, & a two edged Sword - In the middle of the Stars, with the Letters D & Z over each of the Ballance - on the opposite side or reversion is represented the Entry of the princes of in Jerusalem - All the princes ought to have the same Jewel. -

Jewel

The 2 gr.d wardens, which we call the gen.l of the army and the gr.d Treasurer, Sit each under a small Canopy, in the west, at each side of the arch, with the same paraphinalia as the sovereing, except the Crown. - the grand keeper of the seals Called Nehemias is to be on the right hand of the sovereign; and the minister of State Called Esdras on his left; each under a Canopy, with the same decorations -

The other princes are placed to the right and Left by gradation. The door of the gr.d council must always be guarded by the 2 youngest princes, and receive their orders from the gen.l of the army; and they must be with a Spear instead of a Sword, - all the princes that are in office are to be armed with a shield and a Lance. Th apron Lined with yellow, on the Flap of wh. must be painted or Embroider'd a Ballance with the Letters D & Z -

apron

NB: when the council sits on matters of the craft, and any complaints is made to them of Irregularities of Lodges under its Juresdiction (there only one council admitted in each government) and when no reception is to be, there is no occasion for the arch, as Babylon is out the question and the gr.d Council is only formed by itself.

Opening of the grand Council

Q. The Most Illust.s & valorous prince Zurubbabel, says to the gr.d wardens in the west: Thrice valorous princes, how Comes Comes this place divided in two parts, the East yellow, and the west Red?

A. The Eastern part represents Jerusalem, with a yellow or gold colour, a Holy place, where the first Temple of God was constructed - The western part with Red, represents Babylon, and likewise an Emblem of the Blood, that was spilled in the different Combats that were fought on the Road between Babylon & Jerusalem, by the Kn.ts Masons, on their return from Captivity -.

Q. Who presides in our Council?

A. The prince Zurubbabel, under the Title of thrice Equitable.

Q. who are the grand wardens?

A. Two of the princes under the Title of most profound.

Q. if it is so, Thr^{ce} Excell^{t} Brothers princes most Enlighten'd, acquaint the most Excell^{t} & Thrice Valorous here present, that I am going to open the gr^{d} Council.

A. Most Excell^{t} Br^{s}th^{s} Most valorous & most Illus^{s} princes, the sovereign of sovereigns, and Lord of Lords, advertizes you, the gr^{d} Council is open, be attentive, to what he proposes.

Q. what's the clock?

A. 'T is 5 in the Evening –

Then the Sover^{n} Strikes 5 times, on the Step of the Throne, one Slow and 4 quick, and says: most valorous princes the council is open. – which is repeated by the gr^{d} wardens as also the 5 knocks as before – then they are all Seated.

Form of a Reception

After the opening of the gr^{d} Council, 4 Knights and princes accompany Zurubbabel (the cand^{us}) with the ornament of Kn^{ts} of the East, with crapes over their faces, their Sabres drawn in their hands, with shields and Cuirahses; they depart from the East with the Sign of Battle, in a straight Line the road to Babylon with grave countenances; Zurubbabel by himself and ye other 4 behind him. when he arrives at Babylon Zurubbable adrehses King Darius: That he and his 4 companions Kn^{ts} & princes are deputed from Jerusalem as ambahsadors to pray him for Justice against the Samaritans, who refuse to contribute to the rebuilding of ye Temple of the True God; and also refusing what is requisite for the sacrifices etc

After King Darius has heard said ambahsador (wo is the Candidate) he gives him a Roll of paper, being a patent which Contains orders to the people of Samaria, to submit to every thing there in contained – when the Cand^{us} Receives said patent, he makes a Low obedience, kihses the upperpart of the kings right hand, and departs the same Road they came, and in the same manner with the Sign of Battle, but no Crape over their faces, shewing thereby that their ambahsy had succeeded – Then the gr^{d} M^{r} of Ceremonies, Carries the candidate to ye sovereign and he takes the foll^{g} Ob^{n}

"I A: B. promise & Engage most solemnly in the presence of the most Mighty great architect of the universe, and in the presence of the valorous princes of Jerusalem here present, and on the faith of an honest man to be inviolable in my Religion, and to observe the Laws of the State as far as in my power – I promise never to fight my brother prince of Jerusalem, and never to receive or Consent to be received any mason in this Eminent degree, but conformable to the antient Statutes and Regulations of this gr^{d} council of valorous princes of Jerusalem

"I promise to appear at all times at the Councils or gr^{d} Councils that I shall be ordered to attend by my sovereign, unlehs having a good reason to the contrary

I promise at all times to Submit to the orders of the Kn^{ts} of the Sun,

Kn[ts] of Black & white Eagle, and princes of the Royal Secret.

All these I promise under the penalty of being dishonor'd and Loose the glorious Title of Free & accepted Mason, and being deprived of all advantages of masonry in general, So God maintain me in uprightnehs & Justice, Amen.

After this ob: the cand[us] is conducted to the gen[l] of the army who decorates him with the apron and the large yellow order, with the Jewel suspended thereto, and gives him the Sign Token & word. viz[t]

p: w[d] the pahsword is Thebet a hebrew word Signifying the 20th of the Ninth Month, that the princes Enter'd Jerusalem returning from their ambahsy to Babylon

word - the word is adac, also a hebrew word, Signifying the 23[d] of the Eleventh Month, when they returned thanks to God for the reconstruction of the Temple.

1st S: The 1st Sign is, that of Command, the right arm extended to the hight of the shoulder -

2[d] S: The 2[d] Sign is, as defending in Battle, with the left hand on the left hip - after the cand[us] is thus arrayed, he is conducted to the minister of State who gives him the foll[g] History, viz[t]

You represent most Excell[t] Broth[r] Prince in all the Ceremonies you have past through, Zurubbabel, at the head of the ambahsy sent from Jerusalem to Babylon - you are armed Compleatly, and exprehs by your attitude the figure of the combats they had to Encounter in this travels, from the people they were going to complain of, who had posted themselves ready to oppose their pahsage; - you have represented that Celebrated deputation from the people of Jerusalem to king Darius when Zurubbabel appear'd before that great king and acquainted him with the motive of that ambahsy, on which he received the patent from Darius in which was ordered that the people of Samaria should submit to his mandates therein Set forth. on which Zurubbabel return'd to Jerusalem and gave an account to the people of his succehs - who desired him with his 4 companions to go out of the Town again, and return, in order to make his Entry with pomp & magnificence, for the good he, and his Four Companions had done for the people of Jerusalem - you have recovered the knowledge of our mysteries, which in the End, represents to you the power w[h] was given to these ambahsadors by the people; for their glorious succehs in their ambahsy - the lights in the west being 125 by five's, and the numbers of Fires round the city of Jerusalem, represents the number of the ambahsadors were 5. - and the Bonfires round the City exprehsed the Joy of the people of Jerusalem -

Then all the princes shall come and receive the ambahsadors at the west gate, to compliment and Conduct them to the 2[d] part where he is honor'd with the Title of Prince, in remembrance, that all the people went out of the city before the ambahsadors; when Zurubbabel was Elected prince & governor of the city of Jerusalem.

Darius's Letters patent, to the People of Samaria

"We Darius, first king of Kings, sovereign of sovereigns, Lord of Lords being willing to favor in our own gratitude and goodnehs our dear people of Jerusalem, in Example of our most Illustrious & most puihsant predecessor King Cyrus; we having heard their complaints by their ambahsador against the people of Samaria, who have refused to contribute to the reconstruction of the Temple of the Lord, and the necehsaries for the Sacrifices of which they have need. We order by these presents, that they are to Submit to our former order, under the penalty of incurring our highest displeasure and Just vengeance

Given in our grand Court the 4th of the 2d month of the year 3534 - under the Seal of the faithfull Satraps under all Judea, and of our reign the 3d Current of the year five / signed /

Darius Rex

Lecture

Q. Most enlighten'd & most Illus^s prince first gr^d Warden are you a prince of Jerusalem?

A. The Road to Babylon is known to me.

Q. What was you before you travelled that way?

A. Most valorous & Illus^s Prince & Sovereign, I was a Kn^t of the East, which I merited after a Captivity of 70 years - and my ancestors found the precious Treasure of the gr^d Elect perf^t and Sub^{me} Masons, under the ruins of Solomons Temple, w^h was distroyed by Nabuzaradan - general of Nebucadnezars Troops King of Syria.

Q. How came you by the dignity of Prince?

A. By the great Zeal and ardor which I have Shewn on different occasions, and the succehs I met with in my ambahsy to king Darius.

Q. where did you travel, for which you received this dignity?

A. from Jerusalem to Babylon.

Q. For what reason were you Sent?

A. As the Samaritans refused to pay the Tribute, for the sacrifices of the new Temple; therefore an ambahsy was sent to king Darius by the people of Jerusalem, to lay before him their Just complaints.

Q. what was the number of that ambahsy?

A. Five.

Q. who was the chief?

A. The great architect of the universe and myself.

Q. what is your name?

A. Zurubbabel.

Q. were there no Enemies on the road, who obstructed your pahsage?

A. Yes, and we were oblig'd to deffend ourselves from the ahsaults of those very people we went to complain of; and got the better of all obstacles.

Q. what did you obtain from Darius, after your Interview with him?

A. We obtained a Decree from Darius to the people of Samaria, to submit to all the demands of the people of Jerusalem.

Q. how were you received, on your return to Jerusalem?

A. we were Rec^d with great pomp & magnificence - the people of Jerusalem came out to receive us with great Joy, and accompanied us into

Jerusalem Exprehsing their Joys with bonfires displayed by five's all round the City in allusion to our number, and in favor of our succehs, Created us princes.

Q. where did these princes ahsemble, to give Justice to the people?

A. In two Chambers of the Temple.

Q. How were they arrayed in grand Council?

A. In gold.

Q. why in gold?

A. In order to receive people the more respectable, therefore they chose the most Rich and precious vestments.

Q. Did they carry any thing else remarkable?

A. They were decorated with a large gold colour'd Ribbon, suspended from the left shoulder to the right hip, to which hung the Jewel of the order, on which was a Ballance Equally poised, a Two Edged sword, 5 Stars & the Letters D & Z.

Q. How came they to wear that Jewel?

A. To shew, that for their great Zeal, Courage & knowledge they obtained the Title of governors of the people, w^h they were to govern with Equity.

Q. what represents the draft of the princes of Jerusalem?

A. The Temple of Solomon, almost brought to perfection, on the Holy Mountain in an oblong square, and the city of Jerusalem surrounded by Bonfires, displayed by 5's. The people gathering round the ambahsadors with Instruments of Music & those of the craft, some Carrying a sword, shields, an Equilateral, and one Carrying a Ballance all which Signifies the valor & Justice of the princes.

Q. Why do the princes of Jerusalem still wear their aprons?

A. To remember their first origin.

Q. what was the pahsword?

A. Tebeth, a hebrew word w^h signifies the 20th of the 9th month when they Entered Jerusalem.

Q. And what was the word?

A. Adac, w^h Signifies the 23^d of the 11th month, when they returned - thanks to God, for the reconstruction of the Temple.

Q. What was the first Sign?

A. That of command, the right arm extended to the hight of the shoulder.

Q. what was the 2^d Sign.

A. of defending, as if in combat; to put the Left hand on the Left hip.

Q. How ought the Council in the west / which represents Babylon, to be lighted.

A. By 125 lights, distributed by 5^s (NB. 25 will suffice)

Q. Why this number?

A. To represent the number of the ambahsadors, being 5.

Q. How is the gr^d Coun^l Lighted in the East, representing <u>Jerusalem</u>.

A. of Many Lights placed indifferently

Q. why so?

A. to represent the fires of Joy, made, on their return from Babylon.

Q. How came you Introduced in the grand Council?

A. By 25 knocks, Struck by 5's.

Q. In what manner do the princes walk?

A. On their Toes, one Slow, and four quick.

Q. of what colour are the aprons of the princes?

A. A white apron lined and bound with yellow, a deep red ribbon on the outside edge, on the flap an equal Ballance, with the letters D & Z over it. the flap down.

Q. Why is their aprons Stained with Red?

A. Because in their combats with the <u>Samaritans</u>, much blood was spilled and their aprons Stained with it.

Q. In what posture are you to be in a grand Council?

A. With a grave air, the Left hand on the Left hip in a Square.

Q. In what place is the sovereign, & his 4 officers in a grand Council?

A. The sovereign is placed in the East under a yellow Canopy; a small Triangular Table before him, on which is naked sword, a Ballance, a shield, a Crown a Scepter and a Candlestick with 5 branches - The 2 gr^d wardens, which we call the gen^l of the army, and the gr^d Treasurer, in the west, each under a small Canopy, with the same paraphinalia as the sovereign except the crown - and the grand keeper of the Seals Called <u>Nehemiah</u>, is to be on the right hand of the sovereign, and the minister of State Called <u>Esdras</u> on the Left of the sovereign, both also under a small Canopy, with the same Paraphinalia. - The other princes are placed on the right & left by gradation - The door of the gr^d Council must be guarded out and inside by the youngest princes; who receive their orders from the gen^l of the army - These guards are always arm'd with a Spear instead of a Sword, and the other princes with a Shield & Lance.

End of Lecture

To close the grand Council.

sov^n Q. Thr: Excell^t Broth^r & valorous prince, what hour is it actually?

Genl A. Most Illus^s Most Val^s prince, most Equitable Sovereign, the Sun has traversed half his Career, and Justice is done to the people.

Sov^n Thr: Ex^t & m^t Enligh^d pr^e, proclaim that I am going to close the grand council by the mysterious numbers.

gen^l T: E: & Mt Val^s Pr^s the Sov^n of sovereigns, announces ye, that the gr^d Council is going to be closed / then there is a Silence for a minute / and then rise all. The Sover^n knocks 5 with his sword on the Table and says: this grand council is closed - which is repeated by the 2 gr^d officers, who knock the same number with their hands, & the gr^d Council is closed.

Priviledges of Princes of Jerusalem

1st They are the chiefs of all degrees below them, and only give place to the founder of their constitutions, the Knights of the Sun, the Knights of white & black Eagle, & princes of the Sublime Royal Secret -

2d They have a right to disclose every matter, that is not done in a proper manner, in Councils of Knights of the East, Lodges of Perfection and of lower degrees when they visit there, if none of higher degrees are present, as Knts of the Sun etc as above mentioned, as they are the chiefs of all masonic orders -

3d When a prince of Jerusalem visits any Lodge, and it is known that he is a prince, the Master sends deputies to enquire if he chuses to be Introduced with all his Honors! he answers, he expects it by his dignity of his Royal degree, which being reported by the Deputies, that the Brother prince visitor expects to be received with "all his Honors". on which the master Sends 4 of the oldest masters with naked swords to receive him. The prince Enters with his sword in his hand, with his Buckler & spear, and stands between the wardens Salutes the master & bretheren with his sword without taking off his hatt - after wh the master Invites the prince visitor and Sit at his right hand - when he advances to the master, all the bretheren form the arch with their Swords, through which he goes, till he arrives at the Seat, when the master offers him the Hiram and the chair, which he may take or refuse; but if he takes the Seat etc he returns it presently back -

4th If a prince visitor desires to retire out the lodge before it is closed; The Master orders the arch, with the oldest brothers to Conduct him to the door. The Master and all the bretheren Standing whilst he departs -

5th A prince of Jerusalem Cannot receive these honors, when there is present a brother or brothers of higher degrees; when he only goes through the arch, and takes his Seat according to his Rank.

6th When a Prince of Jerusalem visits a Lodge, he has the Title of valorous prince - a Knight of the Sun, Sovereign prince, and prince of the Royal Secret, Thrice Illuss & Sublime prince -

A lodge is obliged to give an Exact account of every of their transactions; shew him their Constitutions if they are valid and good etc and if any coolnehs subsists among the Bretheren he is to reconcile them. and if any are obstinate, he has a power to Expell them Immediatly, if they will not conform to the rules and regulations of masonry.

7th The Princes of Jerusalem have a right to keep their seats in all the opperations of the symbolic lodges, with his hatt on, but Cannot claim these priviledges without his order and decorations -

8th Five princes of Jerusalem can form a grd Council, but not a lehs number. and only one grand Council can be formed in one government. and if any Lodges of R: A: or perfection etc Established, in any province where no grand council is yet established, such Lodges may appeal to Such grd Council, which said grand Council Can finally Judge thereof, and no appeal can be had from Such Judgement they are authorized by the same power that was given by their predeceh-

:ors by the people of Jerusalem, and by their perfect knowledge in
:very matter of the Craft -

These are the Priviledges of the most Excellent and most Illustrious & valorous Princes of Jerusalem - they are honor'd with this glorious Title; because they represent those Illust[S] masons, who by their merit only became to govern the people with peace & Equity, In Imitation of the great Zurubbabel the Hebrew prince, the restorer of the Captive masons of the Race of David, known by the princes masons and by the restoration of Masonry -

End.

17th Degree.
Knights of East & West

Origin -

When the Kn^ts & Princes Called them selves to Conquer ye Holy Land, they took a Crohs to distinguish them, as a mark of being under the Banner, and they took an oath, to spend the last drop of blood to establish the true religion.

The peace being made, they could not fulfill their vow, & therefore returned to their own respective Countries, and resolved to do by theory what they could not do by practice; and never to admit in their Ceremonies any but those who had given proofs of friendship Zeal & discretion

They Joyned at <u>Malta</u> by having a Connection with them relative to masonry, and they took the name of Kn^ts of East & West, princes of Jerusalem, to teach all the world where that order began, and never changed any wise their Customs and receptions.

In the year 1118, the first Kn^ts to the number of Eleven took their vows between the hands of <u>Garinous</u> patriarch & pr^ce of Jerusalem

Ceremony, when a Reception

1st The gr^d Coun^l of Kn^ts of East & West, must be red, Spread with Stars of Gold.

2d In the East a Canopy Elevated by 7 Steps, Supported by 4 Lions or Eagles, and between them an animal of the Human kind with 6 wings -

3d on one side of the Throne the Sun, and on the other the Moon, made light by transperance, and under a Rainbow, and below this a bason with perfumed water, and a Skull.

4th Each Side South & North are 11 Small Canopies Elevated by 3 Steps for the venerable antients - opposite the Throne in the West 2 canopies, elevated by 5 Steps, for the 2 antient officers, who act as wardens -

5th A full gr^d Council must be composed of 24 Kn^ts The venerable master is Stiled all puihsant; the wardens and the 21 brothers are Called Resp^ble antients. if there are more brothers, they are Stiled Resp^ble Knights, and are placed north and south behind the small canopies - the 1st Canopy at the right Side of the Puihs^t is always vacant for the Candidate -

6th all the bretheren are vested in white Robes, with a Cincture of gold round their waists, and each a long white beard, and a gold crown on their heads; the Kn^ts in their ordinary habits, carry a white broad ribbon from their right shoulder to their left hip, with the Jewel Suspended thereto; and carry the Crohs of their order on their breast to a black ribbon -

7th The all puihs^t has his right hand on a large book with 7 Seals hanging thereto, which lays on the Pedestal.

8th The draught of the Council is a Heptagon in a Circle, in each angle are the following Letters, B, D, H, P, C, T, S, - in the middle a man vested with a white Robe, Cinted with a girdle of gold, his right hand extended and surrounded with 7 Stars; he has a long white beard, his head surrounded with a glory, a two edged sword acrohs his mouth, and 7 candlesticks round him with these letters over the Candlesticks: H, D, P, I, P, R & C –

To open the Council.

Q. Vener^{ble} Broth^{rs} Kn^{ts} & Princes what is your duty?

A. To know if we are secure.

Q. See & Search, if we are so?

A. We are so.

Q. Resp^{ble} & ven^{ble} Brothers this gr^d Council of Kn^{ts} of East & West is open, be attentive?

A. We shall always be attentive, to Every thing you will order.

Form of a Reception

The cand^{te} is Introduced by 7 knocks, 6 quick & one Slow. When both the officers go and see, who it is that knocks, on seing the Cand^{te} take him by the hand and says: come my dear brother, we will shew you surprizing things, then leads him 7 times round and Stops at each angle, where he puts his feet in a square, & so proceeds till the last, from which by 7 Steps he advances to the Bason; holds his right hand to the all puihsant, between whose hands He takes the foll^g Ob^n on his knees

"I A: B. promise and Swear to be faithfull in my Religion and to observe the Laws of the State as far as I can. I promise never to reveal the mysteries of Kn^{ts} of East and West, and never to receive nor initiate, or Consent any to be received in this degree, but conformable to the antient Statutes & Regulations, or by a power vested in me for that purpose all under the penalties of this and my former obligations: So God maintain me in uprightnehs and Justice Amen".

after this ob^n the M^r of Ceremonies Rises the Candidate and brings him between the two wardens before the draught. Then the Senr warden says to him brother, Examin with delibration all these things which the all puihsant is going to operate to you. after a little Silence, the Senr warden Continues and says: is the mortal here worthy to open the book and Seals? All the bretheren Cast their Eyes down and Sigh. The Senr warden hearing their Sighs, says to them: Ven^{ble} & Resp^{ble} bretheren knights do not be afflicted, here is a victim (pointing to the cand^{te}) his defete will give you content.

Q. (To the cand^{us}) do you know the reasons why these antients have a long beard?

A. (he being prompted) You know it.

Q. They are those, who came here, after pahsing great affliction, & having dipt and washed their Robes in their own blood. Will you have such Robes, at such price?

A. Yes – on w^h the wardens Conduct him to the Bason, make both his arms Bare, puts a Ligature on both, and orders him to put them both in the water – the wardens have each a Lancet, which retires back with a Spring, having a little red wine to drop from thence, then they give him each a knock on the vein, when the blood that comes from the Lancet is wiped on a white cloth, and each warden Shews it to the Bretheren, and Says: He never was afraid to Spill his blood to see our surprizing thing. Then the Ligatures are taken off but his arms are left bare, when the gr^d orator makes him a Comp^t on his resolution.

Then the All puihs^t open the

1st Seal of the great book, and takes out a Bow and quiver with arrows, and a crown; gives them to one of the old men, and says: go, depart & continue the Conquest.

2^d Then he opens the 2^d Seal, takes out a sword, gives it to the next aged, and says: go and distroy the peace among the profane & wicked bretheren, that they never may have a residence in our Lodge —

3^d Then he opens the 3^d Seal, Takes out a Ballance, gives that to another aged brother and says: Endeavour, that the profane & wicked bretheren might never find Justice but in our Lodge

4th He then opens the 4th Seal, takes out a deaths head, gives it to another aged, and says: go & endeavor that the wicked might never find Life but amongst us —

5th He then opens the 5th Seal, and takes out a cloth stained with blood, gives it to another and says: when is the time that we shall revenge and punish the profane and wicked brothers who have destroyed so many worthy bretheren by their false accusations —

6th Then he opens the 6th Seal, and in that Instant the Sun becomes dark and looks black, and the moon is Stained with blood —

7th He then opens the 7th and last Seal, and takes out Incence and gives that to a brother; and also takes out a vase with 7 Trumpets, which he gives to 7 aged brethern — when the four old men / who must be one of them in each of the four Corners with a bladder full of wind represent^s the four winds / Shew their bladders; when the all puihsant says: Never Strike no profane nor wicked brother, till the moment I have discover'd the true and worthy masons — when the four winds put up their bladders, and one of the Trumpets sounds, when the two wardens go and take the Cand^{te}, Cover his arms, and take from him his apron & Jewel, with which he was decorated.

a 2^r Trumpet Sounds, when the Junr warden gives the Cand^{te} a white Robe, the apron & Jewel of the order.

a 3^d Trumpet Sounds, when the Senr warden gives him a long white beard.

a 4th Trumpet Sounds, The Junr warden gives him a Crown of gold.

5th Trumpet Sounds, the Senr ward^n gives him a Cincture of gold.

6th Trump^t Sounds, when he Receives from the Junr warden the Sign

7th Trumpet Sounds. on w^h all the 7 Trumpets Sound together on w^h the Senr warden Conducts him to the vacant Canopy.

Sign — The Sign is: To look over your right shoulder; the other answers by Looking over his left shoulder.

words. — one says: <u>abadon</u>. the other ans^{rs} <u>Jabulum</u>. Signif^e = angel of <u>abyhs</u>.

- is to touch the left shoulder of a broth[r] with the right hand, the person So touched looks over his right Shoulder. and so visa versa.

- is a heptagon regular of Silver or gold, in every angle on one side a Star of gold and one of the foll[g] Letters, vit[t] B, D, S, H, P, I, G. and on the other side in each angle these Letters, viz[t] B, D, W, P, H, G, I. - and in the middle of those Letters a two Edged sword between an equal ballance, and in the Centre of the other Side with the Stars is a Lamb. - this Jewel is wore by the gr[d] Knight from the centre of the golden Cincture, and by the other Knights from their broad white order and all of them wear a white Croħs to a black ribbon round their necks.

When a kn[t] of East & west visits a symbolic Lodge of the 14 degrees, he cannot dispence with wearing the ribbon & Jewel - they Enter the Lodge with their hatts on, a naked sword in their hands with a Shield as the princes of Jerusalem; and when he is going in the Lodge, the door is thrown open, and he is conducted by 2 masters through the arch, and if the Right worsh[l] is not a kn[t] of East & west, he offers the prince visitor the Hiram & Seat who may accept or refuse it, and always Sits in the right hand of the master.

Lecture of the Knights of the East.

Q. Are you a kn[t] of East & west?

A. I am.

Q. what have you Seen?

A. Marvelous things.

Q. In which manner was you received?

A. By water, & effusion of blood.

Q. Explain this to me?

A. A Mason is never afraid to spill his blood for masonry.

Q. what are y[e] ornaments of the council?

A. Superb thrones, Sun, moon & a bason of perfumed water.

Q. what is the figure of the draught?

A. A regular Heptagon placed in a Circle.

Q. what is the representation of it?

A. A man, vested in white Robes, girded with a gold Cincture, round his right hand 7 Stars; his head surrounded with a glory, a long white beard, a two edged Sword acroħs his mouth, surrounded and lighted by 7 Candlesticks with these Initials H, D, P, I, P: R & C.

Q. what signifies the Centre?

A. As the Centre is finished from one point, in the same manner ough a Lodge to be animated by its union.

Q. what signifies the Heptagon?

A. Our mystic number inclosed in 7 Letters.

Q. what are these 7 Letters?

A. B, D: W, P, H, G & F, Signifying Beauty, Divinity, Wisdom, puihsence, Honor, Glory & Force.

Q. Give me the Explanation of these words?

A. Divinity, teaches us that masonry has Divine principles -
Wisdom - is a quality to Invent.
Puihsence - is necehsary to crush the profane & wicked bretheren and to reduce them in their Calumnies -
Honor - is an indispensable quality to a mason to maintain himself in that respectable order.
Glory - Shews that a good mason is equal to the most High Prince, and
Force - to sustain us.

Q. what signifies the 7 Stars?

A. Seven qualities, by which Masons must be conducted, vizt Friendship, union, Submihsion, discretion, Fidelity, prudence & Temperance.

Q. why ought a mason to be pohsehsed of these 7 qualities?

Friendship - is a sentiment that ought to reign among brothers.
Union - is the Base of Society.
Submihsion - To receive directions from a lodge without murmuring
Discretion - to be upon your guard never to be surprized.
Fidelity - in observing Strictly our obligations -
Prudence - To rule our actions in Such a manner, that the profane be always Jelous of our pleasure, without being able to blame our Conduct, and
Temperance - To Shun excehs, equal against our body & Soul.

Q. what Signif^s the 7 candlesticks & their letters

A. The 7 faults w^h msons ought to Shun vizt Hatred, Discord, Pride, Indiscretion, Perfidy, Rashnehs & Calumny.

Q. What are the reasons, that masons ought to Shun these Crimes?

A. because they are absolute Contrary to the qualities which we have come to and aquired - a good mason even never bears hatred against his brother, though he Should be treated Ill by him
Discord - is contrary to Society for w^h we must Shun it.
Pride must be banished as it is contrary to humanity -
Indiscretion - is Fatal to masonry -
Perfidy - is Horrible to an honest man
Rashnehs - is tiresome to masonry.
Calumny - is a vice below a mason. that he must endeavour to reunite in himself a perfectnehs, and Shun all other Vaults, that are a plague to human nature.

Q. what Signifies the two edged Sword?

A. It exprehses the Superiority over all other degrees.

Q. Are there any higher degrees then this?

A. Yes, there is the respectable order of the Kn^{ts} of the Eagle, and the Sun or chaos dihsentangled. and the Sublime degree which is preceeded by the last Step of masonry -

Q. what Signifies the book with 7 Seals, which non Can open?

A. A lodge of masons which the all puihs^t has a right to convoke & oper

Q. what is inclosed in the 1st Seal?

A. A Bow and quiver with a crown.

Q. what in the 2d?

A. A two edged Sword.

Q. What in the third?

A. A Ballance.

Q. what in the 4th?

A. a deaths head.

Q. what in the 5th

A. A Cloth with blood

Q. what in the 6th?

A. The power to darken the Sun, and tinge the moon with blood.

Q. and what is in the 7th Seal?

A. Seven Trumpets & perfumes.

Q. Explain all these things to me?

A. 1st The Bow & quiver with the Crown Signifys the order of the Lodge, wh ought to be executed with such quicknehs and Exactnehs as the Bow sends forth the arrow, and receive those orders with such submihsion as from a Crown'd head.

2d The Sword teaches that a lodge is always armed to punish.

3d the Ballance is a Symbol of Justice.

4th The Skull is an Image of a brother who is excluded from a Lodge, this Idea must make all tremble, the more when they remember the penalties they have laid themselves under by their Obs

5th the cloth Stained with blood teacheth that we are not to hesitate to spill the last drop of our blood for the good of masonry

6th The power to darken the Sun, & Stain ye Moon is a representation of the power that a visiting brothr with a Superior degree, has over a lodge, in Interdicting the officers in case a lodge works not regular, until they repent of it, by their amendment & submihsion etc

7th The 7 trumpets & perfumes signifies that masonry is Spread over the Earth on the wings of Fame, and She will Sustain it with every mark of honor, perfums occasion odour.

Q. what age are you?   A. very antient.

Q. what are you?   A. a pathmien

Q. From whence come you?   A. from Pathmos.

End of the Lecture -

To Close

Q. what's the Clock?   ansr There is no more time.

Then the All puihsant knocks 7, as at the openg. and Says: this Council is closed, wh being repeated by the two wardens, Closes the Council -

End of Knts of East & West

18th Degree

Knights of the white Eagle or Pelican, known by the name of perfect mason, or knight of the Rose crohs -

This degree keeps the original form of Scotch masonry, until the Last Temple of Jesus christ.

The kn^{ts} of perf^t masons, is in some Lodges the 4th degree of masonry, under the name of Rose crohs. In others by the name of kn^{ts} of S^t andrews, the patron of Scotland and the 7th or last degree; and now under the name of perf^t masons and follows after the Kn^{ts} of East and West.

It is surprising that the purity of an object so perfect as masonry should be Susceptible of so many variations, particularly, in the Title of this degree The reasons will appear to you, when you know that divers nations were too anxious to know the last mysteries of the order, without knowing its original Instructions. If you report it only to some adepts, whom their Ignorance should hardly permit them to know the first symbolic figures; upon their report, that the last knowledge of the order / foreign to the Source / are fabricated by them to Strangers, some degrees a little like the matter, and gives it after that a new Title; which produces this day the great variation on this matter, and a great way from the Truth.

1st This degree is known by the name of kn^t of the Eagle; a Title that every body must know to be most antient, consequently it was adopted by its true name, which origin is taken from masonry, allegoric of the son of the great architect of the universe who comes established on earth and establishes our redemption from vice, which had plunged mankind into it - Independently the son of man was compared to the Supreme puihsence of the father. Symbolicly the Eagle is the Image & foundation of the Supreme puihsance. Masons adopted this like an original Title has produced matter to this degree -

2^d It is Called kn^t of the Pelican, because the son of man is compared to the Pelican, who Strikes his body with his Bill, from thence brings out blood to nourish its young - That Image is compared with the sacrifice of the crohs, which gives rise to this name from the Justnehs of the 2 Comparisons -

3^{aly} This degree is Called kn^t of the Rose Crohs, because the masons of Scotland in the primitive times had medals made on which was a Symbol relative to this Degree Consisting, because the son of the great architect is Compared to an Evangelic Rose, by his exemplary sweetnehs - some of the medals have by posterity pahsed into the hands of Lodges, where the members were Ignorant of their principles. they found that Emblem fine enough to make a distinction and therefore adopted the name of Rose crohs to make their society known By an Elegant Emblem, which has pahsed many ages, without knowing the origin, and took the names of kn^{ts} of Rose crohs, without knowing for what purpose.

4th This degree is also Called under the name Herodim masonry, because the first lodge of it was kept on the summit of a mountain of that name, Situated between the west & north of Scotland - This Circumstance confounded the name of Rose crohs, as they had nearly the same method of working & Ceremonies. There are some of them, that will not know each other by the difference of the name - Most part of the English Lodges, do not know the Herodim others not the Rose crohs. - this last name is much increased in France & other parts. these two last kind of masons are more reported in the administration of their mysteries - they are well enough in their Initiations and agree in the Spirit of the subject. But the large veil was to thick for that mystic object - they worked openly & shew'd the superstition & prejudice of their Morals - they knew nothing of the antient allegory w^h the true masons have always kept Close in their hearts - the reason w^h produced this disgrace to masonry is, that the Herodim & Rose crohs had made great progrehs in great Britain, w^h had multiplied with such confusion, that the most low masons had been Initiated, which was the Lohs of the dignity of the order, and oversat the foundation. The Religious Ceremony has been distroyed by their conduct to profanation, by Ignorance - Those masons who have kept ye Title of kn^{ts} of the Eagle, know but little of the truth; but we can say to their praise that they never have abused it, and have continued their masonry under the primitive Title. They Instruct nothing but an amusing Allegoric moral; they always take Care to guard against Fanaticks that have given occasion to profanation in those lodges known by the name of Harodim and the Rose Crohs.

5th This degree is also Called kn^{ts} of S^t andrews, which origin came through fanatism. in Scotland in the earliest times masonry multiplied more than in any other place - they established many Lodges on the same plan of virtue wisdom and prudence - which presides in said order - one of s^d Lodges had none of these; they had adopted the Costum annually on S^t andrews day to hold their grand meeting, being the patron of that country.

These people being Ignorant of knowing the object of their mystery they only knew that they were Called kn^{ts} masons, and vulgarly so, of S^t andrews. what contributed more to this name in the Eyes of the vulgar was, that their festivals and procehsions in a pompous manner was held on S^t andrews day, which made every strong imprehsion on the people of the Lover clahs who aspired with ardor the remaining part of the year to be Initiated, in order to share in the pomp of the next celebrating day of their Patron - afterwards this same Lodge open'd its door easily to admit the people of the Lower sort, and only kept the name of S^t andrews because they were used to these festivals and said name. Notwithstanding they learned in their receptions that the Title of this degree originally was Called the Kn^{ts} of the Eagle, w^h was its true name.

Afterwards having lost their Jewels, the could not get any Intilligence from any foreign or other Lodges, who had not been exposed to the like Events by changes, Ignorance or mistakes of the antient form

Tranquility having been Established, they took the model of the Crohs of S^t andrews and formed a Jewel of it, on w^h that Saint was laid at full length, tho' there was no relation between the Symbol of this Jewel, and their work. it was sufficient for them, that they had adopted the Crohs. This is the principal reason that those who wear the Crohs of S^t andrews wear it as a badge of masonry - they are for the most part Ignorant why they wear it; and these Errors have been Carried into Germany, where some travellers have constituted Lodges of this kind, such as that at Cologne which has been established few years ago; Except that they govern themselves perfectly well. Notwithstanding this, it has a great many other Improprieties in its instructions w^h is nothing else, but that these Changes has Corrupted the Beauty of this degree and

6^{thly} In fine. it is Called perfect masons, because the masons that we know in the universe under the Title of Perf^t masons, makes of it the highest and most Eminent degree, and the Last of their degrees. which is the 7th. there are some Lodges in England, who gave it to some, who were not even masters; which is not practized but Strictly forbid in Lodges, where perfect Masonry is profehsed, from degree to degree, until the degree or Title of perfect mason; as they dont give the knowledge of these Sciences Out by degrees; they conduct you from the first Temple to the 2^d and from the 2^d to the 3^d, and in short to attain from one to another even to the 7th which they give the name of perfect masons, w^h is the Living Temple, or the allegory of the Redeemer - This is the reason that all the bretheren that are admitted are to be christians - the 6 first degrees may be given to all Sects who have knowledge of the antient Temple - but this 7th cannot be given but to them that Submit to the new Law

The disposition of the Lodge

This Lodge must Consist of two apartments; the 1st represents Mount <u>Calvary</u>. The 2^d represents the Tomb of the Son of the great architect of the universe, which Shews allegorically the death and resurrection of Jesus Christ -

The 1st apartment must be black, 33 lights on 3 branches of 11 each which Shews the age of our Saviour - In 3 angles of the room must be 3 pillars Six feet high, on the Capitals must be wrote, on the 1st in the North East, <u>Faith</u>, on the 2^d in the East <u>Hope</u>, and on the 3^d in the South East <u>Charity</u>.

The draught of the Lodge is an oblong square and figured like Mount <u>Calvary</u>, with the Tools of masonry according to the distinction here after.

The Lodge is marked by treble Lines, in which must be wrote in ye Extremities, <u>Strength</u>, <u>Wisdom</u> & <u>Beauty</u>, in the interim, E: W: N. & S. with a dropping <u>Curtain</u> from a Canopy in the East.

At the East and South angles, are the Sun & Moon, the Heavens spread with Stars, and some very dark Clouds.

In the East is an Eagle rising in the air, a Symbol of the Supreme puihsance. 3 squares in one, in each of them 3 circles, allegorically to represent Mount Calvary - opposite is a mount with a Cubic Stone, as if it was Sweating blood & water, to represent Christ in that situation and on the Cubic Stone a <u>Rose</u>, Signifying great architect or the Expiring words. The spaces between the Circles are clouds to represent those on the Earth at the time of that Sacrifice -

Below are the antient Tools of masonry, and the Columns broke in many pieces, with the pavement all broke, to demonstrate that all the parts depending on the work of Masons is distroyed when ye architect is dead, and Cannot be Carried on, and all the work divided, Every thing Ceased to be, by his death -

A little higher is the veil or Curtain of the Temple, torn in two parts at that time, on the outside of the Columns the 7 knots of union of perfect masons.

Before the master must be a small Triangular Table lighted by 3 lights, The Bible with the Evangelists, Compas, Square & Triangle upon it.

All the breth^n must be drehsed in black, a large black ribbon from the in the first Chamber, where the M^r ward^s & officers must wear a large black ribbon as a collar, to the End of wch is the ordinary Jewel cover'd with black cloth - Said Jewel is a crownd Compas, the points extended to a Circle of 60 degrees, a crohs within the compas, and a Pelican feeding its young who are in a nest at bottom, and on the other Side of the crohs & Jewel, a white Eagle with his wings Extended as rising in the air, on both Sides of the Joints of the Compas a Red Rose. In the 2^d apartment, this Jewel is wore to a red ribbon at the bottom of a small blown Rose - this 2^d apartment represents the moment of the resurrection, and ought to be hung w^h tapistry full of glory, without any human figures, and on 3 Candlesticks 33 lights inclosed in a box, So Cut with holes that the lights look like Stars - the draught of this apartment must be an oblong square with quadruple Lines, between w^h must be wrote in the Exterior Faith, hope & Charity, and E: W: N. & South round the border.

In the East part must be a Crohs surrounded with a glory, filled with clouds and 7 cherubims, in the Centre of the crohs a Rose expanded, and in its Centre the Letter G - below 3 squares on w^h are 3 circles; and on the opposite Side a Small mountain with 3 Triangles inclosed in each other on the Top of a Square Cubic Stone, which is allegorically the Holy Mount where Christ Suffered - above said hill must be a blazing Star with 7 points, in ye Centre of w^h the Let G. That is the allegoric representation of the Son of Man risen in all his glory. -

In the South a Pelican feeding its young in their nest with his own blood; an Image of the Eternal Tendernehs - In the north an Eagle Spread as rising in the air, the Image of the Supreme puihsance - below is the Tomb.

In the Lower part of said square in the middle line from the East to the west is the Trehsel board, cubic Stone, hammer, two foot rule, & Level; on the north Side, the rough Stone & mallet, Setting Tool & plumb, in the Exterior of the East, a white Dove and the 7 knots of union among Masons - .

The 2^d point of a Reception

There must be a 3^d apartment, a little distance from the others, destined to be the Image of Hell, in which must be represented the Horrors of Torments; 7 Candlesticks with large flambeaux lighted, the Sockets of s^d Candlesticks to be skulls and 2 Crohs bones on each; the walls painted with human figures as if damned, So painted, as to shew the most Cruel Tortures and torments in ye faces of the sufferers, which that place can inspire -

In this lodge the M^r represents the personage of wisdom & reflection - which Gives him the Title of most wise & perf^t M^r. The wardens have the Title of thrice Excell^t & perf^t wardens, the rest of the officers, of Th: & Illus^s & perfect masters, and the rest of the Breth^n as perfect Masters -

In the first point of Reception non shall take the name of Perfect but only in the 2^d apartment, and for the 2^d point of reception, there is no other Table, then a small one on the right hand of the master, and that a very small one of a Triangular form with the 3 lights, Evangelists etc upon it, as mentioned before

In this apartment all the bretheren shall wear their Jewel, Ribbon and aprons as before mentioned: the Jewel to a black ribbon

Preparation of the Candidate

The cand[te] must be vested in black, and red ornaments of ribbon and apron, with a Sword & Sash - The M[r] of Ceremonies goes to him in order to prepare him, and Says: All the masons Temples are demolished, the Tools & Columns broke, and the masters word is Lost since your last reception in spite of all precaution, we have taken and endeavour'd not to be surprised, we are deprived of knowing ourselves and the order in general in the greatest Consternation.

After M[r] of Ceremonies has thus spoke to him, leaves him in the darkneſs in that Room, and comes to the Lodge to be present at the opening of the perfect masons - .

To open.

All the bretheren placed in order, the M[r] by the name of the most wise, opens the Lodge as follows -

Q. Thrice Excell[t] wardens, what is the duty of a Mason?

A. To See, if we are well Tiled.

Q. do your duty then - / they go & return / .

Q. what's the clock?

A. The hour of perfect masons.

Q. what is that hour?

A. The instant when the veil of the Temple was laid Low, darkneſs & consternation Spread on the Earth - the light departs from us; the Tools are broken; the blazing Star is obscured - the cubic Stone sweats blood & water - and the masters word is lost. on which the M[r] proceeds:

My dear bretheren, as masonry Seems and proves to be in Just tribulations, let us employ all our time by a new Labour to recover the word - this Lodge of kn[ts] of the Eagle or perfect masons, is open.

The wardens reply Huzzah! Huzzah! Huzzah! after which there is a Silence for some time.

Form of a Reception.

When the cand[te] is ready to be introduced, the master of Ceremonies conducts him to the door of the Lodge, and knocks 7 as the usual manner the Junior warden ans[rs] the same on the mallet of the Sen[r] warden and the Senior on that of the the Jun[r]; on which the Jun[r] warden in duty goes to the door to see, what's there; and then says to the Sen[r] ward[n] there is one at the door, who knocks as a kn[t] of East & west. The Sen[r] warden repeats the same to the master, who orders him to do his duty, who sends the Junior warden to go and See the M[r] of Ceremonies, who tells the Junior warden, that there is a wandring brother mason among the woods & mountains Since the distruction of the Temple, who has lost his reward, & comes here with the desire to recover it by your Consent - on w[h] the Jun[r] warden Shuts the door, and repeats it to the Sen[r] warden, who does the same to the M[r], who then Says: Brothers, do you consent that the wand'ring Brother Shall be Introduced in this Lodge to Satisfie his desire? all the bretheren manifest their approbation by raising their hands. then they all are seated, and shew a great consternation, their right hands on their hearts, and their heads leaning on the left, covering their Eyes the Elbow on the Left knees - The master has his left hand on his forehead his Elbow on the Table, and his right hand on <u>his</u>

heart - when the Candidate is Introduced between the 2 wardens - Then the Sen.r warden warden Says to the M.r Here is the kn.t mason, who desires the masters word - on w.h the M.r addrehses the cand.te thus:

Q. what's the name of the 3 pillars?

A. Faith, Hope & charity.

Q. How shall we do to find these pillars?

A. In travelling and Searching in the most profound darknehs.

Q. and what time will that take?

A. Three days - Then the m.r Says: let us travel my dear brother from the east to the North, from the north to the west, from the west to the south, and not loose the point of view of the good End that leads us -

All the bretheren follow the M.r as discribed above 33 times / but may be reduced to 7 times; after w.h the mast.r goes from that apartment to the next, where they all together take their ornaments of Red, and from thence they proceed to the 3.d or <u>Hell</u> apartment, but leave the Candidate in the 2.d apartment with the M.r of Ceremonies - who is then Conducted to the door of the 3.d apartment, and knocks 7 times on the door, a brother in waiting at the door gives him the pahs of <u>Emanuel</u>, the m.r of Ceremonies orders the Cand.us to pronounce the pahs, when he is coming in, the Tiler demands the pahs? the cand.us Says: that he is one of the brothers who search for the Secrets of the new Law and the 3 pillars of masonry - the Tiler knows by that ans.r that he is the Cand.us, directly Seises hem, and takes from him his black Ribbon and apron, and Says: the marks you are now decorated with, are not the marks of humility, and for recovering what you are looking for, - you must yet undergo more rigorous proofs then before - he then covers him with a black cloth, bespattered with ashes, in such a manner, that he can See nothing, and says follow me, and I will conduct you in the most dark place, where the mysterious word shall arise Triumphant in glory with the great advantages of Masonry, but you must confide in me. After this he conducts the Cand.te in a Room to mount and descend as often as it is pohsible, and then Conducts him to the 3.d apartment, or Hell, and then lifts up the veil or cloth that he may See and perceive all the horrid objects for a minute or two; the he Carries him 3 times round, and Says: this is in memory of the mystic voyage when he was in darknehs for 3 days; and then returns to the door and drops the veil again and Says, All the horrors which you have already received, is nothing in comparison to those you will suffer, if you have not the requisite firmnes - Then the Tiler Carries him back to the 2.d apartment, at the door of which he knocks 7, and tells him remember to answer to all demands that shall be made you, That you come from <u>Judea</u>, that you have past by <u>Nazareth</u>, and if they ask you my name Tell them 't is <u>Rafael</u>, and that you are from the Tribe of <u>Juda</u>, without w.h you cannot guard yourself, from the most unhappy things that will befal you - The Junior warden waits some time after the knocks before he goes to the door to give time to the Tiler to Instruct the Cand.us, and then he opens the door and demands, viz.t

Q. who Comes there?

A. A Knight of East & West, who having travelled a Space of the most profound darknehs, offers you by the fruit of his labor to ahsist in y.e works.

the cand^te to be Introduced — Then the Junr Warden Says to the Mr This is the Knight of East & West, who by his help hopes to recover the word that was lost, and become by that a perfect mason

When the Mast^r asks him the foll^g questions

Q. whence do you come from?

A. from Judea.

Q. which Town did you pahs by?

A. by Nazareth

Q. what is the name of your Conductor?

A. Raphaël.

Q. what Tribe do you belong to?

A. Juda.

Q. give me the Initials of the 4 words?

A. I. N. R. I.

Q. put these letters together?

A. Inri.

Then the Mr Says: Brothers, the word is found, give our brother the Light; when the wardens take off the veil or black Cloth, and all together clap 3 times with their hands and Cry Huzza! huzza, huzza. Then the master tells him, come to me, that I might communicate to you the last mysteries of the order — The Senr Warden conducts him to the M^r who gives him the S: T. & word, and says to him: I wish you Joy my brother on the recovery of our mysterious word, w^h gives you the Title of Perfect mason — .

Sign   1st Sign is, to raise your Eyes to heaven, clinch your fingers of both hands, y^r palms opposite your forehead, then let them fall close to your waist, this is the Sign of admiration.

2^d Sign is, the ans^r to the first, and is to lift up your right hand, put up the forefinger, & clinch the others, w^h signif^s there is only one god, the source of purity & truth —

Token   — The Token is to Crohs your hands, and clap them Reciprocally on each others breast —

P: w^d   The pahsword is Emanuel. etc.

The word Inri.

The discourse

Masons from the Re-edification of the Temple having neglected their works, abandoned to the vicihsitudes of the times the precious Edifice that they had raised with so much pain, the works & the wise workmen corrupted, the force of the materials and the beauty of the architecture gave place to discord & vice.

The great architect of the universe determin'd to manifest his glory, and abandon the Temple, to Elevate by his Supreme Geometry a Spiritual Temple, which Existance would not be attacked by human greatnehs, and w^h might Exist to Eternity; by that puihsant resolution that men have seen, the Miraculous Phenomenon, the prodigie of prodigies, the cubic Stone pointed, Sweating Blood & Water, and Suffered all the anguis of

Soul - This was, when the corner stone of the Edifice was broke by the workmen of the foundation of the Temple; for when the rubbish of the building at that time was thrown, the masonic Rose was Sacrific'd on a crohs planted on the top of a mountain from the Surface to be Elevated to the Celestial globe by 3 Squares, 3 Triangles & 3 Circles cut in Diamonds Human masonry was in an instant distroyed; the veil was Rent, the Earth was cover'd with darknehs, the light was withdrawn; the Tools of masonry were broke, the flaming Star vanished, and the word was lost; you might easily Judge what suffering the good masons underwent; in that moment what consternation & afflictions more can be Exprehsed; the were obliged to Travel in the most profound darknehs, for 3 days, uncertain to know if they were to live longer, or if any new accident should happen to them - they were so far reduced in perplexity of their hearts, that they feared the End of time was come - The will of him that conducts all Events & things, after finishing the time of that universal surprize, caused the light to shine at the End of 3 days, & which was not done without some new Surprising Phenomenon. The Tools of masonry w^h were broke, retook their ordinary Forms, the blazing Star returned in a most Brilliant manner, and the word was recovered. This was the Scourge to the masons for their negligence and obsurity, w^h their neglect had plunged them into - Some of them after travelling for the Space of 33 years in Searching for the word, learned to some others the method to find it was to know the 3 pillars of <u>Hope</u>, <u>Faith</u> & <u>charity</u>, & to embrace the new Law, in order to hope to Enter in the mystic works of the order, and that, that was not by any new principles that masonry appeared to the Eyes of man, but on some Theoric Rules, that conducts them allegorically to the practice of their actions; Since w^h time the masons do not build any material Edifice, but the Spiritual are their works - they inforce their work by Temperance, prudence, Justice and fortitude, and never are afraid of the vicihsitudes of the Times.

I wish my dear Brother these pillars may never fall, and that the great architect of the universe, be your help - .

To Close

The Junr Warden knocks 7. the Senr Warden the Same.

Junr Ward: What's the clock?

S: W^{den} The Hour of perf^t Masons.

J: W^{den} what was that hour?

S: W^{den} The moment the word was recovered, the Cubic Stone was changed to a mystic Rose, the Blazing Star return'd with more Splendour, our Tools have taken their former Shape; the light is come to us, with the greatest Brilliancy, darknehs is quite vanished, and the new Law Shall reign universally among us. -

Junr W: Let us follow that Law which was grounded by the most miraculous Events - Then all Cry, Huzza. 3 times, and close.

NB: There is no Ob^n In this degree.

19th Degree.
Sublime Scotch Masonry, Called by the name of Gr:d Pontif.

1st The hangings of this Lodge must be Blue, Spread with golden Stars.

2d The R:W: Mastr is Stiled Thrice puihsant gr:d Pontif, in vested in a white Satin Robe; and all the bretheren are vested the same, and these go by the name of faithfull & true brothers; they must all have a blue satin fillet with 12 golden Stars on it, tied round their foreheads.

3d The T: Pt Sits under a blue Canopy on a throne, behind wh in a Nich is a transparent light, Sufficient to light the whole Lodge, the T: P: holds a Scepter in his hand - the Threshold board or draught of the Lodge represents, viz:

A Square city, or the Celestial Jerusalem, descending from heaven, to Crush the remains of the present Jerusalem - a Serpent or hydra with 3 heads representing the badnehs of the Infidels, Jews etc yet remaining there - this Celestial Jerusalem has 12 gates, 3 on each Side - and in the middle of Said City you see a Tree, that bears 12 different Sorts of fruit - Said City is Elevated as on the clouds, and under it is the antient City as in Ruins and turned opside down, and the Said Serpent with 3 heads in Chains, and seems as if crushed by the weight of the Celestial Jerusalem: one one Side of ye draught appears a high Mountain

To open the Lodge.

The T: P: Gr:d Pontif, Strikes 12 at Equal distance, and then asks the follg questions, viz:

Q. what's the clock, brother?

A. The hour foretold.

Q. Faithfull bretheren the whole is, <u>alpha</u> & <u>omega</u>, <u>Emanuel</u> let us work.

Then the warden knocks also 12, as above, and Says: Faithfull and true Bretheren, the Lodge of gr:d Pontif is, open.

Form of a Reception.

The candte must be decorated, with the Badges of knt of East & West, and a blue Satin fillet with 12 golden Stars tied round his head, before he Enters; then Introduced directly in the Lodge, when the warden puts him on the Top of the Mountain, and asks him: brother, do you detest and hate the perfidious? do you promise that you will break all communication, correspondence and friendship with them? He ansrs That I promise & Swear. Then the Cande is left on the mountains Top, and the warden Comes down from it backwards; and when down, he measures the 4 Sides of the Colestial City with a surveyers chain, and then returns to the candte on the Top of the mountain, and tells him, brother that City (pointing to it) measures 12000 Stades each Side - he then takes the Candte by the left hand, and both come down Backwards, and Carries him before the draught facing the Thr: Puihst, when he stands at the right hand of the wardens - after a minutes Silence, he makes him go with 3 Square Steps to the chained Serpent, then one Step on each of the 3 heads, then he makes him advance towards the Celestial City, advancing with his left foot only, bringing up his right foot to the heel of the left every Step, and then he kneels 3 times with his right knee, holding at the same time his right hand housontally towards the Thr: puihs^t - NB. This obedience, is in Lieu of the obligation Then the Thr: puihs^t orders him to walk 3 Steps backwards which brings him at the bottom of the draught, when and where the warden gives him the Sign, Token & word - vizt

Sign is, to hold the right hand horisontal, the fingers Extended, and then drop the 3 last fingers perpendicular down.

Token is, to put reciprocally the palms of the right hand on each others forehead.

words - There a 4 words vizt one says: Hallelujah, the other answers Let us pray the Lord - the first says again, Emanuel, & the other answers God grant.

order. The order is a broad Red Ribbon, strewed with 12 golden Stars, to which hangs the Square Jewel of gold, from the right shoulder to the Left hip, one one Side Alpha, and on the other Side omega.

Doctrine of the Sub^{me} gr^d Pontif.

Q. what are you?

A. I am a Sublime gr^d Pontif.

Q. where have you received this degree?

A. In a place that neither wants Sun nor Moon to Light it.

Q. Explain this to me?

A. As the gr^d Pontifs never wants any artificial Light to light them, in the same manner, the faithfull and true brothers the Sub^{me} gr^d Pontifs do not want Riches nor Titles to be admitted into this Sublime Lodge, as they prove themselves in their attachment to masonry and faithfulnehs in their obligations, & true friendship to their bretheren in general

Q. what represents the draught of the Lodge ? -

A. A Square City of 4 equal Sides with 3 gates on each Side, on the middle of which is a Tree bearing 12 different fruits & Said City is Suspended as on clouds, Crushing a Serpent with 3 heads -

Q. Explain this to me?

A. The Square City represents antient masonry, under the Title of grand pontif, that Comes down from Heaven to replace the antient distructed Temple, when the gr^d pontifs come to make it appear, as is represented by the Ruins and the 3 headed Serpent chained.

Q. How comes Masonry fall'n to ruin, as we are tied and attached indihsolubily by our ob^s which Cannot be Equivocal?

A. As it was decreed in all times, which we learn by St John, which we know was the first mason that held a perfection Lodge.

Q. where does St John says this?

A. In his revalations, where he Speaks of Babylon and the Colestial Jerusalem.

Q. what Signifies the Tree with the 12 different fruits in the Center of Said City?

A. The Tree of life is placed there, to make us understand, where the Sweets of life is to be found; and the 12 fruits Signifie, that we meet every month to Instruct ourselves mutually, and Sustain each other against our Enemies.

Q. what Signifies the fillet or Veil, that the Candidate is blinded with, and the 12 golden Stars, thereon?

A. It procures him the Entrance of our lodge, as it did procure the Entrance in Calestial Jerusalem to those that wore it - thus has St John Explained himself. -

Q. what Signifies the 12 Stars, on the fillet of the Candidate, and those of the Bretheren?

A. They represent the 12 angels, who watch the 12 gates of Celestial Jerusalem.

Q. what Signifies the blue hangings, and golden Stars there on?

A. The Blue is the Symbol of Lenity, fidelity and Sweetnehs, w^h ought to be the Share of all faithfull and true brothers. and the Stars represent those masons who have given proofs of their attachment to the Statutes and rules of the order, which in the End will make them deserving of Entering the Celestial Jerusalem

Q. what age are you?

A. I reckon no more.

Q. what remains for you to acquire?

A. The Sub^{me} Truth of the princes adepts and the Royal Secret. -

Q. what is your name?

A. Faithfull and True brother.

To Close.

Q. what's the Clock?

A. Thr: Puihs^t, the hour accomplished.

Then the Thr. Puihsant Says: <u>Alpha</u> & <u>omega</u>, Let us rejoice my brothers - he then Strikes 12, which are repeated by the warden, and the Lodge of gr^d Pontif is closed -

End

20th Degree.

Venerable gr^d M^r of all Symbolic lodges, Sovereign princes of masonry, or M^r ad vitam

This lodge must be decorated with blue & yellow. The gr^d Mr Sits on a Throne Elevated by 9 Steps under a Canopy; before him an altar on which is a Sword, Bible, compas, Square, Mallet etc. the same as in a Symbolic Lodge - between the altar & ~~South a~~ Candlestick with 9 branches, which is always lighted in this Lodge - 2 wardens in the west - The grand M^r represents Cyrus, Darius, artaxerxes etc With all his Royal ornaments with a large & b^e yellow Ribbon acrohs each other -

To open -

The gr^d Mr Says: I desire to open this Lodge. and then goes down on the Lowest Step of the Throne, when he is ahsured that the Lodge is well Tiled; he knock 1 & 2 Separate with his mallet, each warden repeats the Same, w^h makes 9 in all -

Q. where is the gr^d master?

A. In the East.

Q. why in the East?

A. because the Sun rises in the East.

Then the gr^d Mr Says: as I Sit in the East, I open this Lodge; which is repeated by the wardens, and all the bretheren knock 1 & 2.

order of a Reception.

The cand^{te} is Zurubbabel, who Comes by himself, without being introduced; decorated with the Jewels & badges of his highest degrees. the wardens take him by the hand and place him in a blue Elbow chair, opposite the M^r who asks him all the questions from an Enter'd apprentice to a gr^d pontif. and after he has satisfied the gr^d M^r & is found worthy to hold a scepter, they make him travel 9 times the Lodge beginning in the South, and then by 9 Square Steps, he comes to the Throne walking over 2 Swords laid acrohs - there must be a pot with coalfire close to the Throne, that he can feel the heat of it whilst he is taking his ob^n w^h he takes putting his right hand on the Bible, covered by the gr^d M^r's right hand, repeatings as follows - .

"I A.B. promise & swear, even more then by my former ob^{ns}, and on the greatest penalties, to protect masons & Masonry with all my might, and not acknowledge any one for a true masons, who is not made in a Lawfull Lodge. I promise that they Shall Strictly observe all the Statutes & regulations, and further promise never to discover this degree, but by a full power & patent in writing from the gr^d Insp^r or his deputy; and then to no one, but Such as has been master of a Lodge, under the penalty of being dishonored and dispised by the order in general" - he kihses the Bible. -

Exercise of the Signs

The 1st Sign is to make 4 times a Square with your right hand and arm, the fingers close and the thumb up. clapping your hand twice on your breast, then put your left hand on your left hip, the thumb and fingers making also a Square as well as the arm, at the same time put your two heels together forming another Square - .

2ᵈ Sign is that of aaron the high priest, which he made when the Tabernacle was finished; wʰ is kneeling down, with both elbows on the ground, the head reclining to the left Side downwards -

3ᵈ Sign is that of Solomon, when the Temple was finished, wʰ are 5 Squares Crohsing both your hands on your breast, both your thumbs upwards which are 4, then putting the heels together, makes the 5 Squares -

Token is, Take each others right Elbow with the right hand, squeese it 4 times reciprocally then Slip the hand down, and give the masters gripe -

The word is Jeckson, wʰ Signifies I am what I am, this is also the name of that man, who found out the Cavern, where the Lion used to keep, who kept In his Tusks the key of the ark of alliance, wʰ was lost, as is mentioned in the degree of the R:A. - the ansʳ to the word is Nikelots, a pahsword.

2ᵈ pahsword is Jubellum, who is he, that fought the Lion in sᵈ Cavern - the said Lion had a gold Colar, on which was engraved the word Jeckson The rest is an Enigma to you and is only known to the Subᵐᵉ princes of the Royal Secret - a Degree you Cannot require unlehs you Crush the Serpent of Ignorance

The 3ᵈ pahsword is Zanabazare, and is the name of him that laid the first foundation of the Temple, rebuilt by the princes of Jerusalem Jewel is a   medal, in which is engraved the word Secret, to a large blue and yellow Ribbon.

Instructions, by way of Lecture

Q. Are you a gᵈ mʳ of all Lodges?
A. They know me at Jerusalem to be such.
Q. How shall I know, that you are a grᵈ Mʳ of all Lodges?
A. Seing my Zeal, in rebuilding the Temple.
Q. I what manner have you travelled?
A. From the South to the East.
Q. how many voyages?
A. Nine.
Q. why so many?
A. In memory of the 9 grᵈ masters that travelled to Jerusalem.
Q. can you give me their names?
A. Their names were, Esdras, Zurubbabel, Phalehi, Josue, Eliab, Joyada, Homen, nehemias & Malechias.
Q. what are the pahswords?
A. Nikelots, Jubellum, & Zanabazare
Q. What struck you most, when you Entered the grᵈ Mʳˢ Lodge?
A. The candle Stick with 9 branches.

Q. how Come they always to burn in the Lodge?

A. To remember, that there can be no Lehs then 9 M^{rs}, to form a lodge of gr^d. m^{rs} ad vitam.

Q. what was the reason that you desired to be admitted in this Lodge of gr^d. m^{rs} ad vitam?

A. To receive the 2 lights I was not acquainted with.

Q. how have you rec^d these 2 lights?

A. In receiving first the Small light.

Q. Explain this to me?

A. That is to say, that I am received by Steel and fire.

Q. what Signifies the Steel?

A. In remembrance of the Steel by which Hiram abif, lost his life; and I have sworn to make use of it, when ever I can revenge said murder, on Traitors of masonry.

Q. what signifies the fire?

A. That our forefathers have been purified by fire.

Q. By whom have you been received?

A. By Cyrus, Darius etc

Q. How So by Cyrus?

A. Because t was him that order'd Zurubbabel to rebuild the Temple

Q. what have you promihs'd & sworn, when you was rec^d in this degree?

A. I have promihs'd & sworn, that I will See the Laws, Statutes & regulations observed in my Lodge

Q. what's your name?

A. Cyrus.

Q. what was your name before you did receive this degree?

A. Zurubbabel.

Q. what Signsifies the word Jeckson?

A. I am, what I am, and is the name of him that found the cavern, where the Lion used to keep.

Q. why is the Lodge Yellow & Blue?

A. In memory, when the Eternal appear'd on clouds of gold & azur on mount Sinai to dictate the laws to Moses, the great Sacrificer of his people.

Q. where do you find the history of our mystery?

A. It is found in the archives of Kilwinnin in the north of Scotland.

Q. How Comes it that you travel from the South to the East?

A. To prove the power of the great architect of the universe, that he extends himself from one End of the world to the other, without any bounds —

Q. Why do you wash your hands in ye Degree of gr^d El^t & perf^t Subl^{me}

A. To prove our Innocence.

Q. How Comes it that the History of <u>Hiram abif</u>, is so much revered?

A. Because we are Certain, that he rather chose loose his life then give up the Secret of masonry.

Q. How Comes the Triangle with the word Secret on it, to be the most precious Jewel of masonry, with w^h you are now decorated?

A. Because its Justnehs, Equality & proportion, represents our Redemption

Q. What was the mark of the place, where our Mr H. A. was found under ground?

A. The mark was a Sprig of granate.

Q. For w^h reason do the mast^rs masons in Symbolic Lodges talk of a Sprig of <u>accahsia</u>?

A. The Sub^me gr^d. Elect^d discendants from the antient patriarchs, did not think to give the real truth of masonry, therefore agreed together to Say that it was a Sprig of accahsia for reasons, as it Stunk very much.

Q. what is the reasons of the different knockings at the door, to get admittance?

A. To know and be ahsured that they have pahsed the different degrees, w^h different numbers we must understand.

Q. How comes it that we keep our mysteries with so much Circumspection Secret?

A. For fear that some Traitors of the Stamp of the 3 Ruffians that murder'd H. A. might be found among us.

Q. What are the reasons, that the gr^d mast^rs of all lodges, are Rec^d with so much Honor in Symbolic Lodges?

A. Those Homages are due to their virtue and their qualities as princes masons. Their firmnehs which they have Shew on many occasions, Spilling their blood in the support of masonry & their fraternity.

Q. How Comes it that we applaud with our hands?

A. By that we exprehs our happinehs when we do a good thing, and have render'd Justice.

Q. What Subject of meditation offers us, or what can we say of the Conduct of Solomon?

A. That a wise man Can Err, and when he is Sensible of his fault, corrects himself in acknowledging that fault, and thereby claims the Indulgence of his Brothers -

Q. Why do the blue Lodges take the Title of Lodges of St John of Jerusalem?

A. Because in the times of the Crusades the perf^t masons, kn^ts and princes communicated their mysteries to the kn^ts of that order, and then it was resolved that they should Celebrate their fistivals annually on that Saints day being all under the Same Law.

Q. Who was the first architect that Conducted the works of Solomons Temple?

A. <u>Hiram abif</u>. Signifying the inspired <u>Hiram</u>.

Q. Who laid the first Stone?

A. Solomon Cut himself that Stone and laid it, which Stone afterwards Supported the Tabernacle.

Q. was any thing inclosed in That Stone?

A. Yes, Some characters, wh were like the name of the gr^t arch^t of the universe, as it was known to Solomon at that time.

Q. what was that Stone?

A. an agate, of a foot Square.

Q. what was the form of it?

A. Cubic form.

Q. what hour or time of the day was it, when that Stone was laid?

A. Before Sunrise.

Q. what was the reason there of?

A. To Shew that we must be early and vigilant in our good works.

Q. what Cement did he make use of?

A. A Cement composed of the finest and purest of flower, milk, oyl & wine.

Q. Is there any meaning in the composition of this Cement?

A. Yes, for when the gr^t arch^t of the universe was willing to create the world, he employed his Sweetnehs, his bounty, his wisdom & his Strength.

Q. what is the reason the number of 81 is in so great estéem among the princes M^s?

A. Because that number explains the tripple alliance, w^h the eternal operates by the Tripple Triangle, w^h was seen when Solomon conserated Solomons Temple. and also that H. a. was 81 years of age when he died.

Q. What was perceived more at the construction of said Temple?

A. A perfume w^h did not only surround the Temple, but all Jerusalem.

Q. who did distroy that Temple?

A. <u>Nebucadnezar</u>.

Q. how many years after it was built?

A. 470 years, 6 months, & 10 days after its foundation

Q. Who built the 2^d Temple?

A. <u>Zurubbabel</u>, by the grant and help of king <u>Cyrus</u> of Persia, and afterwards in the reign of <u>Darius</u>, as he was known to be a prince of <u>Jerusalem</u> - Cyrus gave him all the Treasures of the first Temple to Embellish the 2^d

Q. what Signifies the Jewel of a R^t W^l gr^d M^r of all lodges, being a Triangle

A. He wears it in remembrance of the presents given by monarchs and the protectors of the order in recompence for our Zeal, fervency & constancy.

Q. Which way have you travell'd or posted to become a R^t W^l gr^d M^r of all Lodges & Sublime Patriarch?

A. by the 4 Elements.

Q. why by the 4 Elements?

A. To put me in mind of the troubles of this world, and cleanse & purifie myself of all my impurity and render myself worthy of perfect virtue.

Q. where was that Lodge of gr^d W^l m^r of all lodges first held?

A. To the East of the Temple in a Sacred vault.

Q. where is that Lodge kept at present?

A. All over the world, comformable to the orders of Solomon; when he told us to travel and to Spread over the universe, to teach masonry to those worthy of it; and Especially to those that received us kindly, and who were virtues men

Q. What did Solomon give you on your departure to remember him?

A. He recompenced the merits of all workmen; and shew'd to the chief mast^{rs} the cubic agate Stone, on which was engrav'd on a gold plate, the name of God.

Q. How was that agate Stone Supported?

A. on a pedestal of a Triangular form, Surrounded by 3 brahs Pillars, w^h pillars were again Surrounded by a Circle of the Same Metal.

Q. what Signifies these 3 pillars?

A. Strength, wisdom & Beauty.

Q. what was in the middle of the Circle?

A. The point of exactnehs, which teacheth the point of Masonry & perfection.

Q. what did Solomon give you more?

A. The great Sign of admiration & consternation, by w^h I am known by my brother. - he also put a ring on my finger in remembrance of my alliance with virtue. & further loaded us with kindnehses.

Q. Why have you a Sun, on the Jewel of perfection?

A. To Shew that we know masonry in all its perfection.

Q. who distroy'd the 2^d Temple, w^h was finish'd by the princes of Jerusalem?

A. Pompey, begans its distruction & king Herod the great finished it -

Q. and who rebuilt it again?

A. Herod the great, repenting the action he had done unjustly, order'd to recal all the masons that were fled and ihsued an order for them to return to Jerusalem, for ye Reconstruction of Said Temple.

Q. who distroyed this 3^d Temple?

A. Tite, the Son of the Emperor Vespasian   The masons who Saw with

Catholicks, and took a resolution never to ahsist in raising another Temple.

Q. what became afterwards of these masons?

A. After residing a long time at Rome, most of them died, and the remaining masons divided themselves into several parts, & the greatest part of the remaining went into Scotland, where they built a Town called Kilwinnin, where at this present time is a lodge of that name.

Q. what happen'd afterwards to these masons?

A. 27000, of these masons resolv'd to ahsist the Christian knights that were at that time at Jerusalem, with leave of the Scotch monarch, to ahsist in ye Crusades.

Q. what happen'd the most remarkable to them?

A. Their bravery, gain'd them the esteem of the Kn^{ts} of St John of Jerusalem, that the general of their order, and all the great officers took the resolution to be admitted in the Secret of their masonry, w^h when they had received, they also admitted those masons into their order, by the name Rose=crohs, or Pelican.

Q. what became afterwards of those masons?

A. After the Crusade was over, every one retired to their respective Countries; at which time masonry was Spread over all Europe, and was for a long time in full vigor in France & England - but after the distruction of the Temple they neglected the Craft for many ages in France England etc and the Scotch to their praise, were the only who kept up the practize of it.

Q. How came it again in Vogue in France?

A. A Scotch nobleman who went to France became for a long time a resident of Bordeaux; where he established a Lodge, and from the members of Said lodge, he Established a Lodge of Perfection In the year 1744, being ahsisted by a French gentleman who delighted much in all the degrees of masonry - and this Said Lodge, is Still kept up in the most Splendid manner by the first people of quality, in the new street there.

Q. what Signifies the fire in our Lodge?

A. My Submihsion, the purification of my Morals, and my Egality among my bretheren.

Q. what Signifies, the Sign of the air?

A. The purity of virtue, and Truth of this degree.

Q. What Signifies the Sign of the Sun?

A. It Signifies that Some of us are more Enlightened in the mysteries of masonry; and for that reason are often Called Kn^{ts} of the Sun.

Q. How many Signs have you in the degree of gr^d Pontif, W: G: m^r of all Lodges?

A. we have 12, and are as follows

   1st the Sign of the Earth - or apprentice
   2^d The Sign of Fellow Craft.   3^d Sign of Terror or the master.
   4th That of Fire - 5th that of air - 6th that of the point in view

7th the Sign of the Sun – 8th that of astonishment – 9th of Horror, 10th that of Strong Smell, 11th of adoration & 12th that of Consternation –

End of the Lecture.

When a Br vested in this degree, visits a Lodge, he must be Examind by the follow^g questions vizt

Q. From whence come you?   ans^r From the Sacred vault of Jerusalem

Q. what Come you to do here? ans^r I come to visit and See your work, & Shew you mine, to work together & Rectifie our morals, & if pohsible to Sanctifie the profane. But this only by the permihsion of a Prince Subl^{me} of the Royal Secret (if one present).

Q. what have you brought? ans^r Glory, Grandeur, & beauty.

Q. why do you give the name or Title of St John to our lodges?

A. Formerly all lodges were under the name of Solomons, as the founder of masonry, but since of the Crusades, we have agreed with the Knights Templars Hospitallers or Kn^{ts} of St John, to dedicate them to St John, as he was the Support of the New & Christian Law –

Q. what do you ask here?

A. Your good will and pleasure, as you find me worthy, obed^t & virtuous.

To close.

G: P Speaks: My brothers, Enter in the Cave of Siloé, work with the great Rafodom. Measure your Steps to the Sun, & then the great black Eagle, will cover you with his wings, to the End of what you desire, by the help of the most Subl^{me} Prin^e gr^d commander – he then Strikes 1 & 2, makes the Sign of the 4 squares, w^h is repeated by the ward^s & the Lodge is Closed –

End

21st Degree.

Pruhsian Kn^t or Noachite, In two Degrees – otherwise Called, The Masonic Key

You must absolutely have been Initiated in the degree of the Kn^t of the white Eagle, to be admitted in this Degree; tho' it is look'd upon only as the Kn^{ts} Servants of the Kadoch, or Kn^{ts} of the white & black Eagle, as it is now called for reasons known. Formerly it was sufficient to be a Mr Mason of Hiram's Lodge to be Initiated in this degree, which Cannot be in the present times for Reasons w^h will be given in due time.

The Origin of this Degree

The Most antient order of Noachite, known this day by the name of Pruhsian Knights Servants, of the Princes of the white & black Eagle, Translated from the German by Brother Berage, Kn^t of Eloquence & gr^d orator of ye Chapter of Brother Gelois, gr^d Inspect^r and Kn^t Lieutenant Commander general of the Pruhsian Council, or Noachite in France, in the year 4664 –

The Gr^d M^r gen^l of the order, who is Stiled Kn^t prince & commander, is the Most Illus^s Frederic of Bronswyck, King of Pruhsia, whose ancestors have for these 300 years been the protectors of said order, and is Celebrated by the pruhsian Kn^{ts} in memory of the building of the Tower of Babel, and the confusion w^h happen'd there.

Formerly, this degree was known by the name of Kn^{ts} Noachite, w^h is descendants of Noah.

The Pagans knew this order under the name of Titans, who attempted to Seale the Heavens and dethrone Jupiter – But the present knights acknowledge no other god, but the great architect of the universe, and our happenehs Consists, in adoring him

We celebrate Every year in the month of March during the full Moon, the confusion of the languages, and the distruction of the Tower of Babel, w^h Tower was one of the greatest wonder of the Creator. and is the Epocha of that day of gods wonders & revenge that we celebrate and meet for that purpose on the aforesaid night in March – Every other month during the full moon, Cand^{tes} may be received; but no other light then the moon & Stars are allowed at a reception, & the holding of a Chapter.

The gr^d officers of the Chapter

1st The M^r of the Chapter is Called Lieut^{nt} Commander, and is decorated with a Large black ribbon in a Triangular form round his neck, an Equilateral Triangle hanging on his breast. –

2^d The Senior Kn^t of the chapter officiates as Senr warden, and is a grand Inspector, decorated with the Same Jewel to a narrow ribbon, to the 3^d buttonhole of his coat.

3^d The Junr Kn^t acts as Junr ward: & is called Introductor, wears the same Jewel.

4th Another Kn^t of the Chapter, is call'd Kn^t of Eloquence or gr^d orator – wears the Same Jewel, but to the 3^d button hole of his waistcoat.

5th another kn^es is chancellor or gr^d Secretary, ye Same Jewel as the gr^d orator.

6th another kn^t is kn^t Treasurer - with d^o Jewel.

7th another kn^t is Kn^t Captain of the guards, with d^o Jewel.

All the rest of the Kn^ts have the Same Jewel to their waistcoats, and Sit bareheaded, but the 7 gr^d officers have their hatts on in the chapter. and the kn^ts are Called kn^ts Pruhsians, or <u>Noachites</u> -

In case of Scarcity of officers, 3 of the above named 7 officers Can hold a chapter, (id est) the Knight Lieutenant Commander and the Two Senior kn^ts, who officiate in the function of wardens.

The draught of the chapter, is only the Firmament, with the full moon & Stars. - on w^h they Eyes must always be fixed.

The place where this Chapter is held, ought to be Situated so, that the full moon & Stars may Enlighten it, Either through windows or other openings as it is especially forbid that any rays of the Sun, or any other light should enlighten it.

To open the Grand Chapter

The kn^t Lieut^nt Commander opens the chapter in the East, by 3 distinct knocks very Slow at equal distance - the Senr kn^t in the west ans^rs by Striking one blow with his Mallet on the pummel of his Sword; on w^h the Lieut^nt Commander Says: to order. on w^h all the knights rise, putting up both their hands to Heaven the fingers Extended, and all look towards the East, where the moon rises, and whilst in this disposition or attitude the Lieut^nt Comm^der asks the foll^g questions:

Q. Brother Senr kn^t, who are you?

A. If you are Curious to know who I am, tell me first, who you are?

Q. do you know the Sons of <u>Noah</u>?

A. I know 3 of them.

Q. Who are they?

A. I will tell you it, in the manner of our Spelling.

Q. Then let us hear?

A. You begin and I answer.

Q. S. -

A. C -

Q. J. - well what Signifie these 3 letters

A. They are Initials of <u>Shem</u>, <u>cham</u> & <u>Japhet</u>.

Q. give me the Sign -

A. Here it is (he makes the Sign) looking up to Heaven.

Q. give me the pahsword -

A. Phaleg / spoke very Slow / - Then the Lieut^nt Command^r Says the chapter is open; and Every body is Seated. when the Lecture Continues.

Q. what name is that?

A. 'T is the name of the architect, who made the plan and Conducted the building of the Tower of Babel -

Q. who learn'd you his name? -

A. The Lieut^{nt} Commander of the Pruhsian Knight.

Q. In what place did he give you his name?

A. In a place where the moon alone gave Light.

Q. Could they get no other light?

A. No.

Q. was the building of this Tower praise worthy?

A. No, as the perfection of it was impohsible.

Q. Why was it impohsible?

A. Because, presumption, vanity and arrogance was the foundation of it.

Q. Is it in imitation of the Sons of Noah, that you keep this in memory?

A. No, on the contrary; and is for this reason to have their vaults always before their Eyes.

Q. Where lies, or is deposed the Body of Phaleg?

A. In a Tomb made of grey Stone.

Q. Has he been rejected, or disown'd for his Sins?

A. No - because by Characters which were engraved on an agate Stone, w^h was found among the Dust of his body, in a durable Coffin of Stone in Said Tomb, we learn that God had forgiven him, as he had repented of his Sins, and was become humble.

Q. In what manner was you Iniciated a pruhsian knight?

A. By 3 genuflections (kneelings) and by 3 times kihsing the pummel of the Lieut^{nt} Commanders Sword.

Q. Why did you make 3 genuflections?

A. To put me in mind of practicing humility.

Q. why do the kn^{ts} wear a Triangle?

A. In memory of the Triangle before w^h Phaleg the penitent did pray.

Q. why is the arrow in the Triangle reversed?

A. That is in memory of what happend at the Tower of Babel.

Q. why a black Ribbon - ans^r, the Black Shews the grief sorrow and repentance of the workmen of Said Tower

Q. did they work by night and day?

A. Yes, in the day by the favor of the Sun, and at night by the light of the moon.

Q. where is the Lieut^{nt} Command^r placed in the chapter?

A. Allways opposite the moon.

Q. where are the gr^d officers placed?

A. opposite the Lieut^{nt} Commander.

Q. where are the other Knights placed?

A. Any where, but their Eyes always fixed on the Lieut^{nt} Commander.

Q. What is the reason there of?

A. Because, a pruhsian kn^t has renouned all pride & ostentation, in order to practize humility, and therefore requires no Rank in a chapter.

Q. Have you any more Signs in particular?

A. Yes, and will answer them if properly questioned.

Q. Where is your Father?

A. (The ans^r & Sign is) he looks up to Heaven, in admiration.

Q. where is your mother?

A. He Looks mournfully down on the ground –

End of the Lecture.

The Form of a Reception

The Cand^{te} is Introduced bareheaded in his ordinary cloaths, without a Sword, decorated with a plain white Symbolic apron – the Junr ward^n Called Introductor, is always the protector of the cand^{te} – he goes to the antichamber and conducts him to the door of the chapter, on which he knocks 3 times – when the Senr officers Says, who knocks there? on which the kn^t Captain of the guards, goes out to the Junr knight and then returns again, and informs the Senr kn^t, that the Junior kn^t wants to enter the chapter, who is then admitted on pronouncing the pahsword Phaleg – and informs the Lieut^{nt} Comm^{der} that he has left out of doors a cand^{te} decorated with the attributes of a Mr Mason of <u>Hiram</u>, who begs the Lieut^{nt} commander to receive him a pruhsian knight – when he is ordered to be Introduced on pronouncing the M^{rs} pahsword <u>Tubalcain</u>, when the Lieut^{nt} Commander questions vizt –

Q. Brother Junr Kn^t, do you ans^r for the Master you present me?

A. I answer for him as for myself.

Q. If so, let him advance to the foot of my Throne.

on which the Cand^{te} advances, and gives the Sign Token & word of a Mr Mason. Then the Lieut^{nt} Commander says: brothers kn^{ts} do you Consent that a perfect mason of Hiram who is desirous of becoming a Pruhsian Kn^t, Shall be received? when all the bretheren draw their Swords and point them towards the Cand^{te} as their consent without Speaking – then the Lieut^{nt} Comm^{der} Says to the Candidate, In the name of all the pruhsian kn^{ts} here present, I consent to your request provided you will renounce all pride & ostentation, during your future Life. answer me, what is it, you Say?

(the cand^{te} ans^{rs}) I consent & promise, that I will from this moment divest myself in my future Life, of all pride & ostentation – Then the Lieut^{nt} Comm^{der} Says: if it is so, and you are sincere, come, and make a beginning of an act of humility – on which he is carried by the Junr kn^t and Captn of the guards to the footstool of the Throne, when he makes 3 genuflections, with his left knee, and the 3^d time he continues on that knee, when the Lieut^{nt} command^r comes to him and presents him the pummel of his sword, w^h the cand^{te} kihses 3 times. – Then the kn^t

of Eloquence or gr^d orator harangs him the Cand^{te} by putting him in mind of the proud and ostentatious attempts of the Sons of Noah, and Likewise of the repentance and humility of Phaleg, that great architect of the Tower of Babel etc. -

After this discourse, all the bretheren knights Sheath their swords, and observing a Silence for a little while - they all make the Sign of the master Mason of Hiram - Then the Lieut^{nt} Commander administers the foll^g ob^n to the Candidate.

Q. 1st Do you promise me, never to reveal the mysteries of our order to any of adam's children, unlehs you are convinced, that he is a pruhsian knight?

A. (cand^{te}) I Swear and Consent.

Q. 2dly do you promise on the peril of your life, that you never will Suffer a Son of adam to wear the Jewel of our order, unlehs you are ahsured that he is a pruhsian knight?

A. (cand^{te}) I Swear and Consent. - on which he is relieved, and the Lieut^{nt} Commd^r orders the Senr ward^n to give the Cand^{te} the S: T. & word.

The Sign is: To put up both your hands, the Thumbs opposite your Ears, and the fingers extended upwards, and making 3 genuflections. -

The pahsword is: Phaleg, pronounced very slow, 3 times.

Token The mysterious words are, Shem, cham, & Japhet - when you give the Token take the 2 forefingers of a brothers right hand, between you thumb and y^r two forefingers, prehs them with your thumb and say: Shem, the other answers, by prehsing in the same manner and says: cham, the first then prehses again, and says, Japhet -

There is an other Sign, Token & word to Enter the chapter, which is called the S. T. & w^d of Entrance, viz: he that wants to Enter Shews 3 fingers, the other ans^{rs} the Sign; then he that made the first Sign, takes the 3 fingers of the other brother in his hand, and says, Frederick the 3^d, the other answers, 3 times Noah, - the last Sign, Token & word Signifies that Frederic king of Pruhsia, is the 3^d of that name. and to him we are beholden for the knowledge of the precious Treasure and Sublime knowledge, w^h is deposited to him in Succehsion from his ancestors - then follows the

Historical discourse by the Brother of Eloquence

The descendants of Noah, (Notwithstanding the covenant with God, which was made by the Sign of the Rainbow, that he would never distroy the Sons of men again with a deluge) Resolved to build a Tower So high, that they thereby would defy the Divine vengeance of the almighty; and chose for this purpose a plain Called Senara in asia - Ten years after the foundation of Said Tower was laid; the Almighty looking down on Earth, and Seing the pride & audacious attempt of this People, he descended to confound their project, therefore caused the confusion of languages among the workmen - w^h is the reason that Said Tower was Called Babel, which Signifies, Confusion.

Sometime afterwards Nimrod, (who was the first that Established distinction among men, and who vindicated the right of duration due to the Divinity, founded a City, which for the above reason, was Called Babylon; as much as to say a Circle of confusion -

It was in the time of full moon, that God work'd this wonder, which is the reason that the kn^ts pruhsians or Noachites hold their festivals, every year in the month march, during the full of ye Moon

As the workmen Could no longer understand one another, they divided themselves and departed - Phaleg who gave the plan of Said building, and was also the chief conductor thereof, finding that he was very guilty, and had greatly Sinned against God, condemned himself to a very Severe penitence - he retired from the Sinfull Spot, and went into the north Called Germany, where he arrived after undergoing a great deal of Trouble & fatigue, in Crohsing dehsarts where he found nothing else for Sustenance but the roots of the Earth & wild fruits - He fixed himself in that part w^h is now called Pruhsia, and with great Labor he constructed Several hutts, where he Sheltered himself from the weather, and in procehs of time he built himself a little Temple of a Triangular form, where he used to Shut himself up very often to implore the forgivenehs of God, for the Sins he had committed.

In the year 1553, in digging for Salt mines / which are frequently found in Pruhsia / they found Ruins of a Triangular Edifice 18 cubits deep; in the center of which Stood a column of white Marble, on the base of which was engraved in Syriac characters, the whole history of the penitent Phaleg. - By the Side of Said column, they found a Coffin or a Tomb of grey Stone, in which they perceived Some dust, and a black agate Stone, on which was Cut also in Syriac Characters "Here lies the ahshes of the great architect of the Tower of Babel; the almighty pitied him, because he became penitent & humble" -

They continued to digg, and found a quantity of other agate Stones, and Some of white marble, which had on them also diverse curious and interesting discriptions; part of which are already translated in the german tongue, and some others, that are not as yet deciphered or translated.

All the discriptions that are engraved on these agate Stones are very Interesting mysterious, which we cannot communicate but to those who have from time to time given the greatest proofs of their discretion; and who have been Initiated, in the highest and most Sublime knowledge of our mysteries; because we are not to doubt of his Sagacity and prudence, when he is come to that perfect point, and all confidence ought and may be reposed to him -

All these Curious pieces of agate, marble, coffin and Column are deposited in the archives of the king of Pruhsia, being a Secret place.

NB. the Epitaph, does not Say, that Phaleg, was the architect of the Tower of Babel; but the Inscription on the Base of the column, instructs us, that Phaleg was the Son of Shem, the oldest Son of Noah.

There my brother kn^t, you have a part of the Secret of our order, which is not known by any of the Sons of adam, (id est) the profane.

I Now have trusted you with this, and with pleasure, but woe be to you if you are So rash to become indisrete - Pursue the Example of that great architect Phaleg, and practice humility, and those lehsons, which the Knights Philosophers have teacheth, that is to Say, the princes adepts, knights of the Sun.

The Noachites, are Called this day Pruhsian kn^ts and are descendants of Phaleg, the gr^d architect of the Tower of Babel - Therefore the origin of this order is long before the Era of Hiram's or Solomons masonry, because every body knows that the Tower of <u>Babel</u> was built many Centuries before the Temple of Solomon - and in former ages, it was not required that a cand^te Should be a master Mason of <u>Hiram</u>, but in the times of the crusades, the knights of the different orders in Europe were Initiated into this degree, by the Christian princes, to conquer the holy land, which was invaded by the Infidels -

The Masons descendants of Hiram, by the affection they had for the <u>Noachites</u> as they were much venerated and Esteem'd, therefore desired to be Initiated into their order, and were admitted pruhsian kn^ts according to the mystery of masonry - and from that time, they cannot admit a Cand^te unlehs he is at least a perfect mason according to the Statutes & Regulations of the order; deposited also in the archieves of the king of Pruhsia.

It is Especially forbid by the Statutes of our order, to make use of any Tables, Eating or drinking or artificial light in this chapter; but the Lieut^nt Commander, the only depositer of the Instructions and doctrine of this degree, has the power, for the Instruction of the Cand^te, to open a Table or fellowcrafts lodge (after the chapter is closed) on which is to be served up of any kind of animal food, but only roots fruits and vegitables, in memory of the penitent <u>Phaleg</u>, who Lived only on vegitables during his penitence

End of the 1st Part.

The 2^d part of the Degree of Pruhsian Knight Called the perfect Pruhsian Knight

To open

Q. where is your Father?

A. (he ans^rs by) looking up to Heaven.

Q. Where is thy mothers?

A. (he ans^s by) looking downwards.

Then the Lt Comm^der Says: this Chapter is open.

Further Explanation

In the grey Stone Coffin of <u>Phaleg</u> among his dust besides the black agate Stone / mentioned in the first part) was also found, vizt

1st one agate Stone of a Triangular form on w^h is engraved in hyroglyphic Characters, w^h was never explained before the Reign of the present Frederic the 3^d of Pruhsia who had them explained and wereby we learn, that 9000 years before the Ara of adam, this world did Exist etc etc

2dly on an other Stone in the Same Characters, was Engraved that our forefathers had built many Edifices under ground, for reasons that they Should not be profaned by infidels etc of which that of <u>Enoch</u> was one & the very first.

3dly there were also Six other Stones of white marble found, engraved also by Certain Heroglyphic's, but these will not be explained, until the True Elected are all Re=united under the Banner of one Sovereign and one Law - which Law is that, which is practiced by the knights adepts; and which will bring us to the knowledge of it. But we must absolutily Crush intirely the Serpent of Ignorance and prejudice in matters of Religion, in hopes and full Expectation of the Eternal Beatitude -

    Closing of the chapter is the Same as the opening -

End

22ᵈ Degree.

Knights of the Royal Ax - or the Grᵈ Patriarchs By the Name of Princes of Libanon

This meeting is Called a Colledge

To open the Colledge

The chief Prince Says to order Bretheren, wʰ is repeated by the Senior and Junior grand officers - after Some Silence is observed, the chief prince holds up both hands, the fingers & thumb extended as wide as pohsible, and Says: the Trees of Libanus are grown up, and fit to be Cut - on which all the bretheren hold up their hands in the Same manner, then let them fall on their thighs, in allusion, that they are fell'd and Cut down, in order to be used for Holy purposes, vizᵗ NB: (this is the Sign in this degree)

1ˢᵗ That they were used for the Building of Noah's ark.
2ᵈˡʸ They had been used for the construction of the ark of alliance
3ᵈˡʸ For the use of Solomons Temple. The chief Prince then Says:

1ˢᵗ Noah } the answer to these { Japhet }   NB there is no Token
2ᵈ Bezelee'l } words are made by { Eliab   }   in this degree
3ᵈ Sidonians } the Senʳ grᵈ officer { Libanus }

Origin of this degree

The origin of this degree was Established on the different occasions When the Cedars of <u>Libanus</u> were cut down for Holy Enterprizes - the Explanation of each of the following Letters will make an abridgement of the follᵍ History, and are the Initials of every name which we retain in our memory. vizᵗ

L.	on one Side of the blade of the Royal ax - Signifies	Libanon.
S.	on the Top of the handle of said ax - - - do - -	Solomon.
A.	on the Same Side, below the S. - - - - do. - -	Abda.
AD.	on ditto Side - - - - - - - - - - - - do. - -	Adoniram.
C.	on ditto Side - - - - - - - - - - - - - do - -	Cyrus.
D.	on ditto Side - - - - - - - - - - - - - do - -	Darius.
X	on ditto - - - - - - - - - - - - - - - do - -	Xerxes.
Z	on ditto - - - - - - - - - - - - - - - do -	Zurubbabel.
A	on dᵒ - - - - - - - - - - - - - - - - - do - -	Ananias.
S.	on the other Side of the blade of Sᵈ ax - Signifies	Sidonians.
N.	at the Top of the handle that Side - - - " - -	Noah.
S.	at & on ditto next the N - - - - - - - " - -	Shem.
C.	on ditto - - - - - - - - - - - - - - - " - -	cham.
I.	on ditto - - - - - - - - - - - - - - - - " - -	Japhet
M.	on ditto - - - - - - - - - - - - - - - - " - -	Moses.
B.	on ditto - - - - - - - - - - - - - - - - " -	Bezelee'l.
E.	on dᵒ - - - - - - - - - - - - - - - - - - " - -	Eliab.

on the Top of Said ax or Jewel of gold must be a Crown, to hang to a ribbon of the colour of a Rainbow, in form of a Collar on the breast - it may be also wore from the right Shoulder to yᵉ left hip. -

The <u>Sidonians</u> were always Zealous for the Holy Enterprize before the Deluge; they employed themselves in Cutting the cedars of mount Libanus for the construction of the Ark of <u>Noah</u>; under the Conduct of Japhet -

the descendants of them Likewise Cut the Cedars that were grown up again, for the Construction of the ark of the covenant - and their posterity also Cut in the Same Forest the cedars again, under ye Conduct of Prince <u>Herodim</u>, for the construction of the First Temple of god by orders of <u>Solomon</u> - the Same Nation ahsisted in bringing the Timber down from Said Mount to the Seaside, to be transported from thence to <u>Joppa</u>.

Those Zealous descendants, have Since be employed to fell the Timbers of Said Mountain, for the construction of the 2^d Temple By the orders of <u>Cyrus</u>, <u>Darius</u> & <u>Xerxes</u>, under the Conduct of <u>Zurubbabel</u>. -

This celebrated Nation formed in the Earliest days and time on Said Mountain, Colledges; and adored always in their works, the great architect of the universe - they had the Same Signs, and their different words were the names of their Inspectors & conductors as <u>Noah</u>, <u>Shem</u>, <u>cham</u> & Japhet - <u>Noah</u> being the first chief and his Sons Conductors -

We owe to these Conductors and antient Patriarchs, that we are come to the knowledge of these events. In Succehsion of times Since the Deluge - In Said Earliest times, Colledges were established on Said Mount, for the construction of Said ark of the Covenant - and in after ages and Epocha afterwards the Same Colledges were held for the construction of Solomon's Temple.

That wise Monarch ordered that a small palace Should be Built on mount <u>Libanus</u>, which when finished, he used to go to, in order to visit the <u>Princes Herodim</u>, and at the Same time to See what progrehs the workmen made in hewing and Squaring the Cedars - .

Thus by their Example, we preserve with the greatest Respect, the names of those venerable Patriarchs, and also the memory of the Sidonians - The Initials of the Jewel form an abridgement of this Interesting history, as well as the figure of the draught -

This Colledge is closed in the Same form, as opend

End

23ᵈ Degree
The Key of Masonry
Philosophical Lodge of the Knᵗˢ of Eagle, or Sun

This grand Council must be Illuminated by only one Single Light, and is enlightend by one Divine Light; because there is but one Single light that Shines amongst man, who have the happinehs of going from darknehs of Ignorance and of the vulgar prejudice, to follow the only light that leads to the Calestial Truth

The light that Shines in our Council, is composed of a glahs globe filled with water, and the light is placed behind it, therefore renders the light more clear through the glahs of reflection - this globe when lighted is placed in the South.

The grᵈ Mr. or Thrice puihsᵗ is named Father <u>Adam</u>, is placed in the East, vested in a Robe of pale yellow, like the morning, his hatt on - holding in his hand a Scepter on the Top of wʰ is a globe of gold, and the handle or Extremity of the Scepter, also gilded -

The reason that <u>Adam</u> Carries the globe above the Scepter in this council is, because he was constituted sovereign master of the world, and created Sovereign father of all men. -

He carries a Sun to a Suspended gold chain round his neck, and on the reversion of Said Jewel is a globe - In this degree no aprons are wore.

There is only one warden, whose name is Brother Truth, he sits in the west opposite Father <u>Adam</u>, and is decorated with the Same Jewel and order as the T: Pᵗ Father <u>Adam</u> - he wears besides a large white water'd Ribbon, as a collar, with an Eye of gold Embroider'd or painted thereon above the gold chain and Sun.

The Number of the other officers are 7, and are Called by the names of the cherubims, (vizᵗ) <u>Zaphxiél</u>, <u>Zabriél</u>, <u>Camaél</u>, <u>Uriél</u>, <u>Michaél</u> - <u>Zaphaél</u> & <u>Gabriél</u>.

These ought to be decorated in the Same manner as the Thr: puihsᵗ father Adam - if there are more than that number of Knᵗˢ of the <u>Sun</u> etc they go by the names of Sylphs, and are the preparers of the Council and ahsistants in all the Ceremonies, or operations of the grᵈ Council. These wear the Same Jewel, to a ribbon of a firy Colour to the 3ᵈ buttonhole of their Coats -

To open the grᵈ Council, the Mighty Father Adam Says:

Q. Brother Truth, what time is it on the Earth?

A. Mighty Father, 't is midnight among the Cowans or Profane, but the Sun shines in its Meridian in this Lodge.

Then Father Adam proceeds and says: my dear children profit of the favor of this austere Luminary, shewing its light to us which will conduct us in the path of virtue, and to follow that Law, which ought Eternally to be engraved on our hearts, and wʰ Law is the only that can conduct us, and by which we Cannot fail to come to the knowledge of pure Truth.

Then Father <u>Adam</u> makes the Sign, and puts his right hand on his left breast: on wʰ all the bretheren put up the first finger of their right hands above the hight of their heads, the other fingers clinched - shewing thereby, that there is but one God, who is the beginning of all Truth - Then Father Adam Says: This Lodge is open.

When Father Adam Says, to order bretheren they all put their right hands on their hearts, and he puts up his first finger and So <u>visa versa</u>.

The Form of a Reception

After the Lodge, or Council is open'd, the candidate is Introduced in an antichamber, where there are a number of <u>Sylphs</u>, each with a pair of Bellows, blowing a large pot with fire, which the cand^{te} Sees, but they take no notice of him. after 2 or 3 minutes the most antient of the <u>Sylphs</u> goes to the Cand^{te} and covers his face with a black Crape or veil (he must be without hatt or sword) The antient <u>Sylph</u> tells him, he must find the door of the Holy Sanctuary, which when he has found it, must knock <u>Six</u> times on it with an open hand - after he has knockd, Brother <u>Truth</u> goes, and opens the door a litle. and asks the Cand^{te} the following questions, which he answers by the help of the antient Sylph (vizt)

Q. what do you desire?

A. I desire to go out of darknehs, to See the true light, and to know the Holy truth in all its purity -

Q. what do you desire more?

A. To divest myself of original Sin, and distroy the Juvenile prejudices of Error, to which all men are Liable, namely the desires of all worldly attachment & pride - on which Brother Truth, comes to Father Adam and relates what the cand^{te} has told him - who then gives orders to Introduce him to true happenehs:

Brother <u>Truth</u>, then opens the door, takes the cand^{te} by the hand and conducts him in the middle of the Lodge or Sanctuary which is also covered with black Cloth, when Fath^r Adam adrehses him -

"My Son, Seing that by your Labor in the Royal art, you are now come to the desire of knowing the pure and holy truth, we Shall lay it open to you, without any disguise or covering. but before we do this, consult your heart, and See in this moment, if you feel yourself disposed to obey her (namely Truth) in all things that She commands? if you are at present disposed as I have desired, I am sure, <u>She</u> is ready in your heart, and you now must feel an Emotion that was unknown to you before? and if it is So, you must hope that She will not be long to manifest herself to you? but have a Care, not to defile this Sanctuary by a Spirit of Curiosity; and take Care not to encrease the number of the vulgar and profane that have for a long time Ill treated her /: Truth:/ until She, was obliged to depart the Earth. and can now hardly trace any of her footsteps. But She always appears in her greatest glory, without disguise to the true, good, honest & virtues masons, that is to Say, to the Zealous Extirpators of Superstitions and Lies. - I hope my dear brother, that you will be one of her Intimate favorites - the proofs that you have given and exercized, ahsure me of every thing I have to expect from your Zeal; for as nothing can be more a Secret between us, I shall order Brother Truth, that he will Instruct you, what you are to do to come to the centre of true happinehs"

After this discourse of Father Adam, the cand^{te} is unveiled and then is

Shewn the form of the Lodge or Council, without explaining any part thereof; - Then Brother Truth proceeds (vizt).

My dear Brother, by my Mouth Holy Truth Speaks to you - but before She manifests herself to you, She requires from you proofs by which She is to be Satisfied - In your Entrance in the masonic order She has appear'd to you in many things, which you could not have comprehended without her ahsistance; but now you have the happinehs of arriving to this Brilliant day, nothing can be a Secret to you. Learn then the Moral use that is made of the 3 first parts of the Furniture - vizt the Bible, compas, and Square.

Bible: By the <u>Bible</u> you are to understand, that is the only Law you ought to follow. 'Tis that, which <u>Adam</u> received at his creation; which the Almighty engraved on his heart - This Law is Called <u>Natural Law</u>, and shews, there is not any other but one God; To adore him without any Subdivision or Interpretation.

compahs   The compas, gives you the faculty of Judging for yourself. That whatever God has created, is well, and that Sovereign author of every thing Existing in himself is neither good nor Evil - Because we understand by this exprehsion, an action done, which is excellent in himself or itself, is relative, and Submits to the human understanding /: Judgement: / to know the price and value of the action - and that <u>God</u> with whom every thing is pohsible, communicates nothing of his will, but Such as his great goodnehs pleases, and every thing in the universe is governed, as he has decreed it, with Just being able to compare it to the attributes of the Divinity - I equally Say that in himself there is no Evil: because he has made every thing with exactnehs; and that every thing Exists according to his will, consequently as it ought to be. the distance of good and evil with the Divinity, cannot be more Justly and clearly compared, than that with a Circle formed with a compahs - from the points reunited form an intire Circumference, and represents the Immensity of God who is the beginning of all things. For as the points form a Circumference by its reunion, which points when Separated, is the beginning of all Solids existing or pohsible; and when any point in particular equally approaches or equally Separates from its point is only a faint resemblance of the distance between good and Evil, which we compare by the points of a compas forming a circle, which Circle, when compleated, is <u>God</u>.

Square   By the Square, we discover, that <u>God</u> has made every thing equal - In the Same manner, as you are not able to dig a body in a quarry compleat or perfect. - Thus the will of the Eternal in Creating the world by a liberal act of his own will, foresaw every matter, that could pohsibly happen in consequence there of; that is to Say: that every thing therein contain'd at the time of the Creation, was good. -

Level.   You have also Seen a Level, a plumb & a Rough Stone

By the Level, you are to learn, to be right and Sincere, and not to Suffer yourself to be drawn away by the multitude of blind & Ignorant people - to be always firm and Steady to Sustain the right of Natural Law, and the pure and real knowledge of that Truth, which it Teacheth -

plumb & rough Stone   By the perpendicular and rough Stone, you ought to understand, the prejudiced man made polished by reason, and put censure away by the Excellence of our master.

You have Seen the threhsel board to draw plans on - this represents to

Threhsel board	you the man, whose whole occupation is the art of thinking and employs reason, to that which is Just and reasonable.
cubic stone	You have Seen the Cubic Stone? The Moral of which and the Sence you are to draw from it is, to rule your actions that they might be Equally brought to the sovereign good. -
2-pillars	The 2 pillars teacheth you, that all masons ought to attach themselves firmly, to become an ornament of the order, as well as the support; as the pillars of Hercules formerly determined the End of the antient world -
Blazing Star	You have Seen the Blazing Star? the moral Sence of which is, a True mason perfecting himself in the way of Truth that he may become like a

blazing Star, which Shines equally during the Thickest darknehs; that is to Say, it is usefull to those that he Shines upon, and who are ready and desirous of profiting by its light -

These first Instructions have conducted you to the knowledge of the Slaughter of <u>Hiram abif</u> and ye enquiries that were made to find him out - you have been informed of the words, Signs & tokens, which were substituted to those we feared to have been Surprized - but of which they afterwards learnt that the Traiterous villains had not been able to receive any knowledge of. - and this ought to be an example and Salutary advice to you, to be always on your guard, and well persuaded, that it is difficult to Escape the Snares that Ignorance Joyn'd to Conceited opinions lay every day against us, to overcome us; and the most virtues men are liable to fall, because their candor renders them unsuspecting - but in this Case, you ought to be as firm as was our Respb^{le} Father <u>Hiram abif</u>, who chose rather to be masacred, than to give up what he had obtain'd. This will teach you, that as soon as Truth Shall be fixed in your heart, you ought no more to Consider, the resolution you Should take. You must live and die to Sustain good - never to expose ourselves to the conversation of Cowans; to be Circumspect even with those, who are our most Intimates in our mysteries and not deliver up ourselves to any, except those whose characters and behaviours has proved to be brothers that are worthy to come and appear in the Sacred Sanctuary, where holy Truth delivers her oracles.

You have past the Secret & perf^t Master, the 4th & 5th degrees of Masonry? You have been decorated with an Ivory Key?, a Symbol of your discretion - You have receiv'd the first pronunciation of the Ineffable name of the great architect of the universe, and have been placed at the first Balustrade of the Sanctuary, and you have had rank among the <u>Levites</u>? after you knew the word <u>Zizon</u>, w^h Signifies a Balustrade of the Levites, where all those are placed, as well as yourself to expect the knowledge of the most Sublime Mysteries -

In the degree of perfect master, they have Shewn you a grave, a Coffin whith rope, to raise and deposit the body in a Sepulchre, made in form of a pyramid, on the Top of which pyramid was a Triangle with in which was the Sacred name of the Eternal, and on the pavement were the two Columns of Jachen & Boaz laid acrohs -

Ivory Key	By the Ivory Key, you are to understand, that you Cannot open your heart with Safety, but at proper times -
grave and coffin -	By the Corps & grave is represented, the State of man, before he had known the happinehs of our order -
	The Rope to which the Coffin is Tied, in order to raise it, is the Sym-

bol of raising and unite, as you have been raised from the grave of Ignorance, to the Calestial place, where truth resides –

Intimate Secretary

The pyramids present the true mason, that raises himself by degrees, till he reaches heaven, to adore the Sacred & unalterable of the Eternal Supreme – This new degree leads you near Solomon and Honor; and after you redoubled your Zeal, you did gain new honours and favors, having nearly Lost your life by y^r Curiosity, which attachment in masonry, gave you the good qualities of your heart, which found you grace and Lead you to the degree of Intendant of the buildings, where you Saw a Blazing Star, a large Candlestick with 7 branches, with altars vases of purification, and a great Brazen Sea –

Intendant

Blazing Star –

By the exprehsion of Purification you are to understand that you are to be cleansed of Impiety and prejudice, before you can require, more of the Sublime knowledge in pahsing the other degrees, to be able to support the brilliant Light or reason enlightend by truth, of which the Blazing Star is the figure –

By the candlestick with 7 branches, you are to remember the mysterious number of the 7, who were named to Succeed <u>one</u>, and from that time it was resolved, that 7 knights of masonry united together, were able to Initiate into masonry, and Shew them the 7 gifts of the Eternal; which we Shall give you the perfect knowledge of, when you have been purified in the Brazen Sea –

Brazen Zea

Urn

You have pahsed from the Secret to the perf^t master, and from that to the Intimate Secretary, prevost & Judge and Intendant of ye buildings in those degrees, they have Shewn you an Ebony box Suspended, a Key, a Ballance, and an Inflamed urn.

Box

The Ebony box Shews you with what a Scruplous attention you are to keep the Secrets that have been confided in you, which you are to reserve in the closest of your heart, of which the box is an Emblem – and when you reflect on the black colour of the Box – it Shews you to cover your Secrets with a thick veil in Such a manner that Cowans Cannot pohsibly have any knowledge there of. –

Key –

The Key demonstrates that you have already obtain'd a key to our knowledge and part of our mysteries, and if you behave with equity fervor and zeal to your brothers; you will arrive Shortly to the knowledge and meaning of our Society – and this Indicates the reason of the Ballance.

Ballance

Inflamed urn –

You are to understand by the Inflamed urn, that as soon as you come to the knowledge of the Royal & Sublime art, you must by your behaviour leave behind you in the minds of your Bretheren, and even the vulgar, an high Idea of your virtue, Equally to the perfume of the Inflamed urn.

Intimate Secretary

In the degree of Intimate Secretary, you have seen and heard 2 kings, who were Entering into their new alliance, and reciprocal promise, and of the perfection of their grand enterprize – They Spoke with regret of the Lohs of <u>Hiram abif</u>, our Excellent Master – you saw guards and a man overseen, and ready to be put to death for his Curiosity of peeping – you also heard a project of a place Called the vault to deposit the precious Treasury of masonry, when the time Should be fulfilled – & afterwards you became their brother – the conversation of the 2 kings is the figure and report that our Laws must have with the natural Law; which forms a perfect agreement with the conveniences and promihses to those, who have the happinehs to be contracted to you in the same manner and perfect alliance, they will afterwards Come to the Centre of the true knowledge.

The Tears, and regret of the 2 kings, are the Emblems of the regret you ought to have when you See or perceive a brother depart from the road of virtue.

By the man, you Saw peeping, who was discovered Seized, and Conducted to death; is an Emblem of those, who come to be Initiated into our mysteries through a motive of Curiosity; and if so indiscrete as to divulge their ob^s, we are bound to cause their death, and take vengeance on the Treason by the distruction of the Traitor - Let us pray the Eternal to preserve our order from Such an Evil - you have Seen here of an Example in the 9th degree, to which you are come by your fervor, Zeal and Constancy -

In that degree, you have remarked, that from all the favorites, that were at that time in the apartment of Solomon only 9 were elected to revenge the death of Hiram abif, - This makes good, That a great many are Called but few are chosen. To Explain this Enigma is, that a great many of the profane have the happinehs to divest themselves of that name, to See & obtain the Entrance in our Sanctuary; but very few are Constant, zealous and fervent, to merit the happinehs of coming to the hight and knowledge of the Sublime Truth.

If you ask me, what are the requisite qualities that a Mason must be pohsehs'd of to come to the Centre of Truth? I answer you, that you must crush the head of the Serpent of Ignorance. You must Shake off the yoke of Infant prejudice, concerning the mysteries of the reigning religion, which worship has been Imaginary, and only founded on the Spirit of pride, which envies to Command and be distinguishd, to be at the head of the vulgar, in affecting an exterior purity, which characterizes a false piety, Joyn'd to a desire of acquiring that, which is not its own, and is always the Subject of this exterior pride, and an unalterable Source of many disorders which being Joyned to gluttonnehs is the daughter of Hypocacy and employs every matter to Satisfie Carnal desire, and raise to these predominant pahsions Altars, upon which he maintains without Ceasing the light of Iniquity, and sacrifices continually offerings to Luxury, voluptiousnehs, Hatred, Envy and Perjury. -

Behold my brother what you must fight against and distroy, before you can come to the knowledge of the true good and Sovereign happinehs. - Behold this monster under the figure of a Serpent that you must conquer - a Serpent which we detest as an Idol; which is adored by the Idiot & vulgar, under the name of Religion.

In the degree of Elect^d of 15, Illust^s Knights, gr^d Mr Architect and Royal Arch, you have Seen many things, w^h are only repetitions of what you have already examined - you will always find in those degrees, Initial Letters inclosed in different Triangles or Delta - you have also Seen the planet Mercury, the chamber Called Mount Gabaon or the 3^d Heaven, the winding Staircase, ark of alliance. The Tomb of Hiram abif facing the ark & urn - the precious Treasure found by the 3 ahsiduous Travellers and 3 zealous bretheren Masons. The punishment of the haughty Mrs Masons, in being burried under the antient ruins of Enoch - and finally you have Seen the figure of Solomon with Hiram of Tyre, and St John the Baptist -

By the Three J.J.J.^{s} you know the 3^d Sacred name of the Eternal and mount Gabaon, where you come to by 7 degrees, which compose a winding Staircase.

The 7 Steps Represent the 7 principles and different degrees, to which you must come to attain the hight of glory, represented by the mount, where they formerly sacrificed to the most high - when you arrive to that, you are to subdue yourself in your pahsions in not doing any thing that is not prescribed by our Laws -

By the Planet mercury you are taught Continually to mistrust, Shun and run from those, who by a false practice maintain Commerce with people of a vicious Life, who Seem to dispise the most Sacred mysteries; that is, to depart from those who by the vulgar fear, or a bad understanding Should be ready to deny the solemn engagements they have contracted among us - .

When you come to the foot of our ark, you are to apprehend that you are come to the Sant^m Sanctorum - you are not to return, but rather persist To Sustain in the glory of our order, & the truth of our laws, principles & mysteries, in like manner as our Resp^{ble} Mr H. a. who desired to have been burried there for his constancy and fidelity - we have also another Example in the firmnehs of Galaad the Son of Sophine, chief of the Levites, under Surman the High Priest, in the History of Perfection or 14th Degree.

Learn in this Moment my dear Brother, what you are to understand by the figure of Solomon, Hiram of Tyre and John the Baptist.

The Two first exert you by their Zeal in the Royal art to follow the Sublime road, of which Solomon was the Institutor and king Hiram the Supporter - a Title Legitimately, due to that king, who protected the order, and Contributed with all his might to the construction of the Temple, which Solomon built to the Honor of the Almighty.

The 3^d or St John the Baptist, teacheth you, to preach Marvelous of this order; which is as much as to Say, you are to make Secret mihsions among men, which you beleive to be in a State of entering the road of Truth that they might be able one to See her (virtue's) visage, uncovered -

Hiram abif was the Symbol of Truth on Earth. Jubulum akyrop, was ac-cursed by the Serpent of Ignorance, which to this day raises altars in the hearts of the profane & fearful: this profanehs backed up by a fanatic Zeal becomes an Instrument to the monasterial and religious reign, which Struck the first Stroke in the heart of our dear father H. a. which as much as to Say, undermined the Foundation of the Calestial Temple which the Eternal himself had order'd to be raised to the Sublime Truth and his glory.

The first Stage of the world has been witnehs to what I have advanced - The Simple Natural Law, rendered our first Fathers the most uninterrupted happines; they were in those times more virtuous; but as soon as the monster of Pride Started up in the air, and disclosed herself to those unhappy Mortals, She promihsed to them every Sort of happinehs, and Stole on them by her Soft and bewitching Speeches (vizt) That they must render to the Eternal Creator of all things, an adoration with more Testimony, and more extensive, than they had done hitherto etc. This Hydra with her Hundred heads at that time mislead /: and will continue to this day to do: / men, who are so weak as to Submit to her Empire - and this Error will subsist until the moment that the True Elected Shall appear and distroy her intirely -.

The degree of Sub^{me} Elect^d that you pahsed, gives you the knowledge of those things that conducts you to the true and solid good this grand Circle figured here, which represents the immensity of the Eternal Supreme, which has neither beginning nor End. -

The Triangle or Delta figures here △(C S U) is the mysterious figure of the Eternal - the 3 letters which you See - first the C at Top, Signifies grandeur of Masons. - the S. Submihsion of the Same order; and the U. union, that ought to reign among the bretheren; which all together make but one body, or Equal figure in all its parts. Thus is the Triangle called Equilateral - The grand Letter G placed in the center of the Triangle, Signifies gr^d arch^t of the universe, w^h is God, and in this ineffable name is found all the Divine attributes. This letter being placed in the middle of the Triangle, is for us to understand, that every true mason must have it profoundly in his heart -

There is another Triangle repeated, wherein is inclosed three letters △(S J n) of which you have had the explanation in the 6th degree. This Triangle designs the connection of the bretheren in virtue, the Solemn promise that they have made to love each other, to help, Succour, and keep Inviolable secret their mysteries of the perfection proposed in all their Enterprizes - It is said that in that degree you are Entered in the 3^d Heaven, that's to Say, you have Entered in the place where pure Truth resides, Since She abandoned the Earth to monsters who persecuted her - .

The End of the degree of Perfection is a preparation to come more Clearly to the knowledge of true happinehs in becoming a good mason, Enlightend by the Celestial Luminary of Truth, in renouncing voluntary all adorations, but those that are made only to one God, the creator of Heaven and Earth - great, good & merciful.

The Knights of East or Sword, prince of Jerusalem, kn^{ts} of East & west, are known to us in our days to be masonry renewed; and all of them lead us to the Same End of Celestial truth, which is to Say finished - .

The knights of black & white Eagle, and the Sublime princes of the Royal Secret, and grand Commander, are the chief of the great Enterprize, of the order in general - .

Then Father Adam Says to the Cand^{te} my dear son. What you have heard from the mouth of Truth, is an abridgement of all the consequences which you have pahsed, in the different degrees you have gone through, in order to come to the knowledge of the Holy Truth contracting in your last engagements. Do you persist in your demand of coming to holy Truth, and that with a clear heart, answer me?

The cand^{te} ans^{rs} I persist. - Then Father Adam Says: Broth^r Truth, as the Brother persists, approach with him to the Sanctuary in order that he might take a Solemn Ob^n to follow our laws, principles and morals, to attach himself to us for ever. -

Then the Cand^{te} falls on his knees, and father Adam takes his hands between his own, and he repeats the following obligation 3 times /vizt/

"I A: B: promise in the face of God, and between the hands of my Sovereign, and in the presence of all the bretheren here present, never to take arms against my King directly or Indirectly, in any conspiracy against him -

"I promise never to reveal any of the mysteries of the Sub^{me} degree of the knights of the Sun, which is now on the point of being Intrusted to me, to any person or persons whatsoever, without being duly qualified to receive the Same, and never to give my consent for any one to be admitted into our mysteries, only after the most Scrupelous Circumspection & full knowledge of his life and conversation, and who has given at all times proofs of his zeal & fervent attachment for the order & Submihsion to the Tribunal of the Sovereign Princes of the Royal Secret.

"I promihs never to confer this degree of knight of the Sun, without having a permihsion in writing from the grand council of Princes of the Royal Secret, From the gr^d Inspector, or his deputy by Patent, known by their Titles & authority -

"I promise and swear to redouble my Zeal for all my Bretheren knights and princes; and if I fail in this my Obligation, I consent for all my bretheren knights & princes that are present and absent, when they are convinced of my Infidelity, to Seize me, and thrust my Tongue through with a red hot Iron, to pluck out both my Eyes, and deprive me of smelling and hearing; To cut off both my hands, & expose me in that Condition in the field, to be devoured by the Ferocious animals; and if non can be found, I wish the Lightning of Heaven might execute on me the Same vengeance - O god! maintain me in Right, Justice and Equity.

"Amen, amen. amen."

After this ob^n, Father <u>Adam</u> raises the cand^{te} and kihses him once, on his forehead being the Seat of the Soul; he then decorates him, with the collar and Jewel of the order, and gives him the following Sign, Token & word (vizt)

Sing - The Sign is, To clap your right hand on the left breast, which the other answers by putting up the first finger of the right hand (the others clinched) to the hight above the head - this shews there is but one <u>god</u>, which is the true Source of real Truth. consequently there can be but one and true religion, and the Same which <u>Adam</u> received from <u>God</u>.

Pahswords are - The first Says <u>Stibium</u>, w^h Signifies <u>Prima Materia</u>, or the principal co=operator of all things - the other ans^{rs} albra=est, which Signifies a king full of glory without blot -

Sacred word Is <u>adonai</u>, A Sacred word, which Signifies Sovereign Creator of all things -

The Sign to know a knight of the Sun, you ask him to give you his hands, which he will put together & put between yours, you kihs his forehead, and Say <u>Alpha</u>, which the other answers by Saying <u>omega</u>.

Then the Candidate goes round, and gives the Sign, Token and word to every one, which he brings back to Father <u>Adam</u>, when he Sits down with the rest of the bretheren; when Brother <u>Truth</u> gives the following Explanation of

The Philosophical Lodge.

Sun — The Sun represents the unity of the Eternal Supreme, the only grand word of Philosophy -

3 SSS^s — The 3 S.S.S. Signifies, <u>Stellato</u> Sedet Solo, or the residence of the Sovereign matter of all things -

3 candlesticks — The 3 candlesticks shews us the 3 degrees of fire.

4 Triangles. — The 4 Triangles represent, the 4 Elements -

7 planets.	The 7 Planets designs the 7 colours, that appear in their original State, from whence we have so many different artificial ones - .
7 Cherubims.	The 7 cherubims represent the 7 Metals (vizt) gold, silver, copper, Iron, Lead, Tin & quicksilver -
conception in the moon	The conception or woman rising in the Moon demonstrates the purity that matter must Subsist of, in order to remain in its pure State, unmixed with any other Body - from which must come a new king and a Revolution in fullnehs of Time, filled with glory, whose name is albra=est. -
Holy Spirit	The Holy Spirit under the Symbol of a Dove, is the Image of the universal Spirit, that gives light to all, in the 3 States of Nature, and are the <u>animal</u>, <u>vigital</u> and <u>Mineral</u>. -
Ent^{ce} of the Temple	The Entrance of the Temple is represented to you by a Body; because the grand work of Nature is compleat, as gold portable and fixed. - .
Globe	The Globe represents the matter in its original State that is to Say, compleat.
Caduceus.	The <u>Caduceus</u>, represents the double mercury, that you must extract from the matter, that's to Say the Mercury fixed - and from thence is Extracted gold and silver - .
Stibium	The word <u>Stibium</u>, is the pahsword of the Philosophical Lodge - and Signifies the antimony, from whence is taken an <u>alkali</u>, which we Employ in our grand work - .
M: L:	The Father Adam Explains the Moral, Lodge
Sun	The Sun represents the Divinity of the Eternal - for as there is but one <u>Sun</u>, to light and invigorate the Earth, So there is but one God, to whom we ought to pay our greatest adoration
SSS.	The 3 SSS^s Shews you that Science adorned with wisdom, Creates a Holy man.
3 Candlesticks	The 3 Candlesticks, are the Image of the Life of man considered, by, youth, manhood and old age. and happy are those, that have been enlightend in those ages by the Light of Truth.
4 Triangles	The 4 Triangles, Shews us the 4 principal duties that create our tranquil Life - 1st Fraternal Love among men in general, and particular among bretheren in the same degree with us - 2dly In not having any thing but for the use & advantage of your Brother - 3dly Doubting of every matter that cannot be demonstrated to you Clearly, by which an attempt might be ensinuated to you as mysterious in matters of Riligion. and thereby lead you away, from the Holy Truth.
7 planets.	The 7 planets represent the 7 principal pahsions of man
7 cherubims.	The 7 cherubims, are the Images of the delights of this Life, namely by, Seeing, hearing, Tasting, Smelling, feeling, Tranquility & health.
onception.	The conception, Shews the purity of Matter, and that nothing Can be impure to the Eyes of the Eternal Supreme.
Temple.	The Temple, represents our body, which we are obliged to preserve by our natural feeling. -
Figure of man & lamb	The figure in the Entrance of the Temple, which bears a Lamb in his arms - Teaches us to be attentive to our wants, as a Shepherd takes

	opportunity of doing good, to Labor honestly and to live in this day, as if it was to be our last.
columns	The Columns of J∴ & B∴ are the symbols of the Strength of our Souls, in bearing equally misfortunes, as well as Succehs in Life. -
7 Steps.	The 7 Steps of the Temple, are the figures of the 7 degrees which we must pahs before we arrive to the knowledge of the true God.
Globe	The Globe, represents the world we enhabit.
Lux Ex Tenebris	The device of Lux Ex Tenebris, Teacheth, when man is enlightend by reason he is able to penetrate the darknehs and obsurity which Ignorance and Superstition Spreads abroad -
River	The River acrohs the globe represents the utility of the pahsions, that are as necehsary to man, in the course of his Life, as water is requisite to the Earth, in order to replenish the plants there of.
Crohs.	The Crohs surrounded by 2 Serpents, Signifies that we must watch the vulgar prejudices; to be prudent in giving our knowledge and Secrets in matters of Riligion

End of the Moral Explanation

To Close the Council.

Q. F. Adam,) Brother Truth, what progrehs have men made on Earth, to come to true happinehs - .

A. B.T.) Men have always fallen on vulgar prejudices, that is full of nothing but fraud and falsenehs; very few have Struggeld, and lehs have knocked at the door of the Holy Place, to attain the full light of real Truth, the pure Source of all perfection -

Father Adam then makes the Sign on his heart, and all the bretheren make the answer by putting up the first finger of the right hand - and by 7 knocks they close the Council - .

Explanation of the Physical ... Lodge in
Manner of Lecture

Q. Are you a knight of the Sun?

A. I have Mounted the 7 Steps and principal degrees of Masonry. I have penetrated into the knowledge of the Earth, and among the antient Ruins of Enoch found the most grand & precious Treasure of the Masons; - I have seen, contemplated & admired the great, mysterious and formidable Name, Engraved on the   . I have broke the pillar of Beauty, and thrown down the 2 Columns that Supported it.

Q. Pray tell me, what is that mysterious & Formidable name?

A. I cannot unfold the Sacred characters in this manner, but the Substituted in its place. (viz∴) the word adonai.

Q. what do you understand by throwing down the Columns, that Sustained the pillar of Beauty?

A. For these two reasons: first, when the Temple was distroyed by Nebucadnezar, I was one of them, that helpt to deface the Delta, on which was the Ineffable name, and broke down the pillar of beauty, that it Shou'd not be profaned by the Infidels - and 2dly, I have deserv'd by my travels bounty of the great adonai the mysteries of masonry in pahsing the 7 principal degrees - .

Q. what Signifie the 7 Planets?

A. They are the lights of the Colestial globe, and their Influence by which Exists every matter formed by the concord of the 4 Elements, design'd by the 4 Triangles, that are in regard to them as the 4 greater Planets. -

Q. what are the names of the 7 Planets?

A. Sun, Moon, Venus, Mars, Jupiter, Mercury & Saturn.

Q. Which are the 4 Elements?

A. Air, Fire, Earth & water.

Q. What Influence have the 7 planets, upon the 4 Elements?

A. Three general Matters, of which all bodies are composed, (vizt) Life, Spirit and body. otherwise, Salt, Sulpher & Mercury -

Q. what Life, or Salt?

A. The life given by the Eternal Supreme, or by the planets the agents of Nature.

Q. what is the Spirit, or Sulpher?

A. A fixed matter subject to Several Productions. -

Q. what is the Body, or Mercury?

A. Matter Conducted, or ripen'd to its form, by the union of Salt & Sulpher or the agreement of the 3 governors of Nature.

Q. what are these 3 courses of Nature?

A. Animal, Vigital and Mineral.

Q. what is the animal?

A. we understand in this life, all that is Divine and amiable.

Q. which of the 4 Elements Serves for its production?

A. All four. among which Neverthelehs, the air and fire are predominant - it is these that render the animal the perfection of the Three governments, which man is Elevated to by the breath of the Divine Spirit, when he receives his Soul.

Q. What is the vigital?

A. All that Seems attached to the Earth, and reigns on the Surface of the Earth.

Q. of what is it composed?

A. A generative fire, form'd into a body, whilst it remains in y^e Earth, and is purified by its Moisture and becomes vigitable, and receives life by air and water, whereby the four Elements / tho' different / co=operate, Jointly or Separately.

Q. what is the mineral?

A. All that is generated and Secreted in the Earth.

Q. What do we understand by this name?

A. That which we call, Metals, Demi=metals & minerals.

Q. what is it, that Composes Minerals?

A. The air, penetrating by the Celestial Influence into the Earth meets with a Body, which by its Softnehs fixes, congeals and renders the mineral matter, more or lehs perfect.

Q. which are the perfect Metals?

A. Gold & Silver.

Q. Which are the Imperfect metals?

A. Copper, Tin, Iron, Lead & quicksilver.

Q. How come we by the knowledge of these things?

A. By frequent observations, and the Experiments made in Natural Philosophy, which has brought to a Certainty, that Nature gives a perfection to all things, if She has time to compleat her operations.

Q. Can art bring metal to perfection, as much as by Nature.

A. Yes, but you must have an exact knowledge of Nature, her operations, the quint Ehsence of the Elements, and the fire of Philosophers.

Q. what will ahsist you to bring forth this knowledge?

A. A matter brought to perfection, and render'd an universal Medicine - this matter is what the Philosophers have Sought for under the name of the Philosophers Stone.

Q. what does the globe represent?

A. An information of Philosophers, for the Conduct of the art in this work.

Q. what Signifies the words <u>Lux Ex Tenebris</u>?

A. That is, the dept of darknehs, that you ought to retire from, in order to gain the true light.

Q. What Signifies the crohs on the globe?

A. The Crohs is the health of the Elected.

Q. What represent the 3 candlesticks?

A. The 3 degrees of fire, which the artist gives, to procure the matter from which it proceeds.

Q. What Signifies the word <u>Stibium</u>?

A. The pahsword of the Philosophers - which Signifies antimony or the first matter of all things.

Q. what Signifie the 7 degrees?

A. The different Effectual degrees of Masonry, which you must pahs to come to the Sublime degree of knight of the Sun.

Q. what Signifies the diverse attributes in those degrees?

A. 1st The Bible, or gods Law, which we ought to follow. -
2d The Compas teaches us, to do nothing unjust. -
3d The Square Conducts us Equally to the Same End -
4th The level, demonstrates to us, all that's Just & Equitable.
5th The Perpendicular, to be right, & Subdue the veil of prejudging
6th The Trehsel board, is the Image of our reason, where the functions are combined to effect, compare and think.

7th The Rough Stone is a resemblance of our vices, that we ought to reform
8th The cubic Stone is our pahsions, that we ought to Surmount.
9th The columns, is Strength in all things.
10th The flaming Star, teacheth us, that our hearts ought to be a clear Sun among those that are troubled with things of this Life.
11th The key teacheth to have a watchfulnehs to those who are Contrary to reason -
12th The box teaches us to keep our Secrets Inviolable.
13th The urn Learns us, that we ought to be like a Delicious perfume.
14th The Brazen Sea, that we ought to purifie and cleanse ourselves, and distroy vice - .
15th The Circles in the Triangle, demonstrates the Immensity of the Divinity, under the Symbol of Truth.
16th The poniard teacheth, the Steps of the Elected, many are called but few are chosen, to the Sublime knowledge of true light.
17th The Word <u>albra=est</u> Signifies a king full of glory, and without any blot.
18th <u>Adonai</u>, Signifies, Sovereign Creator of all things -
19th The 7 cherubims, are the Symbols of the delight of Life known by Seing, hearing, Tasting, feeling, Smelling, Tranquility & Sanctity -

Q. what Represents the Sun?

A. It is an Emblem of the Divinity, which might to be regarded as the Image of God - this immense body represents (as I Say) the Infinity of God wonderful well, as the only Source of light and good - the heat of the Sun produces the Rule of the Seasons; recruits nature, takes darknehs from the winter, in order that the deliciousnehs of Spring might succeed.

End of the Physical Lecture.

Another Lecture - In general.

Q. From whence come you?

A. From the centre of the Earth.

Q. How have you Come from thence?

A. By reflection and Study of Nature.

Q. Who has taught you this?

A. Men in general were blind, and lead others in their blindnehs.

Q. What do you understand by this Blindnehs?

A. I do not understand to be privy to their mysteries, but I apprehend under the name of blindnehs those, who Cease to be ardent after they have been privy to the light of the Spirit of reason.

Q. who are those.

A. Those, who the prejudices of Superstition and fanatism Seduces and renders them Slaves to Ignorance.

Q. what do understand by fanatism?

A. The Zeal of all particular Sects, which are Spread on the Earth in leading, to be persuaded of committing precicely the Crimes of offering to fraud and falsehood -.

Q. And do you desire to be raised from this darknehs?

A. My desire is to come to the Centre of Colestial Truth, and to yourney by the Brilliant light of the Sun.

Q. What represents that light?

A. It is the figure only of one god, to whom we ought to pay our adoration. the Sun being the Emblem of God, we ought to regard it as the Image of the Divinity. For that Immence body represents wonderful well the Infinity of God, and is the only Source of light and of God - He invigorates and produces the Seasons, and replenishes nature Intirely in taking the Horrors from winter & produces the delights of the Spring -

Q. what represents the Triangle, with the Sun in the centre?

A. It represents the Immensity of the Supreme.

Q. What signisfies the 3 S.S.S^s -.

A. <u>Sanctitas</u>, <u>Scientia</u> & <u>Sapientia</u>. That science accompanied with wisdom makes Men Holy.

Q. What Signifies the 3 candlesticks?

A. It represents the Courses of Life, Considered by youth, manhood and old age. -

Q. Has it any other meaning?

A. The Tripple light that Shines among us; in order to take a man out of darknehs & Ignorance, into which they are plugged, & bring them to virtue Truth and Holinehs, a Symbol of our perfection.

Q. what Signifies 4 Triangles that are in the great Circle.

A. It is an Emblem of the four principal views of the Life of Tranquility (vizt) Fraternal Love for all mankind in general more in particular for Bretheren, who are Certainly more attached to us, and who with Horror have Seen the wretchednehs of the vulgar.
2dly To be cautious among us, of things, and not to demonstrate them clearly to any, who are not proper to receive them - and to be likewise cautious in giving Credit any matter however arfully it might be disguised without a Self conviction in the heart.
3dly To Cast from us, every matter where in, we conceive that we may ever repent of doing; taking Care of this Moral precept, to do to every one, as we would be done to, and
4^{thly} We ought always to confide in the Bounty of our Creator, and to pray without Ceasing, that all our necehsities might be releived, as it Seemeth best to him for our advantage; To wait for his blehsings patiently in this Life; To be persuaded of his Sublime decrees, That whatever may fall Contrary to our wishes, will be attended with good consequences, to take his Chastizement patiently, and be ahsured that the End of every thing as proposed by him, is the best & Certainly will lead us to Eternal happinehs here after.

Q. Teach us the 7 planets which are inclosed in a Triangle which forms the Rays of the Exterior Circle, and is inclosed in the grand Triangle?

A.   The 7 Planets according to Philosophy represent the Seven principal pahsions in the Life of man - these pahsions are very useful when they are used with moderation for which the Almighty gave them to us; but grow fatal and distroy the Body when let aloose to, but it is our particular duty to Subdue them.

Q.   Explain these pahsions?

A.   1st The propagation of the Species.
     2d   Ambition of requiring riches.
     3d   ambition, in acquiring glory, in the arts & Sciences, & among men in general.
     4th Superiority of Civil Life.
     5th Joys and pleasure of Society.
     6th amusement & gayity of Life, and
     7th Religion.

Q.   which is the greatest Sin of all that man Can Commit, and render him odious to God and man.

A.   Suicide and homicide.

Q.   what Signifies the 7 cherubims, where their names were wrote on a grand Circle, Called first Heaven?

A.   They represent to corporal delights of this life, which the Eternal gave to man when he created him, and are <u>Seeing</u>, <u>hearing</u>, <u>Smelling</u>, <u>Tasting</u> <u>Feeling</u>, <u>Tranquility</u> & <u>Thought</u>.

Q.   what Signifies the figure in the Moon, that we regard as the Image or Emblem of the conception -

The The Purity of Nature which procures us holinehs of the body, & that there is nothing imperfect in the Eyes of the Supreme

Q.   what represents the figures of the Columns?

A.   They are the Emblems of our Souls, which is the breath of life, proceeding from the all puihsant, which ought not to be Soil'd by the works of the Body, but to be as firm as Columns - .

Q.   What represents the figure in the porch, wh Carries a Lamb in his arms?

A.   The Porch ornamented with the Columns of J. & Boaz, & ornamented and Surmounted by the grand J. represents our body, when we ought to have a particular can in watching our conversation, as it is a Secret deposit, which we ought to confide in our Creator, and also to watch our need as the Shepherd his flock -

Q.   what Signifie the 2 letters J & B. at the Porch.

A.   They Signifie our Entrance into the order of masonry; also the firmnehs of Soul, which we ought to pohsehs, from the moment of our Initiation. This we ought to merit before we come to the Sublime degree of knowing Holy truth; and we ought to preserve and be firm in whatever Situation we might be in, not knowing whether it may turn to our good or Evil in the pahsage of this life.

Q.   what Signifies the large J. in the Triangle on the Crown of the Portico?

A.   That large J. being the Initial of the mysterious name of the great architect of the universe; whose greatnehs we always Should have in our view, as the Sure and only Source of our actions.

Q. what Signifie the 7 Steps that leads to the Entry of the Portico?

A. They make the 7 degrees, which are the principal we ought to Endeavour to arrive to, in order to come to the knowledge of the Sovereign good, which is the real knowledge of Truth.

Q. what represents the Therrestial globe?

A. The world which we inhabit, and wherein true masonry is the principal ornament.

Q. What is the Explanation of the great word of adonai?

A. The word which God gave to Adam, for him to pray by - a word our common father never pronounced without trembling

Q. what Signifies Lux Ex Tenebris?

A. Man made Clear by Light of reason, penetrates through obscurity of Ignorance and Superstition - .

Q. What Signifies the River acrohs the globe?

A. It represents the utility of our pahsions, which are necehsary to man in the Cource of his Life, as water is necehsary to render the Earth fertile -

Q. what Signifies the Crohs Encircled by 2 Serpents on the Top of the globe?

A. It represents to us, not to respect the vulgar prejudices to be prudent, and to know the Bottom of the heart in matters of Religion. To be always prepared, not to be of the Sentiments with Sots and Idiots, and lovers of the mysteries of Religion; to avoid Such, and not holding any conversation with them.

Q. What represents the Book, with the word Biblia on it?

A. As the Bible is differently Interpreted by the different Sects, who devide the different parts of the Earth; thus the true Sons of light, or children of Truth, ought to doubt of every thing at present as mysteries or metaphysics; thus all the decisions of Theology & philosophy teach, not to admit, that which is not demonstrated as clearly as 2 and 2 makes 4, or is equal to it. And on the whole, to adore God, and one God alone, to Love him better then yourself; not to do any thing, that you would not have done to yourself; and to have a confidence in the Bounties, and promihses of our Creator. Amen.

End of the gen$\frac{1}{t}$ Philosopical Lecture.

Form of the obligation taken by Israelites in all the
Degrees from the 15th or knights of the East. /vizt/

"I A. B. do swear by the great god adonai, the God of our Forefathers, Abraham Isaac & Jacob, and between the hands of my Sovereign, That I will be Inviolable in my Religion, and observe the laws of the State as far as I can - I promise that I will never reveal the Secrets of the knights etc etc or its Doctrine to any person Living on the Earth, unlehs by a patent from my Sovereign etc etc conformable to the Statutes & regulations or the order. I promise at all times to appear in the grand Councils by order of the Princes of the Royal Secret, when summon'd, and Submit to their orders and mandates - and if I fail in this my obligation, I wish the plagues of Egypt may Torment my body and may my Soul remain wandring, and never Enter the book of Life, but by cut off as corath and his company, be Excommunicated from the Circumcized, and never be numbered amongst the children of Israel - So help me God with hand truth & faith. Amen -

24th Degree
Apare et Lege, Dice & Tace.
The Ne Plus ultra of Masonry

Chapter of the grand Inspector of Lodges, grand Elected Knights of <u>Kadoch</u>, Now by the Title of Knights of the white & black Eagle -

The chief of this order is, The Thrice Illus^s Frederic the 3^d King of Prussia, under the Title of Thrice Illustrious Knight grand Commander.

Opening of the chapter or Consistory

The chapter of grand Elected must be composed of 5 Brothers, every one vested in this degree. They must be all in black, with white gloves - the order a Broad black ribbon from the left Shoulder to the right hip, to which hangs the attribute of the order, being e Rad Crohs, the same as the Teutonic Knights used to wear, in the middle of 2 swords acrohs like s St andrews - No aprons are wore. -

There are no decorations no any emblems in this chapter - The Curtain being intirely drawn - There is only figured on the Threshold the Mysterious Ladder, w^h must be cover'd untill the Candidate has taken his obligation.

Note: you are never to admit a person to this Eminent degree, unlehs you have full proof of his fidelity

of the 5 brothers who compose this Chapter, 2 must be with the Candidate, in another apartment, until he is Introduced - The other 3 remain in the chapter, to do the Necehsaries for a reception.

NB: In a distant place, a Knight of <u>Kadoch</u>, or of white and black <u>Eagle</u>, cannot Initiate another Brother in <u>this</u> Eminent degree, unlehs he has a power and proper patent. Either from a gr^d Insp^t or a Dep^ty gr^d Insp^t under his hand & Seal.

When a Reception is made, the grand commander Must be So Situated, that the Cand^{te} Cannot See him, as he is not to know who Iniated him

Form of opening the chapter.

Q. Illus^s Kn^{ts} are you Elected?

A. Yes, Thr^e Illus^s Kn^t gr^d Commander, I am.

Q. How come you to be Elected?

A. Fortune decided for me.

Q. what proofs Can you give me of your reception

A. A Cavern has been witnehs of it.

Q. What did you do in that Cavern?

A. I Executed Justice.

Q. Have you penetrated further?

A. Yes, Thr^{ce} Illus^s gr^d Commander.

Q. How Shall I believe you?

A. My name is kn^t of <u>Kadoch</u>, or white & black Eagle, you understand me?

Q. As it is So, give me the Sign to convince me of your knowledge against Surprize - on which they all draw their swords, that being the Sign. and then the grand Commander gives a hard knock on the Table before him and Says: Illus^s knights this chapter is open. -

One of the knights with the cand^us out of door, hearing the great knock, goes to the door of the chapter & knocks once; one of them within goes to the door, and asks what he wants? He replies, a Servant kn^t demands to come to the degree of grand Elected, as he has all the requisite degrees of masonry which are necehsary - which is repeated to the grand Command^r who Says: can we admit this freemason among us, without running any risk of Indiscretion from him? the 2 other knights then answer: we swear and promise for him - Then the Thr^ce Illus^s gr^d Command^r approaches, and they all 3 take one another by the hand, and take the foll^g ob^n to each other first giving a great knock.

"We promise and Swear by the Living God always Supreme to revenge the death of our ancestor. and which of us that Should in any manner Commit the most light indiscretion touching the Secrets of our order, Shall his body have burried under this Throne of this Illust^s ahsembly. - So god protect us in our design and maintain us in Equity & Right, amen.

After this ob^n the candidate is Introduced as follows: Sometime after the two knights who are with the Cand^te have heard the great knock of the gr^d commander, giving time for the necehsary Ceremony within, They both take their swords in their hands and Introduce him in the chapter, leave him alone with the grand Commander /tho' he cannot perceive him / and then they all four retire to guard the door of the Entrance and every other door of the adjacent rooms / if any / the reasons is, there never was any person that ahsisted at the reception of a knight Templar.

The cand^te prostrates his face to the ground, when the grand commander reminds him of the principal points of Masonry from its beginning to the Epocha of the ahsahsination of H. abif; Solomon's desire to punish the Traitors in the most exemplary manner; the method he employ'd to dispose the Masters who went in search of the 3 villains, in order to execute the vengeance - He reports to him the Zeal Constancy and fervency of <u>Joabert</u>, <u>Stolkin</u> & <u>Gibulum</u>, who after this painful search had the happinehs / by Solomons order / in finding among the Ruins of <u>Enoch</u> in the 9th arch, the precious Treasure of the perfect masons - He continues to remind him of the firmnehs of the grand Elected at the time of the Temples distruction, when they ran at all risks through the Enemy till they obtain an Entrance in the Sacred vault to find the pillar of Beauty to hinder / by effacing the Ineffable word / that it should not be exposed to the profane. Then he reminds him of the 72 years Captivity, and the clemency of Cyrus king of Persia, who by the request of Zurubbabel not only gave the children of Israel their freedom, but ordered all the Treasure of their Temple / taken by Nebucadnezar) to be restored them in order to decorate the new Temple, which he ordered them to build to the Infine God, and at the same time Created them knights - Then he repeats the clemency of <u>Darius</u> to <u>Zurubbabel</u> (when at the head of the ambahsy from <u>Jerusalem</u> to <u>Babylon</u>, with their complaints against the Samaritans, who refused to contribute to the Sacrifices of the new Temple, according to the proclamation of his predecehsor <u>Cyrus</u> in favor of the knights of the East:) when they receiv'd Darius's letter to all the governors of <u>Samaria</u> etc & and how the Said ambahsadors were receiv'd on their return at <u>Jerusalem</u>, and Elected princes - Then he reminds him after the 2^d Temple had been distroyed, how the most Zealous masons united under a chief, and worked to the reformation of manners and Elevated in their hearts some Spiritual Edifice and rendered themselves worthy by their works - They were more particular distinguished in the time of Manchin, who was the most remarkable amongst them - a great many orther embraced Christianity, and communicated their Secrets to those christians, whom they found had the good qualities for it, living in common and forming themselves as one family, which shews how the Brilliant order of Masons Sustain'd themselves until the 6th age; and how it fell afterwards as into a Lethargy.

Notwith Standing, there has always been Some faithful masons; which is clearly proved by the brilliant manner in which the order of masonry revived in the year 1110 when Eleven of the gr^d Elect & perf^t masons the most Zealous presented themselves to Garinous, prince of Jerusalem, Patriarch and knight mason, and pronounced their promise between the hands of him - They taught him the Succehsion of the times and progrehs, till the time that the princes went to conquer the Holy Land - The alliance that was formed between those princes, and the obligations they made to Spill the last drop of blood to establish in Jerusalem the worship of the most High -

He further informs the Candidate, that the peace that came after those wars, hendered them to accomplish their designs, and therefore have continued by Theory, what they had sworn to do practically; never admitting into their order, but those who had given proofs of Friendship constancy and discretion.

In fine, the gr^d commander makes a general history in genealogy of the masonic order; its progrehs, its decline and the manner how it hath Sustained, till the Epocha of the Crusades and until the historical Circumstances that has given occasion to the degree which the Cand^{te} expects, a degree that will give him a perfect knowledge of the precedent degrees, and the manner how masonry has Come to us - after w^h the cand^{us} takes the follg^s ob^n his right hand on the Bible and his left hand under the Curtain between the hands of the grand commander. (vizt)

"I A. B. promise and sweer, never to reveal the Secrets of the gr^d Elect^d knights of white & black Eagle to any person - To revenge masonry on the Traitors - and never to receive into this degree any, but only a Brother who has come to the degrees of Prince of Jerusalem, and kn^t Prince of the Sun; and then by an authority given to me by a gr^d Commander under his hand an Seal. - I promise to be raddy at all times to conquer the Holy land, when I Shall be Summoned to appear - To pay due obedience at all times to the princes of the Royal Secret, and if I fail in this my obligation, I desire, that all the penalties of my former ob^s may be inflicted on me, Amen" his then kihses the Bible and Rises -

Then the gr^d commander proceeds and Says: my Dr Brother He, who has bestowed this degree on you, which you now have aspired to, and who is described in this place as grand commander, and grand Inspector of all Lodges & gr^d Elected is Sensible of the importance of the Secret already confided to you; 't is therefore necehsary to recommend a Circumspection, and also to observe to those who take the name of knights of white and black Eagle, to be always attentive, not to give the least Suspicion relative to our mysteries, order, progrehs and End of Masonry The imprudence & Indiscretion of many brothers, have given a knowledge to the world of many of our Emblems, by which masonry has suffered greatly and will be repaired with Difficulty - This Indiscretion has caused the lohs and retreat of many puihsant brother who would have been ornaments and Supporters of the order and Lodges - Such indiscretion in this degree my dear Brother would be without any recovery, as there are no more Emblems, when every matter Shall be disclosed and discovered to you, that will give room for Some events, of which you'll See the consequences, when you Shall have heard all my Instructions -

The words which our brothers place at the End of their obligations (vizt) Amen, which Signifies: <u>because this is no more</u>; <u>That Shall be no more</u>; <u>if this Shall be again.</u> - This ought to be no longer a Secret to you, who is going to have the Explination of the origin of masonry and what has occasioned the Society - - Truth penetrates the clouds and Shades, which we can Leave, to come to the knowledge of that, we were before in quality of knights of <u>Kadoch</u> (or of white and black Eagle, as it is now Called:) and what we now are as Symbolic Masons, and what we can be By the distruction of our Enemies - .

Let us Pray:

"Oh most Eternal, Beneficial and all gracious gracious great architect of the universe, we from the Secret dept of our hearts, offer thee a living Sacrifice - we humbly beseech thee to Inspire our Enemies with a Just Sence of the Evil they have done us, from their having a conviction of their wrongs, they might atone for their manyfold Injuries which doth not belong to us thy Servants to redrehs ourselves; but by their eyes being opened, we might be reconciled, and by a hearty union take pohsehsion of our Blehsed lands, where the original Temple was first established; where we might be gathered into one band, there to Celebrate Thy Holy Praizes once more, on the Holy mount in whose bowels were deposited thy ever glorious, Everblehsed and awful Name, Amen" - .

Then the covering of the draught on the floor is taken off.

Learn that the Slightest indiscretion will infallible undermine us, and throw us into an horrible abyhs, where we Should See burried the whole order of Masonry, the remains of our Illustrious and glorious order by its heroisme in favor of the unfortunate. how great it has been in the time when its power authority and riches were arrived to the highest pitch, when the distinguishing birth of those who were menbers of it celebrated its glory. - it was not lehs So, in its unjust and Tragic End, when by the noble firmnehs, knights appeared in the midle of Irons flames & Torments - what can we think of the Prophecy of <u>James de Molay</u> which was verified a little after - what respect ought we not to have for the couragious Zeal of those who have kept the precious remains of an order, which the blackest treason, Envy and most attrocious malignity has not been able to Extinguish? - what hatred Should not we have to those usurpers who occupie the wealth and dignity of this order - they Cannot be regarded but only as a powerful Enemy, the ashes of which ought to renew that unfortunate period, when the numbers of the knights of <u>Kadoch</u> or black and white Eagle Shall be encreased, to be able under the auspiceous Conduct of a powerful commander, and under the establishment of that order, retake the pohsehsions of all the wealth and dignity which did belong to them formerly, and is now held by those who have no other Title this day but injustice and malignity - .

That this my brother be not Said to Intimidate those that have as well as you aspired to this degree, which we are going to confer on you this day, or to Inspire them with an ardor and discrete Zeal; they ought every one to wait the time in Silence, to become ehsential; and if the trust is the most authentic mark of a Sincere friendship, they ought to wish to augment the number of knights, and fear to confer this degree with too much confidence to an ordinary friend, least his discretion Should not be as ahsured as your own –

You remember my dear brother, the obligation you have taken between my hands at the beginning of the Ceremony to render the Justice that you deserve – I have too good an opinion of you, to fear the least Indiscretion in you Concerning the first Notions I have given you of this last degree in masonry –

If in this discource you have made any remarks that might have taken you off, to pronounce the vow that we are obliged to take from you / : before we can give you greater knowledge of this degree of gr^d Elected of Kadoch :) consult yourself and see if you are disposed to penetrate further, and fulfil Exactly all the points of the obligations that you are going to pronounce with me, and link yourself to us for Ever./: Here is a pause for a minute) NB: and if the candidate is afraid or hesitates to pronounce the further obligations The Illust^{rs} grand commander without going further, Sends him out and closes the chapter; in regard to the notions w^h the cand^{te} may have of this degree, the ob^{ns} by him taken already will ahsure us of his discretion – If on the contrary he persists in going further and will take the 2^d obligation, the gr^d Comm^{der}. Continues the Ceremony in the foll^g manner – The cand^{te} then kneels at the feet of the gr^d commander, puts his right hand on the Bible and his left hand between the hands of the gr^d commander, when in this position the gr^d commander says: you swear and promise on that you hold the most dear and Sacred –

1st To practice the works of corporal Mercy, to Live and die in your Riligion, and never to declare to any man, who received you, or ahsisted at your reception in this degree?

The Cand^{us} ans^{rs} I promise and swear. –

Then the gr^d commd^r. Says: Say with me 't Sed halaad, w^h he repeats.

2dly you promise and swear to have candor in all your actions, in consequence never to receive in this degree any brother who is not your most intimate friend, and then by consent of two grand Elected inspectors if to be met with, or by power of a patent given you for that purpose? – The cand^{te} Says, I promise and Swear – Then he repeats the word Scharlabac.

3dly you promise and swear, at all times a sweetnehs of mind as you are capable of, to love and cherish your brother as yourself, to help them in their necehseties and adversities, to visit and help them when Sick; and never to draw arms against them on any pretext what soever? he answers I promise and swear. – Say with me Moteck.

4^{thly} you promise and swear to regulate your discourse by Truth and to keep with great Circumspection in regard to this degree of grand Elected, and kn^t of Kadoch, or white and black Eagle He ans^{rs} I promise & swear. – Say with me Emunah.

5^{thly} you promise and swear to travel for the Honor & advancement of Heaven, and to follow at all thing and points, every matter that you are ordered and prescribed by the Illust^s knights and grand commander, to whose order you Swear a Submihsion and obedience to, on all occasions without any restriction? – he ans^{rs} I promise and Swear –

Say with me Hamach Sciata.

6thly you promise and swear to me, to have patience in adversity and you Swear never to receive any brother to this degree on any pretence what soever, whose will is not free; as Religious monks, and all those who have made vows without restriction to Superiors? He ans^rs I promise and swear -

Say with me Sabaél.

7thly you promise in the End and swear to keep inviolable Secret that I am going to confide in you - To sacrifice the Traitors of Masonry, and look upon the kn^ts of Malta as our Enemies - To renounce for ever to be in that order, and regard them as unjust usurpers of the rights, Titles & dignities of the knights Templars, in whose pohsehsions you hope to Enter with the help of the almighty?

He ans^rs I promise and swear.

Then Say with me choemel, Binah, Tabina.

After the candidate has pronounced these last words the gr^d commander releives him and says: by the 7 conditions and by the power that is given and transmitted to me, which I have acquired by my discretion, my untired Travels, Zeal fervour and Constancy, I receive you grand Inspector of all Lodges, gr^d Elected knight Templar; but before you take rank among the knights Kadoch which we bear the name of, I desire you not to forget it - It is indispensable for you my brother to Mount the mysterious Ladder which you see it will Serve and instruct you in the mysteries of our order, and which is absolutely necehsary, that you may have a true knowledge of it -

Then the cand^te mounts the ladder and pronounces at each Step he rises, the name belonging to it, and when he is on the 7th and highest and has pronounced the 3 last words, the ladder is lowered backwards, in order that the cand^te pahses over the ladder, because he Can not retire the Same way, as he would be obliged to go back, against which he has taken his obligation, not to retire by the Same way as he came - the views and Interest of the order which is the reason - Then he reads the words at the bottom of the Ladder, Ne plus ultra.

Then the gr^d Commander embraces the cand^us and Says to him My dear Brother, I am going to give you the Sign Token & word with the pahsword of the gr^d Elected and grand Inspector after which I Shall give you the explanation of the mysterious Ladder, which you have ahsended and past over without knowing the reason thereof -

This ladder my dear brother is the most ehsential and analogus to the history which I am going to recite to you. like a ladder it is composed of 2 Supporters, which will give you a Just Idea of the Strength which Philip the Fair king of France Rec^d in his union with Pope Clement the 6th.

The Reunion of the 2 Supporters by the 7 Steps, gives you a Just Idea of the 7 conditions that Philip the Fair imposed on the Bishop Bertrand Got, to make him Pope - the 7 Steps Serve to ahsemble the 2 Supporters, the Same as the 7 conditions which Philip the Fair composed and Engaged the Said Pope in; and is the fundamental Base and union that must have been cemented between the king and Said pope

These 7 Steps are also a Resemblance of the 7 points of your Ob^ns which you have contracted, in the same manner as Philip the Fair; that by the

The draught of the Mystirious Ladder.

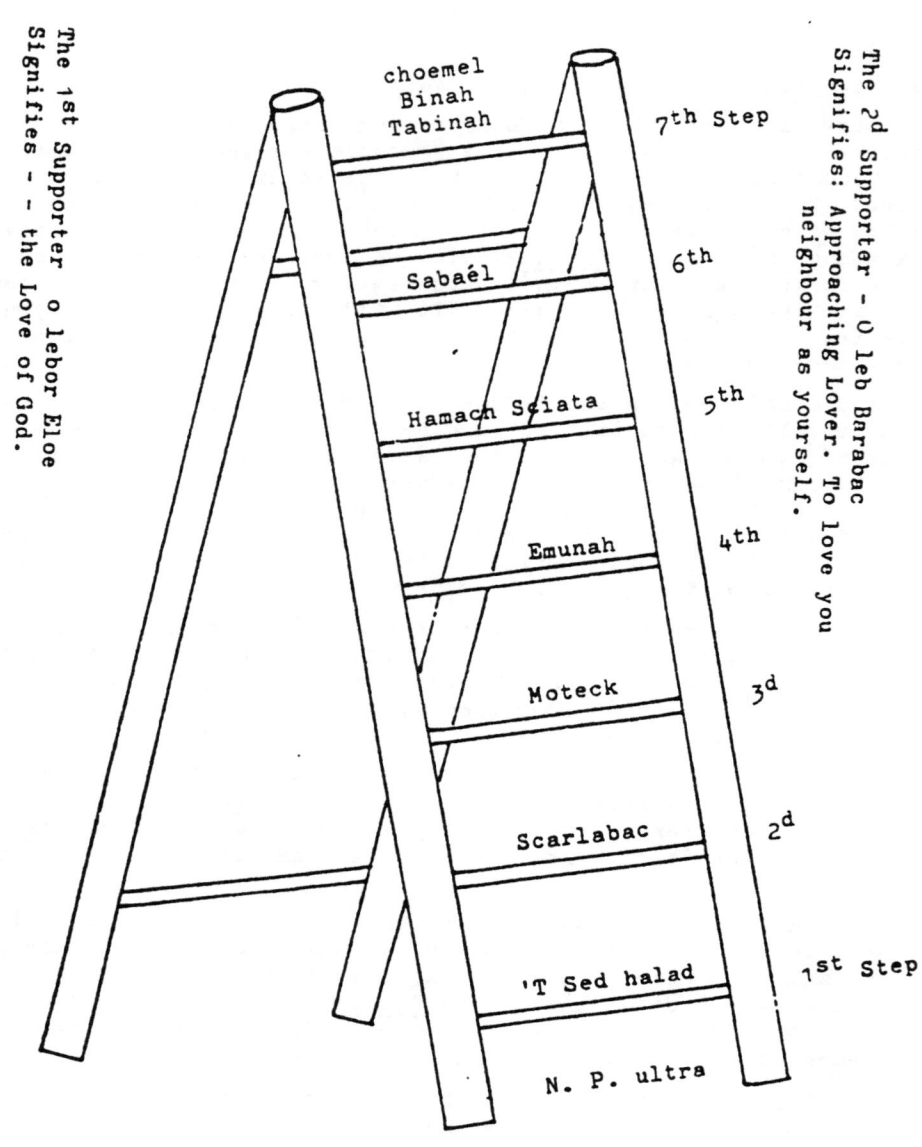

7 articles he imposed on Clement the 6th. He made him Swear the final
distruction of the Templars In the same manner are the 7 points of your
obn where you Swear to bear an Implacable hatred to the knights of
Malta, an Engage yourself to endeavour their total distruction, in order to reclaim the right and dignities they pohsehs. -

Lastly, this moment my dear brother is the time to entrust you in full
in the degree of grand Elected, and give you a true knowledge of the
manner, how masonry has come to us - Have attention to the principal
fate of that History, you then will easily make the application yourself the more you are entrusted -

Listen to the following History.

The History

After the death of Pope Benoit the 13th 1304, the Cardinals met for the
Election of a new Pope, and found themselves in two factions, French
and Italian.

Philip the Fair, king of France had several views which could not be
accomplished without the ahsistance of the pope to be Elected; and as
his party in the conclave fomented these divisions to favour Philips
design (who taking advantage of these Circumstances) He sent for Bertrand Got, then archbishop of Bordeaux / : Son to Bertrand Lord of Villandran in the Same Diocese : / and in the Conference which he had with
him at a pleasant country Seat near St Johns of angely; when he informed
him of his design and the divisions in the conclave; which did put it
in his power to Elect a pope, and that he / Philip / was disposed to
prefer him, provided he would Swear to perform 7 articles, the 7th and
last was even to be a Secret to him / the new pope /, until the time
for the execution of it Should be ripe. according he revealed the Six
first articles, which are foreign to our purpose, but to the 7th, for
the exact performance of which they both took the Sacrament to each
others promise.- The king having found a man to his purpose to be agent
for his revenge, caused him to be Elected Pope and promoted to St Peters
chair - In the year 1305, under the name of Clement the 6th. This Pope
after his Election, established his See at Lyons, where his first Care
was to execute the 6 first Conditions, wh Philip had imposed on him -
The time of declaring the 7th being come, Philip did not delay in declaring to the Pope, that by his oath, he was to Joyn him to intirely
distroy and Exterminate the knights Templars to the extent of Christianity. Here is what has attracted the hatred of Philip the fair, and
what made him take that Barbarous resolution against them all:

He took the the Brother & Nephew of Bertrand Got as hostages for the 7th article.

Vide Vertot, vol: 2d page 65.

Some time before the death of Benoit the 11th the happened a Sedition
in Paris, occasioned by Philip, who had Coined some money, which was
light, mixed and base metal. - on which the Populace were mutinues, who
plundered and demolished the house of Stephen Barbet master of the Mint.
They went afterwards to the kings dwelling and committed a great deal
of indecency, in so much, every matter conspired an Insurrection -

Vide, Vertots h[i]story of Malta vol.2d page 31 & 32. & Poter Dupui's collection

The Templars (: against whom envy had raised many powerful Enemy:) were
Suspected to have been at ye bottom of these outrages, and was the Cause
/: altho' without reason or foundation) that their ruin was determin'd
by the king, for which purpose he Sought the means to ahsist himself by
the death of Benoit the 11th, in order to put in his Stead a Pope on
Certain conditions that Should be imposed on him -

Nothing was now wanting but the pretence (for when force and authority is in hand every matter becomes easy) for which purpose, they prevailed on 2 abandon'd men, that they Should get admittance among the kn^ts Templars, / : these men's names were Gerard Labé, and Benoit Mehui :) and when admitted, in their mysteries to accuse the whole order of the greatest Crimes, which these 2 villains executed exactly - They desired to be admitted and received into the order, which was easy to them, as they had Seemingly honest exterior Titles, and apparent qualities, besides a Supposed Credit at Court.

Every matter conspired in their favour and they were received. But it lasted not long before the Templars repented heartily of having lighted the firebrand, which was the cause of the deplorable and Tragical Scene; when most all the Templars were involved in one common destruction, for these Two wretches, soon after their admihsion accused the whole order of the most dreadful Crimes; demanding to be Separated from them, on occasion of the execrable things Suggested to them -

The Treason is good, but the Traitor is detestable. Thus did they suffer the Same Lot that was kept for the Templars; for they by their treachery, went through the most dismal torments, and not Suffered to live, altho' they had been the Instruments of vengeance to the Templars, by their false accusations -

Vide Vertot vol.2d :64

Upon their report to the king / : who had lately had an Interview with the Pope at Potier : / took the surest measure, to arrest all the Templars in his dominions in one day - this was done on the 13th october 1307, two years after the Imfamous accusation was made. - They Seized on all their papers, Titles, Treasures and generally all their wealth over which were placed overseers -

King Charles of Naples, in the like manner ordered all the Templars to be arrested in Provence - Those taken in France, were locked up in the Tower or Castle of Mehun to take their Trials -

The Pope at the Same time sent for their grand master James de Molay a native of Burgundy (: who was then at war with the Turks in the Island Cyprus :) who, as Soon as he received the orders of the Pope came to Paris with his knights of the order, among which was one Guy, brother to the dauphin, Devienois, Hughes de Peraldes & Theodore Bazille de Monancourt. They were all arrested, and made the most dreadful torments, in order to draw from them a confehsion of the crimes they were accused of, tho' without effect; as they dared bravely every torment, rather than accuse themselves of crimes they were Innocent of. - So that, on no other proof but the accusation of two Imfamous Subtorners they concluded their Trials (being Impohsible to procure the least evidence against them, as never any person ahsisted at the making of a Templar:) and they executed and burnt alive 57 in one day, and the next 59, and so on, until they had compleated almost their Total distruction - They pardoned none, not even those two that Served them in accusing the whole order for as Templars they were included in the general Sentence, and were burnt alive with the others - .

Let the End of these unhappy wretches serve as a lehson to us; that we are not in future to be Seduced by fine promihses, and Initiate any but those, who have given us by a long train of Services proofs of their most Solid worthinehs, least we might be, by their indiscretion dragged once again with all the knights of Kadoch in a Common Fate.

The grand master and the 3 above mentioned Bretheren were neverthelehs not comprehended in the first executions - The Pope for reasons (which no historian has mentioned) kept the Judgement to himself. –

Most all the Templars in this prosecution (which Lasted till the year 1314 :) were arrested in all the Christian States, but were not all put to death –

Philip the Fair was continually hurrying on the Pope, to make an End of James de Molay the grand Master and his 3 companions (: after having groaned 7 years in prison overloaded with Irons :) which was at last executed, when they were burnt alive on the 11th of March 1314, in the Isle of Paris, moving to pity and tears the numerous Spectators who were present, for their Steadinehs, heroical constancy and Solemn vows of their Innocence, which was afterwards apparent Supported by an Event Extreamly memorable –

James de Molay (the grd Master) Seing himself on the Scafford ready to End his life in the flames, (after having Languished ir Irons for Several years :) and which was now become a releive to him to end his life in any manner rather than undergo a longer lingering in this uncertain world – with great composure turn'd himself, and directed to God the following Prayer (vizt)

"Oh almighty and Everlasting God, who knows the Innocence of the victims which have been Sacrificed for Several years; permit us to reflect on the reproach and Imfamous Torments which you permitted Jesus Christ to be covered with at his death, to redeem us from Slavery of our Sins, to give an Example to the Innocent by teaching them by his mildnehs, to Suffer without murmuring the persecutions and Torments which injustice and blindnehs prepare for them – Forgive o God the false accusations and imputations which has Caused the distruction of the whole order, of which your divine providence had established me the chief, and if you are pleased to accept the prayer which we now humbly offer you, permit o God that one day this people dihsabused might know the Innocence of those who have endeavour'd to live in thy Holy fear and Love – .

"We wait your bounty and compahsion the reward of the Torments and death we Suffer; which we offer to you, in order to enjoy your divine presence in everlasting happinehs"

Then addrehsing himself to the people, he Said: "Good people, who See us ready to perish in the flames; you will be able to Judge of our Innocence: for now I Summon Pope Clement the 6th in 40 days, and Philip the Fair, in twelve month to appear before the awful, and tremenduous throne of the Everliving God, to render an account for the blood, they have wickedly Shed". – After which they we hurried to Execution, fearing a Rescue from the Populace. –

The prediction of James de Molay, was accomplished as Pope Clement the 6th died the 19th april the Same year at Rocquemour on the Rhone, and Philip the Fair within 12 month at Fontainbleau.

The news of the prosecution of the knts Templars had already reached the knights, which were left in the Island of Cyprus, and in the absence of the grand Master had been overpowered by the Turks, when they lost acre, with Several other Strong holds, and were oblig'd to retire to the Isle of Rhodes, and the adjacent Islands –

The prosecution against them in open Council at Vienna the 1st of october 1311, when their order was bannished, their Estates confiscated, and left at the disposal of the Pope (: who in the year 1312 gave a part to the knights of St John of Jerusalem - Those, who had escape the prosecution and having retired to the Isle of Rhodes, were oblig'd to disguising themselves, not loosing intirely the hope to See the order re=instated again; they swore an adversion to the kn^{ts} of St John of Jerusalem, who pohsehs yet to this day the greatest part of their Estates. - This adversion makes to this day a part of the Ob^n of the gr^d Elect^d kn^{ts} Templars Called kn^{ts} Kadoch, or of Black and white Eagle, as now Called.

As the number of those who escaped was very Small, rendered that adversion more powerful - they Sought to renew an increase in their order, in admitting persons in whom they beleived that their Behaviour and quality was indisputable, those inshort whom they thought worthy of keeping the most Important Secrets - Instructed of the wonders that had opperated at different times among the good and virtuous masons. Heirs worthy of those whom Solomon had distinguished and favoured after the construction of the Temple, knowing their candor and Intrepidity, which appeared among them, in the greatest dangers: their wisdom, union, charity, Love, Impartiality, firmnehs, discretion and Zeal; they thought, they could do no better, then Endeavour to unite themselves to these masons. Their fathers protectors Support and help, Sought the favor to be admitted into their Society, and to be Initiated into their mysteries - .

Those newly Initiated into their mysteries were informed by these masons, who they were - The barbarous events which they had escaped, and the resolution they had taken, Secretly to increase their number in order to be able one day to reclaim and regain their rights, to Re=establish their order and take pohsehsion again, of their original pohsehsions, rights and Estates. - They offered their bretheren masons their ahsistance in taking their revenge and as a Common cause to accept the tribute from them of the most Just gratitude and thankfulnehs.

The grand Elected kn^{ts} and Princes Masons approved of their designs accepted their offers, and agreed among themselves instead of the characters of the order, which was the Crohs, to make use of the word, Sign & Token of Masons, and by the conformity of several analogies (: Events to their history) persuaded them that the different Signs of the masons, would put them intirely under cover against the maliciousnehs, of those, whom as a Gerard Labé or Benoit Mehuy, Should endeavour to be admitted into an order of which they Should undertake in vain to put oneself under the Shelter, of a like event; that they Should not trust the true Secret of the order, but to those, whom they had perfectly tried, and of which they were as sure as of themselves; after having them made to pahs through the different degrees, which we know in masonry. having taken its birth from the Construction of Solomons Temple, since its origin, till the distruction of the Temple, and characterized writs of the most remarkable events intirely analogous to the distruction of the kn^{ts} Templars, whom as Elects of masonry breeth only, to revenge the death of their Illustrious gr^d Master, and to retake their pohsehsions.

My dear Brother from the degree of Mr Mason that you have Received, and when you have learnt to Shed Tears at the Tomb of Hiram abif, have you not been disposed, in other degrees, to Vengeance? did they not Shew you the Traitor Jubulum akyrop, in the most dreadful colours? would it be exaggerated in comparing the conduct of Philip the Fair, to his? and to compare the 2 imfamous informers Gerard Labé & Benoit Mehuy, to the 2 villains who Joyned akyrop the murderers of Hiram abif? do they not kindle in your heart the Same revenge, which those unhappy fellow Crafts deserved and was executed on them?

The Trials that you have gone through to learn the Historical facts of, and the antient Bible do they not Serve you to understand, and Sound your heart to make a Just application of the death of H. abif, in comparing it with that of James de Molay? By the Degree of 9 Elected, when your heart was disposed to revenge, you have been prepared to the implacable hatred, that you have Sworn to the kn^{ts} of Malta, in whom you ought to ought to revenge the death of James de Molay - as a grand Elected you have acquired by your proved discretion in Symbolic masonry, the light, which leaves nothing more to desire than your Submihsion, to the degree of the Sublime Princes of the Royal Secret, our chiefs and gr^d Elected of the order, who have bestowed on you this Singular Favor.

This is my most Illust^s Brother, how, and by whom Masonry is arrived, and has been transmitted to us. You ought to See what it is to enter into our lawful rights, that we Seek to ahsociate with men, whom merit, bravery and good manners gives them Titles; which only birth right granted to the ancestors of the Templars - you are now a kn^t and on the Side of Envy as persecution; which you may escape by keeping Carefully your Ob^s and Secreting from the vulgar your Estate, and also what you are - .

Having obtained this degree of light which you merit only by the knowledge we have of your manners and Zeal, hath brought you to it - we are prepared and persuaded that our confidence towards you, will be sufficient to make you apprehend how important it is to you not to be the cause of our not repenting in your Initiation - We now know you perfectly, to have the least doubt of you - Thus we did not hesitate to light you in the true Interest of the order, that by your uniting yourself to us, with a Sincere Submihsion; you will Labor to acquire that perfection your Zeal deserves - .

You are now in the rank of those, who Shall be Elected to the grand work - once your name is in the urn of your Election. The delicious perfumes of your actions will bring you to the true happinehs of your desire, Which I Sincerely wish you, amen, amen, amen.

After this History and discource the gr^d Commander gives one great Blow, to call the 4 knights that are out, to enter the chapter; after which the gr^d commander finishes the Reception, and gives the new Elected knight the Sign, Token and word. He arms him, decorates him with the attributes and Communicates to him the name he must take in future, which is uncommon to all others, and is Kn^t of Kadoch, instead of Templar.

The Jewel which was formerly a red Crohs, (: discribed before) is now a black Spread Eagle with 2 Heads, To a bloody red broad order, from the left Shoulder to the right hip, Said Eagle as if going to fly, with a naked Sword in his claws -

The Sign is Sitting, your right hand on the heart the fingers extended, then let the hand fall your right knee, fingers open.

The Token is the Same as the 9 Elected.

The pahsword, Necum or Nikak, otherwise, Manchen

The one Says: Nichamaka, Bulion.

The ans.r is, Bagulkal, Pharaskal, then they embrace and both Say adonai.
The Brothers are desirous of being better acquainted with this interesting History, may Consult the foll.g authors (viz.t)

>   Villaneus's History
>   History of all orders, by Mathei in Parish
>   History of Malta, by Vertot.
>   Ehsay on Paris - by S.t Foix.

Here follows the doctrine of Kadoch, now Called knights of the Black Eagle in manner of Lecture (viz.t)

Q. Are you a grand Elected?

A. I am Thrice Illust.s knight.

Q. who received you in this degree?

A. A worth Dep.ty gr.d Insp.r, by the Consent of two others.

Q. what was done with you?

A. He created me a knight.

Q. How can I beleive you?

A. My name, w.h I bear will convince you.

Q. what is your name?

A. Knight of Kadoch, but now of the black Eagle.

Q. Was any thing else done to you?

A. The Dep.ty Insp.r adorned me with thé habit, order and Jewel of this degree.

Q. Where have you received the prize of your Election?

A. I have rec.d it in a grotto very deep, & in the Silence of night.

Q. What do you apply to?

A. I work with all my might & Strength to raise an Edifice, worthy my brother.

Q. what progrehs have you made?

A. I have required the knowledge of the mysterious Ladder.

Q. what composes that Ladder?

A. Two Supporters and 7 Steps.

Q. what are the names of the two Supporters?

A. O Lebur Eloe & O Leb Barabac.

Q. what design these 2 Supporters?

A. The 1.st, the Love of God, & the 2.d the Love of our neighbour.

Q. what are the 7 Steps of the mysterious ladder?

A. The virtues I must practice, conformable to my obligations

Q. Name them to me?

A. 1.st 't Sed Halad, Practice or works of Mercy
    2.d Scarlabac. Candor of our actions.

3ᵈ   Moteck. Sweetnehs of character, wʰ all the bretheren must follow.

4ᵗʰ   Emunah. Truth in discourse.

5ᵗʰ   Hamach Sciata. advancement to the practice of Heaven.

6ᵗʰ   Sabél. patience in adversity.

7ᵗʰ   choemel, Binah Tabina. prudence wʰ we ought to keep in every Secret confided in us - .

Q. what is your ordinary pahsword?

A. Manchen, the name of the grᵈ Mʳ. most renowned among the Solitaries, known by the name of Kadoch, or black Eagle.

Q. what Signifies that name?

A. Solitary, or Separate.

Q. what was the ansʳ of the Solitaries, when they were asked to what they pretended.

A. averecha, recolgit adonai. Klamed tellesake Sophy, which Signifies, I blehs at all times and will praise him with my mouth.

Q. Do they never Say any thing else?

A. They Say, Begaherad Stibium Hemuy, which is I will ahsist the poor always, & Sustain them with my power & might.

Q. How came the crohs Surmounted, with the Eagle & Sword?

A. For me, to remember that I must employ it in fulnehs of time under the Banner of the black Eagle to Support the order.

Q. Where did you work?

A. In a place of Security to re=establish Secretly the Edifice ruined by the Traitors -

Q. What Succehs do you expect from it?

A. The Reign of virtue, accord of brothers, and the pohsehsions of our fore fathers; and everlasting happinehs.

Q. have you Shed Tears?

A. I have.

Q. Have you wore mourning?

A. Yes, and I wear it Still.

Q. why?

A. Because virtue is disposed, & crimes will continue unpunished as long as vice reigns, and Innocence will be opprehsed.

Q. Who is 't, that will punish vice, and reward virtue?

A. The great architect of the universe alone.

Q. How So?

A. To favor our designs and desire. NB here every brother Says 3 times, God favor our design.

Q. Have you any other name then knᵗ of black Eagle?

A. Yes, I have that of <u>adama</u>, to teach me that from the most Low, I must go to the most high.

Q. give me the Sign of knowledge against Surprize?

A. Here it is. He gives it in the foll$\bar{\text{g}}$ manner; he puts his right hand on the heart of a brother, in the Same manner as with the poniard in the 9th degree, and the Token of the same degree - then both Strike y^{e} right knee.

Q. How Came you to Carry your right hand extended on your heart?

A. That my trust is in god.

Q. why do you extend you hand afterwards?

A. To Shew my brother, that he is welcome to all in my power, and to encourage him, to revenge -

Q. How come you to let your hand fall on your right knee?

A. To Shew, we must bend our knee, to adore god. Amen!

End of the Lecture

To close.

Q. what's the clock?

A. The break of day, demonstrates.

Q. If the break of day demonstrates, let us depart for revenge - after which the gr^{d} command^{r}, puts his hand on his heart, and then lets it fall on his right knee - w^{h} is answ^{d} by them all. Then the gr^{d} commd^{r} embraces all, and they each other all round, and this closes the Chapter.

Note: The grand Inspector, <u>Stephen Morin</u>, founder of the Lodge of Perfection etc In a consistory of Princes of the Royal Secret at Kingston In Jamaica, In the year of Masonry 7769, of which at that time Hen^{y} And^{w} Francken / Senr Dep^{ty} Insp^{r} general / was grand Commander; advertized the princes Masons That lately a commotion had been at <u>Paris</u>; and that enquiry had been made, if those masons who Stiled themselves knights of <u>Kadoch</u>, were not in reality kn^{ts} Templars? It was therefore resolved, in the gr^{d} East of <u>Berlin</u> and <u>Paris</u>, that S^{d} degree in future Should be Stiled, knights of white & black Eagle, and the Jewel, to be a black Spread Eagle etc as mentioned in this 24th degree, and that notice Should be Sent to all the Inspectors abroad -

End.

The Ne plus ultra
or 25th degree Called
The Royal Secret, or the knights of St Andrews, and the Faithful guardians of the Sacred Treasure

Preparations and decorations for fitting out the apartment Necehsary for holding of a grd chapter, or Council of the Sovereign princes of the Royal Secret

This grd chaptr must be held some where in an open Country on a rising ground, and in a building of at least two Stories high. on the 2d floor of which must 3 apartments, where in the grand chapter is to be held, & such meeting in day time, & not at night - 1st The 2 Tilers, are to be on the first floor, or ground, one to Tile Every where, and the other on the Stairs. The first chamber up Stairs is for the guards; The 2d apartment for preparing the candte, and the 3d is that for the chapter, or reception.

This apartment is to be hung with black Sattin, bestrewed with silver Tears. Skeletons, Thigh bones acrohs and dead heads.

2dly There must be a Throne Erected, in the East, under which is a chair of State, for the Sovereign of Sovereigns o. grd Ills Prince who is the commander in chief. - This Throne is to be ahsended by 5 Steps, and lined also with black Sattin, with firy flames instead of Tears, and before the Sovereign is a table, cover'd with black Satin with Tears; and on the forepart of the cloth a deadhead an 2 bones acrohs with the Initials IM, the I over the head, and the M under the bones. -

3dly The Sovereign grd Commander is to be armed with a Bucler and a naked sword, the Sceptre and a ballance on the Table before him, without any books except our Laws.

4thly In the west facing the grd commdr are placed the 2 grd wardens by the Title of Lieutnt commdrs They are to wear buclers, and their hats on as well as the grd commdr, their Sword acrohs on a Table before them; and this Table must be cover'd with a crimson Satin border'd with black ditto, bestrew'd with silver Tears; and on the forepart of Said cover, these Initials NKMK - Embroidered in golden Letters - .

5thly The Minister of State Stands on the right hand of the Sovereign.

6thly The grd chancellor, on the left of the Sovereign.

7thly Next the minister of State, Stands the Grd Secretary.

8thly Next the chancellor, Stands the grd Treasurer

9thly Below them on one Side is placed the Ensigneur who at the Same time is the grd Mr architect - and opposite him on the other Side, the Captain of the guards -

10thly Six members Stand below these, drehsed in Red, without aprons; but all of them wearing the Jewel of the order on their breast, Suspended to a Large broad black ribbon in a Triangular form.

The Royal Secret, or the Rendevous of the Sublime Princes - .

Instructions for the Re=union of the Brothers knights, Princes and Commanders of the Royal <u>Secret</u> or <u>Kadoch</u>, which Signifies the Holy <u>Brothers Separated</u>

Frederic the 3d king of Pruhsia, grand Master and Commander in chief,

Sovereign of Sovereigns etc etc etc With an army composed of the knights Princes of the white and black Eagle, Including Pruhsians, English and French; likewise Joyned by the Princes of Libanus or of the Royal Ax; The knights of Rose crohs, or S^t andrews, kn^ts of East & west, the Princes of Jerusalem, kn^ts of East, The gr^d Elect^d perfect & Sublime, kn^ts of the Royal arch kn^ts Subl^me Elected etc etc etc.

The discription of the draught or Camp -

The Equilateral Triangle in the Center of the draft represents the Centre of the army, and Shews where the knights of Malta are to be placed / : who have been admitted into our mysteries,) who have Shewn themselves faithful guardians to the order   - They are to be Joyned with the knights of white and black Eagle -

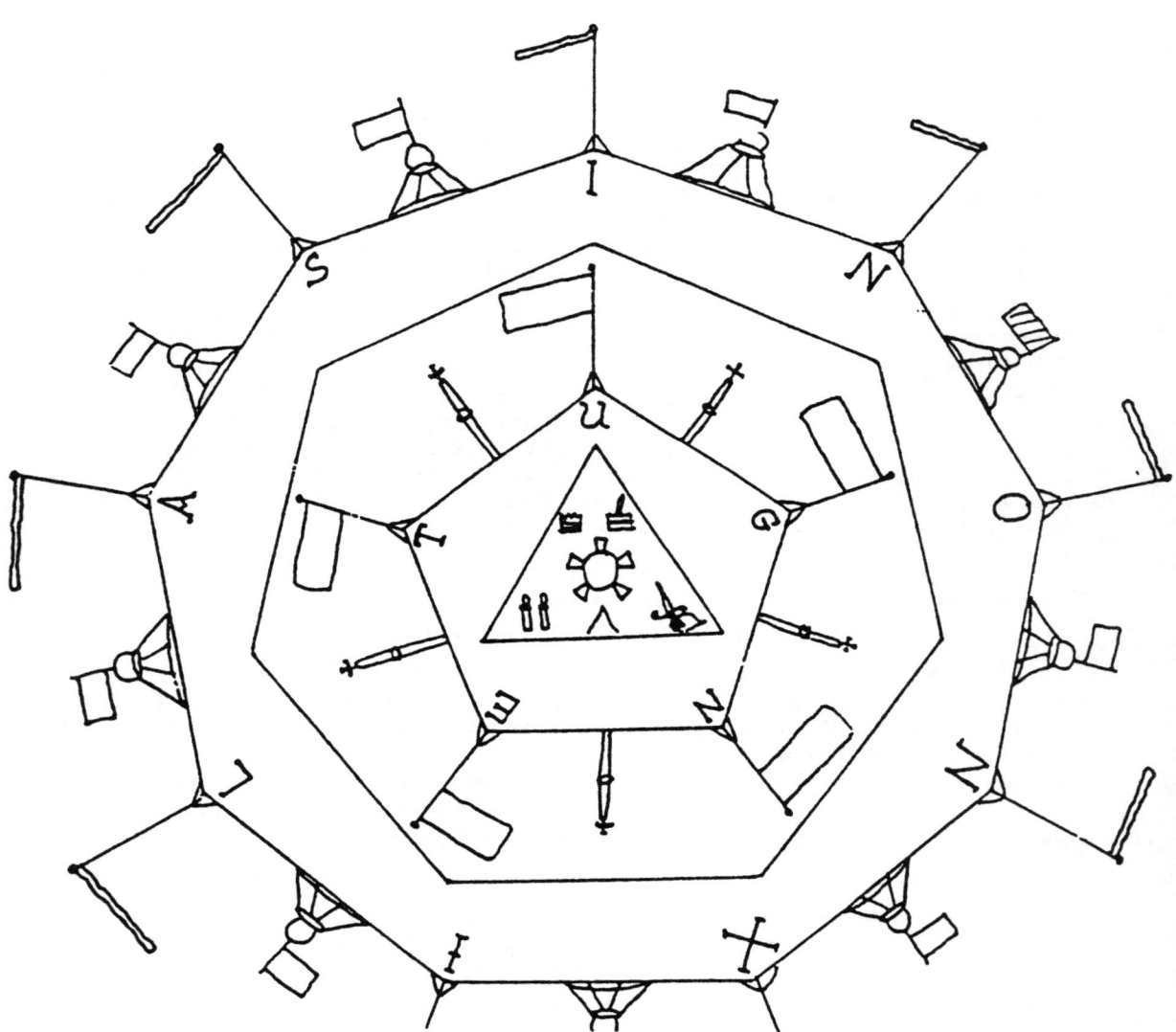

The corps in the Pentagon, is to be commanded by 5 princes Who are to take the command, Joyntly, or by Rotation, according to their degrees; and receives their orders immediatly from the Sovereign of Sovereigns, gr^d M^r or Commander in chief.

These 5 Princes Shall fix their Standers in the 5 angles of the Pentagon, represented in the above draught in the following manner (vizt)

1st The Standard or Flag T, bearing arms a golden Lion, holding In his Mouth a Golden Key, and wearing a golden Collar with these Letters on Said collar, S. Q. S. - Said Lion in an azure field; at the bottom of Said flag these words: <u>ad majorem, Dei gloriam</u>.

2^d The Standard or flag E, bearing arms an Inflamed heart with gules, Sable winged, crowned with a Laurel Syncope - The field argent.

3^d The Standard or flag N, bearing arms a Spread Eagle with two heads, a golden Crown Connecting both heads in the form of a Collar. Said Eagle holding a naked Sword in his right Claw the point downwards, and a bloody heart in his left claw - The field a light green -

4th The Standard or flag G. Bearing an ox Sable, in a field of or. / or gold /.

5th The flag or Standard U, bearing arms the Ark of the covenant, with two light green palmtrees, in a Purple Field; at the bottom of the flag these words: Laus Deo -

The Heptagon represented above, points out the Encampment of the Princes of Libanus & Jerusalem who are to receive their orders from the princes above mention'd

The Eneagon represented above, is the encampment of the masons of all denominations as Shall be explained here after - Note: That every Tent represents a whole camp; and the Flags & Pendants points out the different degrees of Masonry; and each letter distinguishes the flags is taken from these words which we make use of in this Sublime degree - Thus the degree of the Rose=crohs, or S^t andrews, or white Eagle will be distinguished by a white flag and pendant Stained a little with red and is represented by the Tent S.

1st Tent S. Called <u>Malachias</u>, and Shews the camp of the knights of East and west, <u>& Princes of Jerusalem</u>

2^d Tent A, Called <u>Zurubbabel</u> has a light green flag & Pendant and Shews the Camp, of the kn^{ts} of the East or Sword.

3^d Tent L, Called <u>Nehemias</u>, Has a red flag and Pendant, and represents the Camp of the gr^d El^d Perf^t & Sublime

4th Tent I, Called <u>Homen</u>, has a black & red flag & Pendant, and represents the Camp of the kn^{ts} of the Royal arch.

5th Tent X, Called <u>Phaleg</u>, has a black flag and Pendant and represents the Camp of the Elect^d of 9, of 15 and the Illus^s knights -

6th Tent N, Called <u>Joyada</u>, has a red and black flag and pendant & represents the Camp of the Prevosts & Judges -

7th Tent O, Called <u>Eliab</u>, has a green & Red flag & Pendant and points out the Camp of the Intends of the buildings & Intimate Secretaries -

8th Tent N, Called <u>Jusue</u>, has a green flag & pendant, & Shews the camp of the Perfect & Secret masters -

9th Tent S, Called Esdras, has a blue flag & Pendant, and Shews the Camp of the Symbolic masons, and the volunteers - .

The hour fixed on, Shall be the 5th after Sun Set, and Shall be known by the firing of 5 great guns, one first by itself, and 4 more at equal distance and briskly -

The 1st Rendevous Shall be at the port of Naples, from then to the 2^d to the port of Rhodes, and from Rhodes to Cyprus & Malta where the whole Naval Force of all nations is to assemble - The 3^d at Joppa, and the land forces rendevous is to be at Jerusalem, when they will be Joyned by our faithful guardians there

The names of our Standard bearers are Bezeleel, Eliab Menchen, Garinous & Emerk

The watch words for Every day in the week are as foll^s and they are not to be changed but by the exprehs orders from the king of Pruhsia -

			pahswords
Sunday	Cyprus	Ezekiel	Q. Polcat, w^h Signifies which means, Separated -
Monday	Darius	Daniel	
Tuesday	Xerxes	Habacuck	A. Pharaskal w^h means, Reunited to accomplish -
Wednesday	Alexander	Sophonias	
Thursday	Philadelphia	Aggeus	
Friday	Herod	Zacharias	Then they both Say: Nika, Mika, Signifying, I will be the revenger -
Saturday	Ezechiar	Malachi	

Explanation of the Tents and their Letters

The Tent S of the kn^{es} of East & west etc at the Top of the draught, go from that round, against the Sun, and read on When you will find the words Salix Nonis.

The camp of the Pentagon, read as above, and you'll find the word Tengu.

These Three words Joyn'd, from the Initials of the following Prophecy in French. /vizt/ Soutenons apresent L Invencible, Xerxes, Nous offres Notres Incomparable Sacré Trésor, Et nous gagnerons, Victorieusement.

Which is attempted in English by H. A. Francken thus Support adversity Lo Invencible Xerxes, Now offered Near Incomparable Sacred Treasure Engaged, Now gives Victory.

To open, and Close, the gr^d chapter, or Consistory

The President Says Salix, The 2^d gr^d officers Say Nonis. Then all together Say Tengu, which Signifies the Rallying of the wise bretheren, who have been hitherto Separated. -

The Sign is, you put your right hand on your heart, then hold it up, and then let it fall on your right Side, which Sign is made by them all together.

The Sublime Princes, will have the pohsehsion of our Treasure, as being the old Treasures of the order; and the knights of Malta who will Joyn us, Shall have and Enjoy the Same honors & Priviledges -

The Princes of Jerusalem, Shall be honoured with the degree of white & black Eagle, and will command the knights of the East, the Scotch, the Symbolic's and the volunteers, with the pahsword Tripple Pronounced and Elchadai, w^h word Signifies Delta.

Let us Imitate our grand Master Hiram abif, Who, to the last placed all his hopes in the great architect of the universe, and pronounced the following words, Just as he past from this transient life into Eternal Blihs -

    Spes mea, In deo Est - .

                  Finis

                            H. A. Francken. Pr: of the R: S:t
                            and Senior Dep:ty gr:d Insp:r over
                            all Lodges, Councils, chapters etc
(S E A L)   over the two Hemispheres - .

                            In Kingston Jamaica, In the year
                            of light near the B: B: 7783 - .

Form of Submihsion to be Signed by all the bretheren
Initiated, as Soon as they in the Perfection or 14th degree

Lux Ex Tenebris -

By the glory of the Great Architect of the universe

We the underwritten Bretheren of Free and accepted Masons etc etc etc Do hereby acknowledge, that we have been Enlightend, Initiated & Raised into the higher degrees of antient and Modern Free Masonry, by the Thrice Illustrious Brother David Small. Prince of Masons, and Deputy gr^d Insp^r general over all lodges, chapters, Councils and gr^d Councils etc etc etc In the west Indies & North America -

And we hereby acknowledge our Submihsion to ye Supreme Tribunal and Sovereign gr^d Council of Princes of the Royal Secret according to the Tenor meaning and true intent of our different oblig^{ns} taken at our different Initiations -

Kingston Jamaica
Done at the great East, where shines the great Light, and where reigns Silence Concord and Peace, under the Celestial Canopy of the Zenith Deg: Min = 17, 30 - Near the B..B. the 5th day of the 2^d month Called He.... 5544 - of the Restoration 2314. Equal to the 30th day of october 1783 -

(S E A L

	Laws & Regulation for the government of a Lodge of Perfection
These By Laws Substantially the Same as these given at pages 5 to 13	

Health, Stability & Powers.

preamble

As all wel regulated Societies, have Certain rules and regulations for their better Support and Government, and as Free and accepted masons are bound in a more particular manner, to practice the Social, and inforce the Moral virtues; especially in the Lodge of Perfection

The persons hereafter Subscribed their names, and members of the Lodge of Perfection Called   do ahsent to the following Laws and regulations, for their better government, under the penalties here after mentioned - .

First

Institution

That those members mentioned in the Constitution Shall meet by order of the Master / So appointed by the constitutor or a council of Princes etc etc if any, or a Dep^{ty} gr^d Insp^r general) when he Shall open the Lodge of Perfection, and after Saying Prayer, Read himself the constitution, these Laws; and then appoint his officers; after which they Shall agree by a Majority when and where to meet, as Shall be Judged most convenient.

2^d

Numbers of the members 27

if but one nay not Elected -

Jewel order etc to be provided by the body

That the members of this lodge, never exceed the Number of 27, including the master, and that no person be received in this Lodge, unlehs he can be vouched to be a regular made Master Mason, and is a member of a regular constituted Lodge of the 3 first degrees, and is also, or has been an officer in this Lodge, and to become a member, Shall by Petition be proposed by one of the members, when he is to be ballotted for the next ensuing night, and if but one black bead or <u>nay</u> Shall appear in ballotting, Said petitioner can never be proposed again in Said lodge - But if he is chosen by unanimous Consent, he is to be raised the next ordinary lodge night - when on his reception, the Lodge is to furnish the Jewel apron & order etc for Said degree, the expences of which the Initiated brother is to be acquainted with, before hand, that he may come prepared to pay the same when the Ceremony is over -

3^d

payments of each degree

That the bretheren who Shall be admitted into this Body Shall pay for the initiation of each degree, of the first <u>Nine</u> from the Secret M^r to the gr^d M^r architect the Sum of ... and for the Perfection the Sum of   and also for the Jewels aprons orders etc for every degree as mentioned in the foregoing article -

4th

periods of raising

That no member of this lodge can be raised higher unlehs he has at least been two succeeding ordinary lodges present, and is very perfect in his former degrees, for the first <u>Nine</u>, and between the gr^d M^r arch^t & Royal arch at least 3 ordinary lodges; and between the R: A. and the Perfection, at least 4 ordinary Lodges - and if the cand^te Should be found dificient, in the Ceremonies requisite, in the last degree, he is to be admitted by discretion of the Master or remanded back to the Studies of his former degrees - and in case Such cand^te Should murmur against Such proceedings of the master, and not make proper atonement for his behaviour he Shall be excluded as a member of Said lodge, of which a minute is to be kept in the Lodge book -

5th

As Soon as a cand^te becomes a member of this Body the Secretary Shall read these Laws / Standing /, to which Said member Shall Subscribe his name. The Secretary it to keep fair and regular accounts, of all the monies he may receive and disburse in a lodge, and State the cash & personal acc^ts. The ledger to be posted, and the cash accounts Ballanced once a quarter, and paid over to the Treasurer, whose receipts Shall be a voucher for the Secretary - and whoever refuses or wilfully neglects to pay his dues or fines when demanded, will be excluded the Lodge - The minute book is to Contain the transactions of the lodge - and entries of all receipts and disbursements - the minutes to be made, and read, before the lodge is closed - .

The Secretary to keep all the accounts

6th

A visiting brother who produces a Certificate from the Constitutor of this Lodge, or from a regular Constituted Lodge of Perfection, Shall be permitted their first visit gratis; for each Succeeding night pay to the contingent fund, and his proportion of the expences of the night - there are particular times of businehs when no visiting brother Can be admitted - But in case a visiting brother a knight of the East, Prince of Jerusalem etc Shall visit this lodge, and by producing a proper Certificate of his high Degrees, he is to be received according to his rank and dignity, on the Same terms as mentioned in the beginning of this article.

visiting brothers

visiting Princes

7th

Each member of this body, is to contribute towards its Support the Sum of   per annum by four equal payments (vizt) on the feast of St John the Baptist, the 24th September, The feast of St John the Evangelist, and the 25th of March. The whole of each quarters due to be payable from the first day of the quater. So that if a member Should remove from the Society any time after the commencement of a quarter, he is to pay the whole thereof, and a new member is to pay the due of that quarter in which he Joins - each member in case of absence or Sicknehs, on the above mentioned quater days, Shall appoint a person to pay for him, under the penalty of   for each neglect, or excluded this lodge - The quarter days to be deemed Stated meeting, and remembred accordingly

quarterly payments

8th

If the master or any of the officers of this Lodge Shall misbehave or render himself unworthy of the lodges worship and Submihsion; he Shall at the Election of the members be duly tried according to the nature of the Crime - and if the Master Shall neglect or refuse to fine delinquents agreeable to these laws; he Shall at the Election

master or officers refusing to do their duty

of the members present, pay the fines So neglected, himself; Provided that the body is to Judge whether the fines are Justly incurred, or not -

9th

Any member of this Lodge, that Shall be present aiding or ahsisting, at the raising of a mason in any of the Superior degrees clandestinely, Shall be expelled the Lodge for ever, and never be permitted to become a member of any Lodge of Perfection; an Entry there of to be made in the minutes - those minutes to be Sent to all other known Lodges of Perfection

10th

If any member of this lodge Shall forget himself So far, as to come drunk in the Lodge, get drunk during lodge hours, make any disturbance or uproar in the Lodge Shall be expelled for that evening, and afterward dealth with as the present members Shall think proper.

11th

Swearing, and disobedience

A member adrehsing the chair, must do it Standing, and only one person Speak at a time; and only once on the Same Subject, unlehs Called upon by the chair - and whoever shall presume to Swear or Curse or Blaspheme during Lodge hours, Shall be find for each Such offence the Sum of   for the use hereafter mentioned - and he, that refuses Silence after the 3^d Stroke of the mallet, Shall forfeit the like Sum -

12th

not attending the lodges -

Any member who Shall duly attend the lodge, agreeable to the masters orders, Shall pay the Sum of   the night of each Stated Lodge, and the Sum of   each extraordinary lodge he neglects; and no excuse whatever to be taken, exept Sicknehs, Lamenehs or absence from Town

13th

The keys of the chest to be kept by three -

The keys of the chest is to be kept by the master. Senior warden and gr^d Treasurer, one key each; and in case any of them Should be from home or absent from Town, they are to leave their respective keys So, that they may easily had, when ever the Lodge may have occasion to ahsemble, under the penalty of for each neglect, besides repairing the chest, in Case that lock Should be broke open - The chest never to be opened but in the presence of the Body, and no monies disposed of out of it, without the consent of the majority of the members - .

14th

That in case any member desirous of being raised higher (without waiting the limited time mentioned in the 4th article) and being well skilled in his former degrees, or in case of departing for another part of the world, shall by the unanimous consent of the M^r, the officers and the gr^d El^d Members of this lodge, and even receive one two or three degrees at an ordinary Lodge night ...

(Page missing)

appropria- tions of the monies	... payments, Initiations, fines etc Shall be appropreated for the decorations of this Lodge, and Such other uses, as the body Shall Judge proper - .

<u>19th</u>

a R: arch mason, being desirous of becomming a member	That a brother that has been made a Royal arch Mason, in a regular Lodge of that degree, knowing nothing of the foregoing regular degrees, and being desirous of Joining this Lodge, Must go through the various degrees preceeding the 13th, but is to pay nothing for that degree, except for the Jewels orders etc Suitable which he will be presented with -

<u>20th</u>

(T H E   E N D)

CPSIA information can be obtained
at www.ICGtesting.com
Printed in the USA
BVHW011039130619
550939BV00004B/421/P